$3\frac{25}{}$

TEACH YOURSELF BOOKS

ARABIC

The would-be student of Arabic is not faced with an easy task. He has to master a strange script and a structure which is quite unlike that of any of the European languages, and thus has none of the familiar landmarks to guide him. This book, however, reduces his difficulties to a minimum. It is a carefully graded course of lessons specially prepared for students working on their own by an Oriental scholar who has many years' experience of teaching Arabic. Both the script and the grammar are explained clearly and in detail, with many examples and exercises. The reader should find that he is able to make good progress.

You really can teach yourself Arabic from this little book. It is well printed, very cheap, pocket size and just over 300 pages. I am aware, from an experience of a number of years in teaching languages of this group, that Dr. Tritton's method of attack is sound and productive of good results.

Professor Norman Snaith

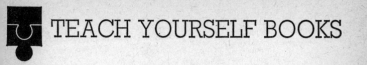

TEACH YOURSELF BOOKS

ARABIC

A. S. Tritton, D.Litt.
Professor Emeritus of Arabic, School of Oriental and
African Studies, University of London.

ST. PAUL'S HOUSE   WARWICK LANE   LONDON EC4P 4AH

First printed 1943
This impression 1974

This volume is published in the U.S.A. by David McKay Company Inc., 750 Third Avenue, New York, N.Y. 10017

ISBN 0 340 05771 8

Printed and bound in Great Britain
for The English Universities Press Ltd. by
Hazell Watson and Viney Ltd., Aylesbury, Bucks

INTRODUCTION

Arabic is a Semitic language and so different from those usually studied in Europe; this is perhaps the main difficulty, there are none of the familiar landmarks. The verbs 'have' and 'be' do not exist; when 'be' is indispensable, 'become' is used as a substitute and it does not take the same case after it as it does before it. The verb has no tenses, only two forms indicating completed and incomplete action. Normally the 'finished' form is used to describe past events but it is also used to express wishes and prayers where the action is only ideally finished. To make up for this poverty the verb is developed in other ways, thus 'be good', 'do well', 'approve' are all expressed by modifications of the same verb.

Most words are derived from roots which consist of three consonants called radicals; it is obvious that these roots are not words. The addition of vowels, prefixes, suffixes to the root makes words. In this way some seventy word patterns are made, each with its own meaning. In English 'man', 'ran', 'fat' are all of the same pattern, a short vowel between two consonants but one is a noun, one a verb, and one an adjective; this is impossible in Arabic. As there are so few word patterns the language sounds rather monotonous; a poem must have the same rhyme throughout and it is common to find nearly one hundred lines with a complicated rhyme like *a:muha:*.

An illustration will make the next point clear. *KaTaBa* has a vowel between the first and the second radical, *yaKTuBu* has not. The beginner, especially in trying to hear the language, finds it hard to believe that the syllable *yak*, which ends in *k*, has anything to do with words which begin with *k*.

The Arab grammarians used the root *fʕl*, a real root, with its derivatives, as the type of all words; they called *ka:tibu* the *faːʕilu* of *ktb* not the active participle and *maktuːbu* the *mafʕuːlu* instead of the passive participle.

maktabu and *maka:nu* are the *mafʕalu* of *ktb* and *kwn* respectively; we should call them nouns of place. In *maka:nu* the *w* of the root has combined with the short vowel to form a long one.

They recognized only three parts of speech, noun, verb, and particle. This classification is useful because, (1) it is not often needful to distinguish the noun from the adjective, what is true of the first is usually true of the second; and (2) there are some words which have no equivalents in English and are lumped together with prepositions and conjunctions as particles. In most languages the commonest words are irregular; this is also true of Arabic, but it has fewer irregularities than most languages. The structure of sentences is simple; elaborate periods are few; clause is joined to clause by 'and' while it is left to the imagination of the reader to supply a more precise link. Effects are obtained by the combination of simple words; 'what is in me' may mean 'my abilities' or 'my feelings' according to the context.

The primary sense of the root usually develops derived meanings. To push money to someone is to pay him; to try to push his enemy from him is to defend him. 'Total' and 'eloquence' both come from 'arrive'; by the addition of small sums you arrive at a total, by persuasive words your ideas arrive at the minds of your hearers. It is obvious that the primary meaning of the root must be picked out from the mass of derivatives.

Print and handwriting are essentially the same. The script unites at least two stages of history. At first only the consonants were written, though in the earliest known inscriptions three of them, *alif* (which was then the glottal stop), *w*, and *y* were also used to indicate the long vowels. The first book to be written was the Koran and this fixed the spelling of the language because the text was too sacred to be tampered with. Unfortunately, Muhammad spoke the dialect of Mecca which did not use the glottal stop, replacing it near *u* and *i* by the consonants *w* and *y*. Other dialects kept the glottal stop and were considered more elegant. So a special sign for the glottal stop was invented, written like the new vowel signs outside the consonantal framework. It was introduced into the Koran and now appears in all Arabic sometimes alone and sometimes in conjunction with *alif* or *w* or *y* but representing only one sound.

Apart from school books all vowels are written only in the Koran ; elsewhere they are used sparingly.

The Arabic of a newspaper is in essentials that of the Koran ; the main difference is the large new vocabulary, partly old words with new meanings, partly loan words. The syntax is slightly simplified. The spoken tongue varies from place to place and differs from the written by the loss or degeneration of inflections and a different vocabulary. It is written only in jokes in comic papers, dialogue in novels, and sometimes in short stories.

Formerly the Arab sat on the floor, ate with his fingers and at meal or bed times his food or bed was brought to him. The result is that many words, indispensable in English, scarcely occur in accounts of native life. For ' table ' Syria uses an Italian, Egypt a Greek, and Mesopotamia a Persian word.

This book is an introduction to written Arabic which is understood from the Atlantic to the frontiers of Persia. It will not help a man to talk to a crossing-sweeper the day of his arrival but it will quicken his progress in talking after the first month or so.

Words, which have been fully explained in the lessons, are left out of the vocabularies.

Proper names, which come in the examples, have not been transliterated in the phonetic alphabet.

In the transcription *j* and *y* have their English sounds.

Owing to the nature of the type in this book many of the vowels are to the left of the consonants instead of being directly above them.

ACKNOWLEDGMENT

The author and publishers gratefully acknowledge the assistance given by Mr. J. R. Firth, M.A., in connection with the sections on the sounds of the language.

CONTENTS

xi

CONTENTS

THE ALPHABET

Writing runs from right to left and the letters consist of strokes or strokes and dots. Vowels are not counted letters. At the end of a word or when standing alone many letters end with a flourish (compare the figures in a doctor's prescription 11ا). There are two classes of letters; those which can be joined on both sides and those which can only be joined to the preceding letter. The first class has four forms, initial, medial, final, and independent; the second has two, final and independent. The essential part of the letter remains unchanged as is shown here :—

independent	final	medial	initial
ب	ب	‍ب‍	ب‍

when there is a final flourish the dot or dots are often put in the middle of it.

Name.	Independent.	Final.	Medial.	Initial.	Equivalent.
alif	ا	ا			ʾ
bā	ب	ب	‍ب‍	ب‍	b
tā	ت	ت	‍ت‍	ت‍	t
thā	ث	ث	‍ث‍	ث‍	θ
jīm	ج	‍ج	‍ج‍	ج‍	j
ḥā	ح	‍ح	‍ح‍	ح‍	ḥ
khā	خ	‍خ	‍خ‍	خ‍	x
dāl	د	‍د			d
dhāl	ذ	‍ذ			ð
rā	ر	‍ر			r
zā	ز	‍ز			z

Name.	Independent.	Final.	Medial.	Initial.	Equivalent.
sīn	س	س	ـسـ	سـ	s
shīn	ش	ش	ـشـ	شـ	ʃ
ṣād	ص	ص	ـصـ	صـ	ʂ
ḍād	ض	ض	ـضـ	ضـ	ɖ
ṭā	ط	ط	ـطـ	طـ	t
ẓā	ظ	ظ	ـظـ	ظـ	ð
'ain	ع	ع	ـعـ	عـ	ʕ
ghain	غ	غ	ـغـ	غـ	γ
fā	ف	ف	ـفـ	فـ	f
ḳāf	ق	ق	ـقـ	قـ	q
kāf	ك	ك	ـكـ	كـ	k
lām	ل	ل	ـلـ	لـ	l
mīm	م	م	ـمـ	مـ	m
nūn	ن	ن	ـنـ	نـ	n
hā	ه	ه	ـهـ	هـ	h
waw	و	و			w
yā	ى	ـى	ـيـ	يـ	y

Even in old Arabic the feminine termination *at* was often pronounced *ah* and written with *h*. When they began to study their own grammar they rectified the existing spelling by putting the two dots of *t* over the *h* ة or ة —and this hybrid must be pronounced *t*.

In writing it is often convenient to put one consonant above another:—

بح *bḥ*; لمح *lmḥ*; لجم *ljm*; حج *ḥjj*. In a book printed in Europe this last might appear as حجج.

CONSONANTS

Twelve of the consonants form correlative pairs.

	Tip of Tongue				Back of tongue towards soft palate	Throat and larynx
	Between teeth	Touching upper teeth	Behind lower teeth (see below)	Behind upper teeth		
Breathed unsingable .	θ	t	ŧ	s	x	ħ
Voiced singable .	ð	d	đ	z	ɣ	ς

The rest, including liquids and semivowels, stand in the next table in the order of their articulation, beginning with the lips and ending with the glottis, i.e. the space between the vocal cords, which may close the glottis completely in a stop ʔ or remain apart allowing the passage of breath in *h*.

	Labial	Labio-dental	Dental	Gums	Palatal	Velar	Uvular	Glottal
Voiced .	b		ð		j			h
Breathed .		ʃ		ʃ s		k	q	ʔ (h)
Liquids and semi vowels (voiced)	m w		l	r n	y			

The six pairs :—

θ as English ' th ' in ' think '.

ð as ' th ' in ' this '.

t as ' t ' in ' eighth '.

d as ' d ' in ' width '.

ŧ voiceless, đ voiced ; counterparts of ' t ' and ' d '.

> Emphatics.—Tip of tongue behind lower teeth, blade behind upper teeth touching gums. There is a depression or hollowing of the tongue just behind this and a raising of the back of the tongue. The sides of the tongue make a sort of inverted lid for the upper jaw, overflowing the back teeth and just touching the inside of the cheeks. The back of the tongue is raised in the same way for the other two emphatics ŝ and ð.

s breathed, z voiced.

s is a strong clear sound as in ' hissing ' to be sharply differentiated from the emphatic ŝ ; the tip of the tongue is behind the upper teeth.

z is a clear buzzing sound as in whizzing.

x breathed, ɣ voiced.

x is like the ' ch ' in the Scottish ' loch ' or the German ' ach ' but more scrapy. The difficulty is not so much in the sound as in the positions in which it can occur —e.g. initially. Pronounce ' loch ' and then try to pronounce it backwards.

ɣ bears a similar relation to x as z does to s. Try to voice x, that is, make it a singable sound, put the buzz of voice into it. Make it a little further back than x ; do not roll it, thus making it a back r.

ħ breathed, ʕ voiced.

ħ differs from h, which is frequently voiced, and has a sharper friction of an entirely different resonance caused by the forced depression of the back of the tongue and the tightening of the throat, the larynx being raised at the same time. The back of the tongue is as low as when the doctor presses it down with a spoon. With a it is very like the stage whisper 'ha!' It must not be produced with scrapy friction which confuses it with **x**.

ʕ is the voiced correlative of **ħ** pronounced with more tightening of the throat and forcing up of the larynx. The feeling in the throat is suggestive of slight retching. If you pronounce English vowels with a tightened throat and squeezed larynx, producing a metallic, rather low-pitched voice, they will be near to Arabic vowels in the neighbourhood of this consonant.

The two remaining emphatics :—

ṣ is the counterpart of **s** and is made with the blade of the tongue against the teeth ridge, the tip being behind the lower teeth.

ð̣ is the counterpart of **ð**; it is interdental but the tip of the tongue points upwards to the upper lip.

The four emphatics and **q** give to the vowel 'a', when it precedes or follows them, special dark qualities like the vowel in 'not'.

q is the furthest back **k** sound you can make, with the back of the tongue closing the arches of the back of the mouth, which are laterally squeezed nearer together to make the closure easier.

ʃ as in 'ship'. In Arabic **s** and **h** can come together without producing the ʃ sound.

ʔ the glottal stop. This sound is commonly used in Cockney instead of 't' in words like 'better', 'bottle' and also in standard English when a word which begins with a vowel is strongly emphasized, ʔ absolutely ʔ awful.

r is rolled as in Scotland; never fricative as in southern England.

The other consonants need no remark.

VOWELS

Three, which occur both short and long, are recognised in writing. Doubtless there were many variations in speech but only one is mentioned here. The consonants *alif*, ' w,' and ' y ' were used to indicate the long ' a ', ' u ', and ' i '. The signs are put above or below the consonant which precedes the vowel.

NAME.	SIGN.	SOUND.	SYMBOL.
i, short	‾	as in ' sin '	*i*
long	ي ‾	as in ' yeast '	*i:*
u, short	́	much as in south English ' foot '	*u*
long	و ́	much as in ' food ' . . .	*u:*
a, short	́	as in south English ' bat ' .	*a*
long	ا ́	as in south English ' man ' (drawled)	*a:*

There are two diphthongs :

ai	ي ́	much as in south English ' fight '	*ay*
au	و ́	much as in south English ' shout '	*aw*

Near an emphatic consonant ' a ' short is like the vowel in ' not ', ' a ' long is like that in ' was ' (drawled) ; represented by *v* and *v:*; and *ay* becomes more like the sound in ' boy '. There is no English equivalent of *aw* under these circumstances ; the ' a ' component becomes *v*.

OTHER CONVENTIONAL SIGNS

Sukûn.—Every consonant, which has no vowel immediately following it, is marked by sukûn ˙ This of course does not apply when the consonant is a letter of prolongation, only indicates a long vowel, as in سُو *suː*, contrasted with سَو *saw*, or when it is written but not pronounced, as

اَلدَّارُ *addaːru*, where the 'l' is assimilated to the 'd'.

Shadda.—If the same consonant is repeated and no vowel comes between the two, it is written once and the sign shadda ّ put over it. This may be due to assimilation, as in *addaːru* above, or it may be part of the word form; thus كَسَرَ *kasara*, 'he broke,' but كَسَّرَ *kassara*, 'he smashed,' when the first syllable ends with 's' and the second begins with 's'. Apparent exceptions are due to the fact that the two consonants belong to different words as اَللَّيْـلُ *allaylu*. The first 'l' belongs to the article and the second to the noun. The first 'l' does not take sukûn because it has been assimilated to the second and is indicated by shadda.

Nunation.—The word nunation is formed from the Arabic name of the letter 'n'. In one class of nouns the final vowel, which is the case ending, is written twice to indicate the pronunciations *un*, *an*, *in* respectively. With 'u' the upper sign is usually reversed ٌ or ~ is used instead.

مَكِينَةٌ *madiːnatun*; مَكِينَةً *madiːnatan*; مَكِينَةٍ *madiːnatin*.

Hamza.—This is the glottal stop (see Introduction). The sign ء is usually written with one of the three consonants *alif, w,* or *y,* which is called its bearer. *y,* when written with hamza, always loses its dots.

Hamza always has *alif* at the beginning of a word and, after the vowel 'a', at the end.

After a long vowel it has no bearer except in the sequence *a:ʔi* when it usually has ' y '.

After sukûn it may be written over a line connecting two letters.

أَقْرَأُ *ʔaqraʔu* ;   إِبِلٌ *ʔibilun* ;   أُذُنٌ *ʔuḏunun*

كِسَاءٌ *kisa:ʔun* ;   سَاءَلَ *sa:ʔala* ;   مَسْؤُولٌ *masʔu:lun*

أَبْنَائِهِ *ʔabna:ʔihi* ;   سُؤَالٌ *suʔa:lun* ;   أَسْئِلَةٌ *ʔasʔilatun*

To find out how to write hamza.—Pronounce the word as if the hamza were not there, write the result, and add hamza. Take the word *fuʔa:dun*. Without hamza it becomes *fuwa:dun*, which is the correct way to write it,

فُوَادٌ then add hamza فُؤَادٌ .   The plural of this word is *ʔafʔidatun*; without hamza it becomes *ʔafi:datun*. This is

أَفِيدَة remove the dots from the ' y ' and add hamza,

and remove ' i ' one step to the left, أَفْئِدَة is the right spelling.

Madda.—This takes the place of hamza when *a:* follows the glottal stop. This sound group may be original or it may be derived from the group *ʔaʔ*, which to Arabs is

unpronounceable. In both cases it is written آ. So

آكَلَ *ʔa:kala* may stand for *ʔa:kala* ' he ate with ' and *ʔaʔkala* ' he fed ' (transitive).

Syllable.—Every syllable must begin with one consonant ; the glottal stop is a consonant. A syllable may consist of consonant and vowel or of consonant vowel consonant.

Liaison.—Some words should begin with two consonants. From what has been said about the syllable it is clear that this is impossible so a helping vowel is put before the first consonant when the word stands alone. This vowel is indicated by *alif* always. If such a word stands alone the helping vowel is ushered in by the glottal stop. In connected speech the helping vowel is dropped and the final vowel of the preceding word takes its place. If there is no final vowel, a short one, usually ' i ', is inserted.

In connected speech the sign ´ is written over the *alif*.

In liaison a final long vowel is shortened in pronunciation and a diphthong is resolved into its component parts.

The best manner is never to write hamza over the liaison *alif* and that is followed in this book.

The words

اِبْتِدَاءِ *ibtida:ʔi*   اِنْهِزَام *inhiza:mi*   اَلْعَدُوِّ *alʕaduwwi*

when connected, read

فِي اِبْتِدَاءِ اَنْهِزَام اَلْعَدُوِّ

fibtida:ʔinhiza:milʕaduwwi (note that *fi:* is shortened).

يَدَىْ *yaday* becomes *yadayi*

يَدَى اَلْكَلْب *yadayilkalbi*

رَمَوْا *ramaw* (*alif* is purely graphic) becomes *ramawu*

رَمَوُا اَلْعَدُوَّ *ramawulʕaduwwa*

The Arabs call this هَمْزَةُ الْوَصْل *hamzatulwasli*.

ACCENT

The accent rests on—

(1) The penultimate syllable when it is long ; i.e. has a long vowel or two consonants. *ki'ta:bun, ya'ku:nu.*

(2) On the antepenultimate when it is long and the penultimate short ; when a word has three short syllables. *'ka:tibun, 'kataba.*

(3) On the long syllable before the antepenultimate when the penultimate and the antepenultimate are both short *mu'ka:tabatun*; on the first syllable if there is no such long vowel *'katabatuhuma:.*

Note that monosyllables and the definite article which are joined in writing to the following word do not affect the accent.

wa-'kataba ; al-'madadu

NUMBERS

The figures are read from left to right and are combined as in English :—

1	2	3	4	5	6	7	8	9	10
١	٢٢	٣٢	٤٢	٥	٦	٧	٨	٩	١٠

١٧٨٩ = 1789

Letters, when used as numbers, follow the order of the Hebrew alphabet, those peculiar to Arabic coming last, they represent the units, tens, hundreds, and a thousand. They are divided into these barbarous words :—

اَبحد هوز حطى كلمن سعفص قرشت ثخذ ضظغ

Usually a line is drawn over the number.

غضعد = 1874

EXERCISE IN READING

كَانَ خَمَّارٌ يُسَافِرُ بِخَمْرٍ لَهُ وَمَعَهُ قِرْدٌ وَكَانَ يَمْزُجُ

الْخَمْرَ بِالْمَاءِ نِصْفَيْنِ وَيَبِيعُهُ بِسِعْرِ الْخَمْرِ وَالْقِرْدُ

يُشِيرُ إِلَيْهِ أَنْ لَا تَفْعَلْ فَيَضْرِبُهُ فَلَمَّا فَرَغَ مِنْ بَيْعِ

الْخَمْرِ وَأَرَادَ الرُّجُوعَ إِلَى بَلَدِهِ رَكِبَ الْبَحْرَ وَقِرْدُهُ

مَعَهُ وَخَرَجَ فِيهِ ثِيَابُهُ وَالْكِيسُ الَّذِي جَمَعَهُ مِنْ ثَمَنِ

الْخَمْرِ فَلَمَّا سَارَ فِي الْبَحْرِ اسْتَخْرَجَ الْقِرْدُ الْكِيسَ

مِنْ مَوْضِعِهِ وَرَقِيَ الدَّقَلَ وَهُوَ مَعَهُ حَتَّى صَارَ فِي

أَعْلَاهُ وَرَمَى إِلَى الْمَرْكَبِ بِدِرْهَمٍ وَإِلَى الْبَحْرِ

بِدِرْهَمٍ فَلَمْ يَزَلْ ذَلِكَ دَأْبَهُ حَتَّى قَسَمَ الدَّرَاهِمَ

نِصْفَيْنِ.

Phonetic Transcription

 kaːna xammaːrun yusaːfiru bixamrin lahu wamaʕahu
qirdun wakaːna yamzuju lxamra bilmaːi nisfayni
wayabiːʕuhu bisiʕri lxamri walqirdu yuʃiːru ʔilayhi ʔan
laː tafʕal fayadˤribuhu falammaː faraya min bayʕi lxamri
waʔaraːda rrujuːʕa ʔilaː baladihi rakiba lbaħra waqirduhu
maʕahu waxurjun fiːhi θiyaːbuhu walkiːsu llaði jamaʕahu

min θamani lxamri falamma: sa:ra fi lbaħri staxraja
lqirdu lki:sa min mawðiˁihi waraqiya ddaqʋla wahuwa
maˁahu ħatta: sʋːra fiː ʔaˁlaːhu warama: ʔila lmarkabi
bidirhamin waʔila lbaħri bidirhamin falam yazal ða:lika
daʔbahu ħatta: qʋsama ddara:hima nisfayni.

Translation

a wine merchant used to travel in wine he had and a
monkey was with him. He mixed the wine with water
half and half and sold it at the price of wine. The monkey
signed to him ; don't do that, so he beat it. When he had
finished selling the wine and wanted to go back to his
town, he rode on the sea having with him the monkey
and saddle-bags in which were his clothes and the purse
which he had collected from the price of the wine. When
he was well at sea, the monkey pulled the purse from its
place and climbed the mast, it being with him, till 'he
reached the top. He threw one dirham into the ship and
one into the sea and that continued to be his practice till
he had divided the dirhams into two halves.

LESSON I

NOUN AND ARTICLES

The distinction between a definite and an indefinite
noun is fundamental.

The indefinite article *n* is put at the end of the noun,
is not expressed by a consonant, but is indicated in one
class of nouns by nunation. For inflection the noun falls
into four classes but, as two of them are indeclinable,
they cannot be called declensions. This lesson deals with
one class only.

نَهْر *nahrun* a river ; مَلِك *malikun* a king

The *u* is the nominative inflection.

One way of making a noun definite is to give it **the**

definite article اَلْ *al*, which is written in front of the noun

and joined to it. The vowel of the article is only a helping
vowel, liaison, so in connected speech it is replaced by the
final vowel of the preceding word. If the noun begins with
a dental, sibilant, *r, l,* or *n*

ن ل ظ ط ض ص ش س ز ر ذ د ث ت

that letter assimilates to itself the *l* of the article in pronunciation though the *l* is still written. The assimilating
consonant takes *shadda*. No noun can be both definite
and indefinite at the same time, so nunation must be

dropped when the definite article is present. اَلْبَيْت

albaytu the house ; اَلشَّمْس *aʃʃamsu* the sun. Arabic uses

the definite article where English does not ; abstract
nouns usually have it ; and it also indicates the class.
'Man is a reasoning animal' must be translated 'The man'.

An adjective, which qualifies a noun, follows it, agrees
with it in gender (if it is singular), in case, and in definite-
ness.

بُسْتَان كَبِير *bustaːnun kabiːrun* a big garden.

اَلْبَحْرُ الْوَاسِع *albaħrulwaːsiʕu* the spacious sea.

The verbs 'is' and 'are' are not expressed ; so 'the
man is handsome' is literally 'the man handsome'. Arabic
grammar took its technical terms from logic, so 'the man'
is subject and 'handsome' (the complement of the verb
to be, as we call it) is the predicate. The subject must be

definite, unless the sentence is negative or interrogative, and the predicate must be indefinite.

اَلرَّجُلُ حَسَنٌ   *arrajulu ħasanun* the man is handsome.

اَلْبَحْرُ وَاسِعٌ   *albaħru waːsiʕun* the sea is spacious.

Questions are asked by prefixing one of the particles

أ   *ʔa* or هَلْ   *hal* to the sentence; *ʔa* is connected with the word it precedes.

أَرَجُلٌ   *ʔarajulun* . . . is a man . . . ?

هَلِ الْبَحْرُ وَاسِعٌ   *halilbaħru waːsiʕun* is the sea spacious ?

ʔa drives out the *alif* of the definite article;

أَلرَّجُلُ حَسَنٌ   *ʔarrajulu ħasanun* is the man handsome ?

Personal Pronouns

	Singular.	Dual.	Plural.
3. Masc.	هُوَ *huwa*	هُمَا *huma:*	هُمْ ـ هُمُ *hum, humu*
Fem.	هِيَ *hiya*		هُنَّ *hunna*
2. Masc.	أَنْتَ *ʔanta*	أَنْتُمَا *ʔantuma:*	أَنْتُمْ *ʔantum*
			أَنْتُمْ *ʔantumu*
Fem.	أَنْتِ *ʔanti*		أَنْتُنَّ *ʔantunna*
1. Com.	أَنَا *ʔana*.		نَحْنُ *naħnu*

Note.— أَنَا has two short syllables, in spite of the spelling. Arabic uses the second person singular. هُمُّ *humu* and أَنْتُمُّ *Pantumu* are used before liaison.

Vocabulary 1

The words in brackets are the customary plurals which are all feminine. Five of the commonest plurals are indicated by letters from the second vocabulary onwards ; they are :

أَقَال a — فُعُول b — فِعَال c — فُعَل d — أَفْعُل e

(بُيُوت) بَيْت house.	(أَنْهَار) نَهْر river, canal.
(بِحَار) بَحْر sea.	(مُلُوك) مَلِك king.
(رِجَال) رَجُل man.	(نَسَاتِين) بُسْتَان garden.
لَحْم flesh, meat.	خُبْز bread.
(قُصُور) قَصْر castle, palace.	(شَوَارِع) شَارِع street.
(أَوْلَاد) وَلَد child, boy.	(نَاس) إِنْسَان human being.
صَغِير little.	كَبِير big.
وَسِخ dirty.	نَظِيف clean.
غَنِي rich.	فَقِير poor.
قَبِيح ugly, bad.	حَسَن good, beautiful.
حَبِيب beloved, friend.	عَرِيض wide.
صَادِق truthful.	وَاسِع spacious.
قَدِيم old (of things).	لَطِيف gracious. طَيِّب good.

Exercise 1

نَهْرٌ كَبِيرٌ ـ اَلْمَلِكُ اَللَّطِيفُ ـ اَلْبَيْتُ نَظِيفٌ ـ بُسْتَانٌ
حَسَنٌ ـ خُبْزٌ طَيِّبٌ ـ اَلرَّجُلُ الْفَقِيرُ ـ إِنْسَانٌ قَبِيحٌ ـ
اَللَّحْمُ طَيِّبٌ ـ اَلشَّارِعُ عَرِيضٌ ـ أَنَا غَنِيٌّ ـ وَلَدٌ
وَسِخٌ ـ أَهُوَ حَبِيبٌ ـ قَصْرٌ قَدِيمٌ ـ هَلْ أَنْتَ صَادِقٌ.

Transcription

nahrun kabi:run — almalikullati:fu — albaytu nað:fun —
busta:nun ħasanun — xubzun tɒyyibun — arrajululfaqi:ru
— ʔinsa:nun qɒbi:ħun — allaħmu tɒyyibun — aʃʃa:riʕu
ʕari:ʤun — ʔana ɣaniyyun — waladun wasixun —
ʔahuwa ħabi:bun — qɒsrun qɒdi:mun — hal ʔanta
sɒ:diqun.

2

a small house — the house is small — a poor man — the
friend is truthful — he is ugly — I am a man — you
(masc. sing.) are gracious — the spacious garden — a wide
river — the sea is beautiful — the ugly street — the little
boy is dirty — the bread is good.

LESSON 2

GENDER

There are two genders, masculine and feminine, so gender
is not co-extensive with sex as it is in English.

The commonest feminine ending is *at*, with case ending

and nunation, which is written with the dotted h ة.

Some nouns and all the adjectives, which have so far been mentioned, form a feminine in this way; though most feminine nouns have no masculine correlative.

كَبِيرَة *kabi:ratun* big ;   مَلِكَة *malikatun* queen ;

جَارِيَة *ja:riyatun* girl ;   قِطْعَة *qitˤatun* piece.

Two nouns have *t* as feminine ending :—

بِنْتٌ *bintun* daughter, girl ;   أُخْتٌ *ʔuxtun* sister.

Names of males are masculine even when they have the feminine ending. Otherwise all nouns with the feminine ending are feminine. Names of females, those of towns and countries and some collectives are feminine.

Some feminine nouns have no feminine ending : names of females :—

أُمّ *ʔummun* mother ;   عَرُوس *ʕaru:sun* bride ;

عَجُوز *ʕaju:zun* old woman ;   أَتَان *ʔata:nun* she ass.

Names of towns and countries :—

مِصْر *misru*, Egypt, Cairo (no nunation) ;

الشَّام *aʃʃa:mu*, Syria, Damascus.

Parts of the body which occur in pairs :—

يَدٌ *yadun* hand ;   عَيْنٌ *ʕaynun* eye ;

قَدَم *qʊdamun* foot, leg ; رِجْل *rijlun* foot, leg ;

سَاق *saːqun* leg.

Some everyday words though no reason can be given :—

أَرْض *Parðun* earth ; شَمْس *ʃamsun* sun ;

خَمْر *xamrun* wine ; نَار *naːrun* fire ;

دَار *daːrun* house ; نَفْس *nafsun* soul ;

رِيح *riːħun* wind ; سُوق *suːqun* street of shops, bazaar.

The feminine ending has other uses. From collective nouns it forms a noun of unity, a singular :—

شَجَر *ʃajarun* trees ; شَجَرَة *ʃajaratun* a tree.

It forms emphatic nouns :—

عَلَّام *ʕallaːmun* a learned man ; عَلَّامَة *ʕallaːmatun* very learned ; perhaps under this head comes خَلِيفَة *xaliːfatun* deputy, caliph. (Other feminine forms are given in Lesson 10).

Vocative.—If the noun has the article, it is put in the nominative and أَيُّهَا *Payyuhaː* is prefixed ; أَيُّهَا الْمَلِكُ *Payyuhalmaliku* O king ; before a feminine noun أَيَّتُهَا

Payyatuha: is used. If the noun stands alone, it is put in the nominative without nunation and the exclamatory particle is يَا *ya:*.

يَا وَلَدُ *ya: waladu* O boy ; يَا جَارِيَةُ *ya: ja:riyatu* O girl. Proper names, which have the definitive article, lose it after *ya:* ; يَا شَامُ *ya: ʃa:mu* O Syria.

Vocabulary 2

(جَوَارٍ) جَارِيَةٌ [1] girl.	(أَخَوَاتٌ) أُخْتٌ sister.
مَدِينَةٌ (d) town.	(آدُرٌ) دَارٌ house.
(أُمَّهَاتٌ) أُمٌّ mother.	(عَجَائِزُ) عَجُوزٌ old woman.
رِيحٌ (c) wind.	سُوقٌ (a) market.
(جَزَائِرُ) جَزِيرَةٌ island.	(نِيرَانٌ) نَارٌ fire.
(أَرَضُونَ) أَرْضٌ earth, land.	شَمْسٌ sun.
شَجَرٌ (a) trees.	شَيْخٌ (b) old man, chief.
جَدِيدٌ new.	شَدِيدٌ strong, violent.
بَعِيدٌ far, distant.	قَرِيبٌ near.
حَارٌّ hot.	عَزِيزٌ mighty.
طَوِيلٌ long, tall.	نَفْسٌ (b) soul.
(بَنَاتٌ) بِنْتٌ daughter.	عَيْنٌ (b) eye.
رِجْلٌ (e) foot, leg.	(سِيقَانٌ) سَاقٌ leg, stalk.
قَدَمٌ (a) foot, leg.	(خُلَفَاءُ) خَلِيفَةٌ deputy, caliph.

[1] Plurals of this form are explained in Lesson 26; till then there is no need to use them.

Exercise 3

جَارِيَةٌ صَغِيرَةٌ ــ أُخْتٌ كَبِيرَةٌ ــ اَلْمَدِينَةُ نَظِيفَةٌ ــ اَلْأُمُّ

حَسَنَةٌ ــ دَارٌ جَدِيدَةٌ ــ اَلرِّيحُ شَدِيدَةٌ ــ عَجُوزٌ صَادِقَةٌ ــ

اَلشَّيْخُ الطَّوِيلُ ــ اَلسُّوقُ بَعِيدَةٌ ــ اَلشَّجَرَةُ صَغِيرَةٌ ــ

جَزِيرَةٌ وَاسِعَةٌ ــ هَلِ الْبِنْتُ حَبِيبَةٌ ــ اَلشَّمْسُ حَارَّةٌ ــ

يَا وَلَدُ ــ أَيَّتُهَا الْمَلِكَةُ الْعَزِيزَةُ ــ أَرْضٌ قَرِيبَةٌ ــ

أَأَنْتِ غَنِيَّةٌ .

Transcription

ja:riyatun ꜱɒɣi:ratun — ?uxtun kabi:ratun — almadi:natu
naθi:fatun — al?ummu ħasanatun — da:run jadi:datun —
arri:ħu ʃadi:datun — ʕaju:zun ꜱɒ:diqɒtun — aʃʃayxutᴛɒ-
wi:lu — aꜱꜱu:qu baʕi:datun — aʃʃajaratu ꜱɒɣi:ratun —
jazi:ratun wa:siʕatun — halilbintu ħabi:batun — aʃʃamsu
ħa:rratun — ya: waladu — ?ayyatuhalmalikatulʕazi:zatu
— ?arđun qɒri:batun — ?a?anti ɣaniyyatun.

4

the hot sun — the island is distant — a tall mother —
the big (elder) sister — the old woman is kind — the fire
is hot — the powerful chief — the house is new — the
ancient palace — is she poor ? — you (fem. sing.) are kind.

LESSON 3

CASE

There are three cases; the familiar names, nominative, accusative, and genitive fit them well though the use of the accusative and genitive is wider than in English. Nouns of both genders which have nunation, have three case endings: u nominative, a accusative, and i genitive. Indefinite masculine nouns add *alif* to the accusative unless the word ends in *?* preceded by *a:*. This *alif* is a letter of prolongation and is due to the fact that in Mecca a final *an* was often pronounced *a:*.

	Nominative.	Accusative.	Genitive.
moon	قَمَرٌ	قَمَرًا	قَمَرٍ
	qʊmarun	*qʊmaran*	*qʊmarin*
	ٱلْقَمَرُ	ٱلْقَمَرَ	ٱلْقَمَرِ
	alqʊmaru	*alqʊmara*	*alqʊmari*
clothing	كِسَاءٌ	كِسَاءَ	كِسَاءٍ
	kisa:ʔun	*kisa:ʔan*	*kisa:ʔin*
garden (now paradise)	جَنَّةٌ	جَنَّةً	جَنَّةٍ
	jannatun	*jannatan*	*jannatin*
	ٱلْجَنَّةُ	ٱلْجَنَّةَ	ٱلْجَنَّةِ
	aljannatu	*aljannata*	*aljannati*

Construct state.—When one noun governs another in the genitive, the first is said to be in the construct state. The governing noun comes first and loses nunation:

بَيْتُ رَجُلٍ *baytu rajulin* a house of a man ;

بَيْتُ الرَّجُلِ *bayturrajuli* the house of the man.

The second noun being definitive makes the first definitive also. Most Europeans find it hard to accustom themselves to this. The first noun, being definitive by position, does not need and cannot have the definitive article.

Nothing can come between the construct and its genitive ; hence the name. An adjective agreeing with the first noun must come after the second. If the construct is definite, the adjective must be definite also ; there is only one way of making an adjective definite, giving it the definite article.

شَعْرُ الْبِنْتِ الْجَمِيلُ

ʃaʕrulbintiljami:lu the beautiful hair of the girl.

دَار الْبِنْتِ الْجَمِيلَة is ambiguous if the vowels are not

added as the feminine adjective may refer to either noun.

A sentence like ' a house of the man ' cannot be translated directly into Arabic, you must go a roundabout way :

بَيْتٌ لِلرَّجُلِ *baytun lirrajuli* a house (belonging) to the man. (Another mode of expression in Lesson 19.)

Emphasis.—' The house is big ' may be translated in two ways :—

اَلْبَيْتُ كَبِيرٌ *albaytu kabi:run.*

إِنَّ الْبَيْتَ كَبِيرٌ *ʔinnalbayta kabi:run.*

To an Arab the second is slightly more emphatic than the first but it is a degree of emphasis which cannot be

represented in English. *Pinna* puts the subject into the
accusative but it is best left untranslated. A degree of
emphasis, which can be translated, is got by using *Pinna*
with the particle *la*. This *l* also appears in the definite
article and in some demonstrative pronouns.

إِنَّ ٱلْبَيْتَ لَكَبِيرٌ

Pinnalbayta lakabi:run the house is indeed big.

This *la* must not be confused with the negative *la:*.
Prepositions. (For a full list see Lesson 36.)
All prepositions, with one partial exception, govern the
genitive. Those, which consist of one consonant, are
written as one word with the word they govern.

بِ *bi* by, with ; لِ *li* to, for ; كَ *ka* as, like.

After *li* the *alif* of the definite article is omitted and,
if the noun begins with *l*, the *l* of the article also.

بِالْيَدِ *bilyadi* by the hand ; بِالْلَّيْلِ *billayli* by (the) night ;

لِمَالِكٍ *limalikin* to a king ; لِلْمَلِكِ *lilmaliki* to the king ;

لِلَّبَنِ *lillabani* for the milk.

There is no verb 'have'; the idea is expressed by a preposition. 'The man has a book' can be said in three ways
with shades of meaning :—

لِلرَّجُلِ كِتَابٌ *lirrajuli kita:bun* (the fact of possession).

عِنْدَ ٱلرَّجُلِ كِتَاب *Sindarrajuli kita:bun*   ⎱ he has it
مَعَ ٱلرَّجُلِ كِتَاب *maSarrajuli kita:bun*   ⎰ on him.

The subject can be indefinite because the predicate is a prepositional phrase.

God. إِلَاهٌ or إِلَاه *ɂila:hun god* (pl. آلِهَةٌ *ɂa:lihatun*)

اَلْإِلَاهُ *alɂila:hu* is sometimes used for *God* but usually

it is shortened to اَللَّهُ *alla:hu*. Note the spellings بِاللَّه

billa:hi and لِلَّه *lilla:hi*.

مِنْ *min of, from* becomes مِنَ *mina* before the definite

article and مِنِ *mini* in any other liaison.

With مِنْ *min* and عَنْ *ʕan*, the *n* is assimilated to the

m of a following monosyllable ; مِمَّنْ *mimman, from*

whom ; مِمَّا *mimma:, from what.* After لِ *li,* مَا *ma:* is

often shortened ; لِمَا — لِمَ *lima or lima:, for what, why.*

Vocabulary 3

بَابٌ (a) door, chapter.	حَفْظٌ keeping (abstract noun).
(أَكْسِيَةٌ) كِسَاءٌ clothing, covering.	عِزٌّ might.
(مَفَاتِيحُ) مِفْتَاحٌ key.	(حِكَمٌ) حِكْمَةٌ wisdom, wise
(أَلْسِنَةٌ) لِسَانٌ tongue.	saying.
(رُفَقَاءُ) رَفِيقٌ companion.	(تُجَّارٌ) تَاجِرٌ merchant.

طَرِيق (d) road.

سَلَامَة safety.

رَأْس (b) head.

مَخَافَة fear.

صَحْن (b) courtyard, dish.

شَعْر (a) hair.

جَمِيل beautiful.

ثَقِيل heavy.

شَرِيف (a) noble.

لَا no, not.

كِتَاب (d) book.

ظِلّ (c) shade, shadow.

خَفِيف light.

كَرِيم noble, generous.

مَفْتُوح opened, open.

شُبَّاك (شَبَابِيك) window.

قُفْل (a) lock.

وَجْه (b) face.

جَار (جِيرَان) protected alien, neighbour.

Exercise 5

بَابُ بَيْتٍ ـ بَابُ الْبُسْتَانِ ـ شُبَّاكُ الدَّارِ مَفْتُوحٌ ـ
إِنَّ الْأَرْضَ وَاسِعَةٌ ـ الْقَبِيلَةُ غَنِيَّةٌ ـ هَلِ الْكِتَابُ
لِبِنْتِ الشَّيْخِ ـ لَا هُوَ لِأُخْتِ التَّاجِرِ ـ شَارِعُ
الْمَدِينَةِ عَرِيضٌ ـ صَحْنُ بَيْتِ الْمَلِكِ الْكَبِيرِ ـ إِنَّ
مِفْتَاحَ الْبَابِ فِى الْقُفْلِ ـ إِنَّ كِسَاءَ الشَّيْخِ
نَظِيفٌ ـ إِنَّ وَجْهَ الْبِنْتِ حَسَنٌ ـ سَلَامَةُ الْإِنْسَانِ
فِى حِفْظِ اللِّسَانِ ـ الْجَارُ قَبْلَ الدَّارِ وَالرَّفِيقِ

قَبْلَ الطَّرِيقِ ـ اَلْعِزُّ لِلَّهِ ـ رَأْسُ الْحِكْمَةِ مَخَافَةُ

اَللَّهِ ـ اَلْخَلِيفَةُ ظِلُّ اللَّهِ عَلَى الْأَرْضِ.

Transcription

ba:bu baytin — ba:bulbusta:ni — ʃubba:kudda:ri maftu:-
ħun — ʔinnalʔarða wa:siyatun — alqɒbi:latu yaniyyatun —
halilkita:bu libintiʃʃayxi — la: huwa liʔuxtitta:jiri —
ʃa:riʕulmadi:nati ʕari:ɖun — sɒħnu baytilmalikilkabi:ru
— ʔinna mifta:ħalba:bi filqufli — ʔinna kisa:ʔaʃʃayxi
nɒði:fun — ʔinna wajhalbinti ħasanun — sala:mtulʔinsa:ni
fi: ħafðillisa:ni — alja:ru qɒbladda:ri warrafi:qu qɒblattɒ-
ri:qi — alʕizzu lilla:hi — raʔsulħikmati maxa:fatulla:hi —
alxali:fatu ðillulla:hi ʕalalʔarði.

6

a royal garden — the strength of a man is in the tongue
— the beautiful face of the beautiful girl — the key of the
door is heavy — the little house is in the shade of a big
tree — a (the) good companion is the beginning of safety
on the road — the merchant is the strength of the land —
the little book is indeed light — the girl has light clothing
and the old woman heavy clothing.

LESSON 4

NUMBER

There are three numbers, singular, dual, and plural.
The dual is formed by cutting off the case ending from

the singular and adding أَنْ a:ni for the nominative and

ـَيْنِ ayni for the accusative or genitive. There is no

nunation. When a noun has only one form for these two cases, it is convenient to call it the oblique case.

عَيْنٌ ʕaynun eye, spring (of water); عَيْنَانِ ʕayna:ni;

عَيْنَيْنِ ʕaynayni.

قِطْعَةٌ qitʕatun piece; قِطْعَتَانِ qitʕata:ni; قِطْعَتَيْنِ qitʕatayni.

The construct state is made by cutting off the ni :—

عَيْنَا الْبِنْتِ ʕaynalbinti the (two) eyes of the girl. The a: is shortened in liaison.

عَيْنَى الْبِنْتِ ʕaynayilbinti. The diphthong resolved in liaison.

Plural.—There are two ways of forming the plural, the sound or external and the broken or internal.

The external plural of nouns with the feminine ending is made by lengthening the a before the t which is then written as t, not as h with dots.

خَادِمَةٌ xa:dimatun maid servant; خَادِمَاتٌ xa:dima:- tun, maids. This plural has two cases, u for the nominative, i for the oblique. It takes nunation.

Masculine plural.—Most participles and a few nouns make an external plural by cutting off the case ending and adding u:na for the nominative and i:na for the oblique case. There is no nunation. Note the alternation of vowels in the dual and the masculine plural.

خَادِمٌ xa:dimun servant; خَادِمُونَ xa:dimu:na;

خَادِمِينَ xa:dimi:na.

The construct state is formed by cutting off *na*.

خَادِمِى الطبيب   *xa:dimuttvbi:bi*   خَادِمُو اُلطَّيِب

xa:dimittvbi:bi the servants of the doctor. The long vowels are shortened in liaison. Adjectives agreeing with the external masculine plural usually take the external plural themselves.

Broken plural.—Nearly all masculine and many feminine nouns use the broken plural. This is made by a change in the word. No rules can be given for the simplest nouns and the plural must be learnt with the singular, it is all memory work. Many nouns have more than one plural; as a rule one form is the favourite or one form may be allotted to a special meaning.

عَبْدٌ *ςabdun* slave, servant ; عَبِيدٌ *ςabi:dun* slaves ;

عِبَادٌ *ςiba:dun* slaves of God, worshippers, men.

All. There is no adjective meaning *all* which has to be expressed by كُلٌّ *kullun*, totality. Of course, this governs the genitive.

كُلُّ رَجُلٍ *kullu rajulin* every man ;

كُلُّ اُلرِّجَالِ *kullurrija:li* all the men.

As the accusative is the adverbial case so :—

كُلَّ يَوْمٍ *kulla yawmin*, every day, daily ;

كُلَّ اُلْيَوْمِ *kullalyawmi* all day long.

وَ *wa* 'and' is written with the following word. It was

enough for the Arabs to join two contrasting phrases by
' and ' where we must use ' but '.

Vocabulary 4

قِطْعَة (قِطَعٌ) piece.	صَاحِبٌ (a) companion, master, owner.
خَادِمٌ (خُدَّامٌ) servant.	طَبِيبٌ (أَطِبَّاءُ) physician.
نَجَّارٌ carpenter.	خَبَّازٌ baker.
فَرَّاشٌ domestic servant.	طَبَّاخٌ cook.
خَيَّاطَة sempstress.	خَيَّاطٌ tailor.
حُجْرَة (حُجَرٌ) room.	أُذُنٌ (a) ear.
فَرَسٌ (a) horse, mare.	بَقَّالٌ greengrocer.
لَاعِبٌ playing (participle).	حِمَارٌ (حَمِيرٌ) donkey.
جَالِسٌ sitting.	مَشْغُولٌ busy, busied.
مُظِلٌّ giving shade, shady.	قَصِيرٌ short.
نَعَمْ yes.	غَنَمٌ sheep (collective).
كَثِيرٌ many, much.	قَلِيلٌ few.

Exercise 7

هَلِ الْخَبَّازُ غَنِيٌّ ـ لَا هُوَ فَقِيرٌ ـ اَلْخَبَّازُونَ
وَالنَّجَّارُونَ مَشْغُولُونَ ـ إِنَّ فِي الْمَدِينَةِ خَبَّازِينَ
وَنَجَّارِينَ كَثِيرِينَ ـ اَلْعَيْنَانِ وَالْأُذَنَانِ فِي الرَّأْسِ ـ
اَلْوَلَدَانِ لَاعِبَانِ ـ بِنْتَانِ لَاعِبَتَانِ ـ يَدَا الْوَلَدِ وَسَخْتَانِ ـ

اَلشَّيْخُ وَالْعَجُوزُ جَالِسَانِ عِنْدَ شَجَرَةٍ قَصِيرَةٍ وَمِظَلَّةٍ ـ

فَرَسَانِ وَحِمَارَانِ ـ إِنَّ أُخْتِي التَّاجِرِ فِي الْحُجْرَةِ

الصَّغِيرَةِ ـ هَلْ أَنْتُمَا صَادِقَانِ ـ نَعَمْ نَحْنُ صَادِقَانِ ـ

إِنَّ الْغَنَمَ الْقَلِيلَةَ لِصَاحِبِ الْبَيْتِ الصَّغِيرِ . .

Transcription

halilxabbaːzu ɣaniyyun — laː huwa faqiːrun — alxabbaː-
zuːna wannajjaːruːna maʃyuːluːna — ʔinna filmadiː-
nati xabbaːziːna wannajjaːriːna kaθiːriːna — alʕaynaːni
walʔuðunaːni firraʔsi — alwaladaːni laːʕibaːni — bintaːni
laːʕibataːni — yadalwaladi wasixataːni — aʃʃayxu
walʕajuːzu jaːlisaːni ʕinda ʃajaratin qɒsiːratin wamu-
ðillatin — farasaːni waħimaːraːni — ʔinna ʔuxtayittaːjiri
filħujratissɒɣiːrati — hal ʔantumaː sɒːdiqɒni — naʕam
naħnu sɒːdiqɒni — ʕinnalɣanamalqɒliːlata lisɒːhibilbaytis-
sɒɣiːri.

8

the two doors of the house are open — he is the owner
of two horses — she is the owner of a house and a garden
in the town — the donkey is the poor man's horse — there
are two doctors in the town — each room in the house has
two windows — are you domestic servants ? — no, we are
cooks — two pieces of meat and much bread are in the
house — the garden belongs to two friends of the king —
they are busy sempstresses.

LESSON 5

BROKEN PLURAL

The commonest forms for the plural of short nouns are :—

أَفْعَالٌ — فُعُولٌ — فِعَالٌ — فُعْلٌ — أَفْعُلٌ — examples

have been given in the vocabularies to earlier lessons.

For some forms of the plural rules can be given.

أَفْعِلَاءُ : فَعِيلٌ is a plural of صَدِيقٌ — أَصْدِقَاءُ :

نَبِيٌّ prophet أَنْبِيَاءُ : غَنِيٌّ — أَغْنِيَاءُ .

فُعَلَاءُ is plural of فَعِيلٌ when it has become a noun:

أَمِيرٌ prince, commander أُمَرَاءُ : شَرِيكٌ partner شُرَكَاءُ .

أَفْعِلَةٌ is plural of nouns with three consonants and a

long vowel in the second syllable : جَنَاحٌ wing أَجْنِحَةٌ :

طَعَامٌ food أَطْعِمَةٌ — رَغِيفٌ loaf of bread أَرْغِفَةٌ —

عَمُودٌ pillar أَعْمِدَةٌ .

مَفَاعِلُ is plural of مَفْعِلٌ or مَفْعَلَةٌ whatever the

vowels may be :—

مَكْتَبٌ school, office, library مَدْرَسَةٌ — مَكَاتِبُ

C

مِنْجَلٌ – مَسَاجِدُ مَسْجِدٌ mosque – مَدَارِسُ school

sickle مَنَاجِلُ . أَقْرَبُ relative أَقَارِبُ .

مَفَاعِيلُ is plural of nouns with four consonants, two syllables and a long vowel in the second whether they have the feminine ending or not. مِفْتَاحٌ key مَفَاتِيحُ –

– مَمْلُوكٌ slave مَمَالِيكُ – صُنْدُوقٌ box صَنَادِيقُ

تَصْوِيرٌ picture تَصَاوِيرُ .

فَاعِلٌ is plural of فَاعِلَةٌ and sometimes of فَوَاعِلُ

فَاكِهَةٌ fruit (considered as food) فَوَاكِهُ – صَاحِبَةٌ

companion فَارِسٌ rider فَوَارِسُ – صَوَاحِبُ .

فَعَائِلُ is plural of feminine nouns with three consonants and a long vowel in the second syllable.

رِسَالَةٌ letter رَسَائِلُ – فَضِيلَةٌ virtue فَضَائِلُ –

رَذِيلَةٌ vice رَذَائِلُ .

فِعَلٌ is plural of فِعْلَةٌ .

قِطْعَةٌ piece قِطَعٌ – سِيرَةٌ manner of walking, character سِيَرٌ.

فُعَلٌ is plural of فُعْلَةٌ.

تُحَفٌ gift تُحْفَةٌ – رُكَبٌ knee رُكْبَةٌ.

All broken plurals are grammatically collective nouns in the feminine singular; consequently they may be construed with feminine singular adjectives.

نِسَاءٌ حَسَنَةٌ or نِسَاءٌ حَسَنَاتٌ fair women

رِجَالٌ كَبِيرَةٌ – كَبِيرُونَ – كِبَارٌ important men

(كِبَارٌ) is a broken plural of كَبِيرٌ generally used of persons.)

Second declension.—Several of the broken plurals end in *u* without nunation. These and similar nouns form the second declension which has two case endings, *u* for the nominative and *a* for the oblique, when they are indefinite. When definite, they have the three terminations of the first declension.

Nominative.	Accusative.	Genitive.
مَدَارِسُ		مَدَارِسَ
اَلْمَدَارِسُ	اَلْمَدَارِسَ	اَلْمَدَارِسِ

(The second declension has *a* in the oblique case while the sound feminine plural has *i*.)

All proper nouns, which end in ة, belong to the second declension.

Nouns which end in a:, whether written with *alif* or *y*, are indeclinable.

شكْوَى complaint ; دُنْيَا world.

The *a:* in these words is a feminine ending which is spelt with *y*, unless the third radical is *y* when *alif* is used for variety. The same ending occurs in the ' elative adjective '.

Vocabulary 5

مَطْبَخٌ kitchen.	قَلْبٌ (b) heart.
(وَرَثَةٌ) وَارِثٌ heir.	(عُلَمَاءُ) عَالِمٌ learned man.
(حُرَّاسٌ) حَارِسٌ a guard, watch-ful.	(عَقَارِبُ) عَقْرَبٌ scorpion.
(دَكَاكِينُ) دُكَّانٌ shop.	كَلْبٌ (c) dog.
عَامٌّ general.	فَلَّاحٌ peasant.
(عَوَامٌّ) عَامَّةٌ the common herd.	خَاصٌّ special.
حِنْطَةٌ wheat.	(خَوَاصٌّ) خَاصَّةٌ the upper ten.
شَعِيرٌ barley.	قَمْحٌ wheat (ripe).
صَدْرٌ (b) breast, chest.	ذُرَةٌ millet, maize.
(أَصَابِعُ) إِصْبَعٌ finger.	كَتِفٌ (a) shoulder.
(مَرَافِقُ) مِرْفَقٌ elbow.	(أَبَاهِيمُ) إِبْهَامٌ thumb.
عُنُقٌ (a) neck.	ظُفْرٌ (a) finger nail.
	بَارِدٌ cold.

Exercise 9

اَلْأَقَارِبُ عَقَارِبُ ـ اَلْعُلَمَاءُ وَرَثَةُ اَلْأَنْبِيَاءِ ـ لِلنَّجَّارِ

شُرَكَاءُ ـ اَلْأَطْعِمَةُ عِنْدَ اَلطَّبَّاخِ فِي اَلْمَطْبَخِ ـ

شَبَابِيكُ اَلْبَيْتِ اَلْكَبِيرِ كَثِيرَةٌ ـ إِنَّ فِي اَلْمَدِينَةِ مَدَارِسَ

كَثِيرَةً ـ هَلْ مَفَاتِيحُ اَلْمَدِينَةِ عِنْدَ اَلْحَارِسِ ـ لَا هِيَ

عِنْدَ اَلْأَمِيرِ ـ اَلشُّيُوخُ وَالْعَجَائِزُ جَالِسُونَ [جَالِسَةٌ]

فِي ظِلِّ اَلْأَشْجَارِ ـ اَلْكِلَابُ كَثِيرَةٌ عِنْدَ قَبِيلَةٍ مِنْ

قَبَائِلِ اَلْعَرَبِ ـ إِنَّ رَذَائِلَ اَلْخَاصَّةِ فَضَائِلُ اَلْعَامَّةِ ـ

إِنَّ اَلْأَرْغِفَةَ مِنْ دَكَاكِينِ اَلْخَبَّازِينَ ـ اَلْأَشْرَافُ

شُرَكَاءُ اَلْأُمَرَاءِ فِي حَفْظِ اَلْمُدُنِ ـ دَكَاكِينُ

اَلْبَقَّالِينَ فِي سُوقٍ خَاصَّةٍ .

Transcription

alʔaqʋːribu ʕaqʋːribu — alʕulamaːʔu waraθatulʔanbiyaːʔi —
linnajjaːri ʃurakaːʔu — alʔatʕimatu ʕindattʋbbaːxi filmʋt-
baxi — ʃubaːbiːkulbaytilkabiːri kaθiːratun — ʔinna
filmadiːnati madaːrisa kaθiːratan — hal mafaːtiːhulmadiːnati
ʕindalhaːrisi — laː hiya ʕindalʔamiːri —
aʃʃuyuːxu walʕajaːʔizu jaːlisuːna [jaːlisatun] fiː ðillilʔaʃ-
ʃjaːri — alkilaːbu kaθiːratun ʕinda qʋbiːlatin min qʋbaːʔilil-
ʕarabi — ʔinna raðaːʔilalxaːsʋʋti fʋdʋʔilulʕaːmmati —

ʔinnalʔarɣifata min dakaːkiːnilxabbaːziːna — alʔaʃraːfu
ʃurakaːʔulʔumaraːʔi fiː ħafðilmuduni — dakaːkiːnulbaqqnː-
liːna fiː suːqin xaːssptin.

10

the farmers and merchants are the pillars of the land —
the boy's fingers are dirty — the slaves are servants (of
God) — wheat is the food of the nobles and barley the
food of the poor — the owners of fine clothing are in
king's palaces — Syrian fruits are good — the children
of the nobles are in special schools — the girl's nails are
clean but (and) the boy's nails are dirty — dogs are the
watchmen of the Arabs — the winds on the islands are
cold — the hearts of men are between the fingers of God.

LESSON 6
PERSONAL PRONOUNS

The independent personal pronoun can be used only in
the nominative case. When a pronoun is in an oblique
case, it is expressed by a suffix added to a verb, noun, or
particle. The same suffixes are used for both the accusative
and genitive except in the first person singular.

	Singular.	Dual.	Plural.
third masc.	هُ hu		هُمْ hum
third fem.	هَا haː	هُمَا humaː	هُنَّ hunna
second masc.	كَ ka		كُمْ kum
second fem.	كِ ki	كُمَا kumaː	كُنَّ kunna
first	ي or ـِي ya, iː		نَا naː

As direct object appended to a verb the first person
singular is niː.

The suffixes are very like the independent pronoun but with *k* instead of *t* in the second person.

After *i* and *ay* the *u* of the third person becomes *i* by assimilation.

Before liaison -*hum* and -*kum* become -*humu:* and -*kumu:*.

For the first person singular *ya* is used after *i:*, *a:*, and *ay:*; everywhere else *i:* is used.

With nouns the suffixes are added to the construct state; that means that nunation is dropped and, of course, the *alif* of the masculine accusative. The *ni* of the dual and the *na* of the sound masculine plural are also dropped.

The *i:* of the first singular swallows up the case ending.

These suffixes make the noun definite so an adjective agreeing with it must be also definite. An adjective is defined by giving it the definite article.

قَدَمِي *qvdami:* my foot (all cases) كَلْبُهُ *kalbuhu* his dog (nom.).

جَارِهِ *ja:rihi* his neighbour (gen.) وَلَدَهُ *waladahu* his son (acc.).

عَيْنَايَ *Sayna:ya* my two eyes (nom.) أُذُنَىَّ *Puðunayya* my two ears (oblique).

خَادِمِىَّ *xa:dimiyya* my servants (all cases; the *u:* of the nominative is assimilated to the *y* of the suffix).

مَدْرَسَةُ مَدِينَتِهِ الْجَدِيدَةُ The new school of (in) his town.

يَدِهِ الْقَوِيَّةِ his strong hand (gen.).

فَضَائِلِكُمُ الشَّرِيفَةَ your noble virtues (acc.).

These suffixes are added to prepositions. Note the following :—

me	thee	him	them
لِ لِي	لَكَ	لَهُ	لَهُمْ
بِ بِي	بِكَ	بِهِ	بِهِمْ
مِنْ مِنِّي	مِنْكَ	مِنْهُ	مِنْهُمْ
عَنْ عَنِّي	عَنْكَ	عَنْهُ	عَنْهُمْ
إِلَى إِلَيَّ	إِلَيْكَ	إِلَيْهِ	إِلَيْهِمْ

Note that before all suffixes except the first singular

لِ becomes لَ.

Sometimes the object suffix cannot be appended to a verb so, as it cannot stand alone, it is added to *ʔiyya:* which has no meaning but serves as a base for the suffix.

إِيَّاهُنَّ — إِيَّايَ — إِيَّاكَ — إِيَّاهُ

The suffixes are also added to إِنَّ and particles like it.

إِنَّا or إِنَّنَا — إِنِّي or إِنَّنِي but — إِنَّكُمْ — إِنَّهُ.

كَ as, like does not take suffixes ; the construct of the noun مِثْلٌ *miθlun* ' likeness ' is used instead, or the compound كَمِثْلِ *kamiθli*.

لَهَا أَجْنِحَةٌ مِثْلُ ٱلْخُفَّاشِ .they have wings like the bat.

(The feminine pronoun in *laha*: refers to a broken plural.)

Arabic is fond of bringing a word or phrase to the front and referring to it by a pronoun in the actual sentence. ' Zaid's native land is Egypt ' can be translated literally :—

. وَطَنُ زَيْدٍ مِصْرُ

It is quite as likely to be :—

زَيْدٌ وَطَنُهُ مِصْرُ

Zaid, his native land is Egypt.

مِصْرُ هِيَ وَطَنُ زَيْدٍ

Egypt, it is Zaid's native land.

وَطَنُ زَيْدٍ هُوَ مِصْرُ

Zaid's native land, it is Egypt.

The difference between these modes of expression is less than it is in English.

بَعْضٌ *baʿḍun*, ' someone, some ' (sing. or pl.). Usually with a following genitive.

بَعْضُ ٱلنَّاسِ فِى ٱلْبَيْتِ وَبَعْضُهُمْ فِى ٱلْبُسْتَانِ

Some of the folk are in the house and some (of them) in the garden.

شِعْرٌ لِبَعْضِ ٱلشُّعَرَاءِ

A poem by some poet.

Vocabulary 6

وَطَنٌ (a) native land.   شِعْرٌ (a) poetry, poem.

شَاعِرٌ (شُعَرَاءُ) poet.   قَوِىٌّ strong.

وَزْنٌ (a) weight.   قُوَّةٌ (قُوَى) strength.

سَرِيعٌ swift.   عَقْلٌ (b) reason, intelligence.

شَرَفٌ honour.   هِمَّةٌ (هِمَمٌ) care, anxiety.

لَبَنٌ (a) milk.   تَجْرِبَةٌ (تَجَارِبُ) experience.

ضَعِيفٌ weak.   كَثْرَةٌ multitude, abundance.

جَمَلٌ (c) male camel.   مَعْلُومٌ known.

نَاقَةٌ (نُوقٌ) female camel.   شَاةٌ (شَاءٌ) a sheep.

مَعْزٌ goats.   بَقَرٌ cattle (sing. بَقَرَةٌ).

ثَوْرٌ (ثِيرَانٌ) bull.   خَيْلٌ horses, horsemen.

زَيْتُونٌ olives, olive trees.   جَامُوسٌ (جَوَامِيسُ) buffalo.

زَيْتٌ olive oil, oil.

Exercise 11

يَدِى نَظِيفَةٌ ـ يَدَاكُمْ نَظِيفَتَانِ ـ أَفْرَاسُهُ الْحَسَنَةُ سَرِيعَةٌ ـ
زَيْدٌ بِنْتُهُ حَسَنَةٌ ـ إِنَّ بَقَرَهُ لَهَا لَبَنٌ كَثِيرٌ ـ وَزْنِى عِنْدَهُ
كَوَزْنِ الْكَلْبِ ـ قُوَّةُ الْإِنْسَانِ فِى عَقْلِهِ وَلِسَانِهِ ـ
شُعَرَاءُ الْعَرَبِ وَفَوَارِسُهَا كَثِيرَةٌ ـ لَهُ وَلَدَانِ كَبِيرُهُمَا
قَصِيرٌ وَصَغِيرُهُمَا طَوِيلٌ ـ شَرَفُ الرَّجُلِ أَوْلَادُهُ

وَهِمَّتُهُ دَارُهُ وَجَارُهُ ـ أَشْعَارُ كُمُ اللَّطِيفَةِ مَعْلُومَةٌ بَيْنَ
النَّاسِ كُلِّهِمْ ـ لِصَاحِبِى الْفَقِيرِ حِمَارَانِ وَلِصَاحِبَتِكُنَّ
أَفْرَاسٌ كَثِيرَةٌ ـ صُنْدُوقُكَ الْكَبِيرُ خَفِيفٌ وَصُنْدُوقُهَا
الصَّغِيرُ ثَقِيلٌ .

12

my wheat and my barley are in my big chests — her two
hands are indeed clean — our native land is dear to us —
boys, have you your books ? — your gracious letters are
in the keeping of my master — my two hands. and my
two feet — your sister and her maids are sitting beside
my cook — their chiefs are masters of wisdom — the
two hands and two eyes of the old woman are weak —
the weight of a man is the weight of his intelligence —
the wisdom of the chief is from the multitude of his
experiences.

LESSON 7

VERB

The verb has no tenses. Apart from the imperative,
there are two finite forms which denote respectively completed and incompleted action. It is convenient to call
them the perfect and imperfect, some prefer perfective
and imperfective, remembering that these terms do not
mean what they mean in English. Normally the perfect
indicates a finished and therefore past act while the imperfect denotes an unfinished and therefore present or future
act. The simplest part of the verb is the third masculine
singular of the perfect which is used as the name of the

verb; we speak of the verb ' to write ', Arabs speak of
kataba ' he wrote '.

The verb is highly developed but on lines foreign to us.
By additions to the root modifications of the original
meaning are expressed. The plain root is called the simple
or first and the enlarged stems are also called by numbers.

It is convenient to call the vowel, which follows the
second radical whether in the perfect or imperfect, the
characteristic.

In this book a strong verb is one which comes from a
root having three different radicals, neither of them being
ʔ, *w*, or *y*.

Perfect of the Strong Verb, Stem I

Before reading the following notes, study carefully the
perfect in Table I.

The perfect is made by the addition of suffixes to the
root. Those of the second person are the same as
the endings of the personal pronoun, and closely resemble
the pronominal suffixes.

In the third feminine singular and dual the *t* is the
feminine *t*.

a: is the sign of the dual as in the nominative of the noun.

u: is masculine plural as in the external nominative
plural of the noun. The *alif* following this *u*: has no
meaning but is always written after a plural *u*: in the
finite verb; in some weak verbs it is useful for distinguish-
ing the plural from the singular. It is dropped before a
pronominal suffix.

In Stem I there are three classes of perfect فَعَلَ — فَعِلَ

— فَعُلَ ; the inflections are the same for all. فَعِلُ فَعُلُ are
usually intransitive. Many verbs have more than one
form.

هَلَكَ — هَلِكَ he perished.

With verbs denoting a state, the perfect must be translated by the English present. شَبِعَ ' he is satisfied (with
food) ', i.e. he has eaten enough and now does not want
to eat more.

The third person singular of the verb may contain its
own subject. شَبِعَ ' he is satisfied ', شَبِعَتْ ' she is
satisfied ' are complete sentences. You can also say,
شَبِعَ زَيْدٌ ' Zayd is satisfied ' ; شَبِعَتْ زَيْنَبُ ' Zaynab
is satisfied '. All other parts of the perfect or imperfect
contain their subjects.

One grammar gives twenty-one rules for the agreement
of subject and verb. You can write correctly if you
remember this much :—

If the verb comes before the subject, it is third masculine
singular unless the subject is a woman or women and
follows the verb immediately when it is third feminine
singular.

If the subject comes first, the verb agrees with it.

Other agreements are possible but not necessary.

دَخَلَ ٱلرَّجُلُ ٱلدَّارَ وَخَرَجَ مِنْهَا

The man went into the house and came out of it.

دَخَلَ ٱلرِّجَالُ ٱلْبَيْتَ وَخَرَجُوا مِنْهُ

The men went into the house and came out of it.

لَبِسَتِ ٱلْعَجُوزُ ثِيَابَهَا وَخَرَجَتْ مِنْ حُجْرَتِهَا

The old woman put on her clothes and came out of her room.

لَعِبَتِ الْبَنَاتُ ثُمَّ رَجَعْنَ إِلَى بُيُوتِهِنَّ [بُيُوتِهَا]

The girls played, then returned to their houses (homes).

both right
{ كَتَبَ إِلَى أُخْتِهَا زَيْنَبُ
كَتَبَتْ إِلَى أُخْتِهَا زَيْنَبُ }
Zaynab wrote to her sister.

Arabic does not distinguish between being and becoming ; thus لَبِسَ means both ' to wear clothes ' and ' to put them on '.

The addition of pronominal suffixes makes no difference to the parts of the perfect except the second masculine plural and, sometimes, the second feminine singular.

The object suffix of the first person singular is *ni*.

كَتَبَهُ he wrote it ; بَعَثَتْنِي she sent me ;

دَخَلْتُمُوهُ you (pl.) entered it ; ضَرَبُوهُ they hit him ;

لَبِسْتِيهِ you (fem. sing.) put it on, or لَبِسْتِهِ.

A nominal sentence begins with a noun.

A verbal sentence begins with a verb.

This distinction is important because some particles must be followed by a noun and others by a verb.

The verb comes first unless there is a reason for some other order. The direct object of a transitive verb is in the accusative.

Most verbs, which are transitive in English, are so in Arabic ; many, which are intransitive in English, are transitive in Arabic.

Vocabulary 7

(The vowel after a verb is that of the imperfect; the noun is the infinitive.)

ضَرَبَ i. ضَرْبٌ hit, strike.   فَهِمَ a. فَهْمٌ understand.

طَلَبَ u. طَلَبٌ seek, look for.   فَتَحَ a. فَتْحٌ open, conquer.

خَرَجَ u. خُرُوجٌ go, come out.   دَخَلَ u. دُخُولٌ enter.

ذَهَبَ a. ذَهَابٌ go away.   رَجَعَ i. رُجُوعٌ return.

كَسَرَ i. كَسْرٌ break.   نَزَلَ i. نُزُولٌ come down, dis-

بَعَثَ a. بَعْثٌ send.   mount, camp.

سَمِعَ a. سَمْعٌ hear.   شَرِبَ شُرْبٌ drink.

كَتَبَ u. كِتَابَةٌ write.   قَطَعَ a. قَطْعٌ cut, cut off.

لَعِبَ لَعِبٌ play.   حَفِظَ حَفْظٌ keep, guard.

ذَكَرَ u. ذِكْرٌ remember, mention.   صَعِدَ صُعُودٌ go up.

شَبِعَ شِبَعٌ be satisfied (with   صَرَخَ u. صُرَاخٌ cry for help.
food).   صَوْتٌ (a) voice, noise.

كَلَامٌ speech, what is said.   لَبَنٌ (a) milk.

جَبَلٌ (c) mountain.

Exercise 13

ضَرَبَ ٱلشَّيْخُ رَأْسَ ٱلْوَلَدِ ـ فَهِمَتِ ٱلْعَجُوزُ كَلَامَ
ٱلْجَارِيَةِ ـ أَطَلَبْتُمْ طَعَامًا مِنَ ٱلْمَطْبَخِ ـ طَلَبْتُ
لَحْمًا مِنْ دُكَّانِ ٱلْجَزَّارِ ـ خَرَجَ ٱلْأَوْلَادُ مِنَ ٱلْمَسْجِدِ

وَدَخَلُوا فِى ٱلْمَدْرَسَةِ ـ ذَهَبَتِ ٱلْخَيَّاطَاتُ مِنْ مَدِيَتِنَا

وَرَجَعْنَ إِلَى وَطَنِهَا [وَطَنِهِنَّ] ـ يَا بَنَاتُ هَلْ

شَرِبْتُنَّ ٱلْمَاءَ ـ بَلْ شَرِبْنَا ٱللَّبَنَ ـ هَلْ سَمِعْتُمَا أَصْوَاتَ

ٱلطَّيْرِ عَلَى ٱلشَّجَرِ ـ قَطَعْتُ ٱللَّحْمَ قِطَعًا صَغِيرَةً ـ

بَعَثْتِنِى أُمِّى إِلَيْكَ ـ نَزَلَ ٱلرِّجَالُ مِنْ رَأْسِ

ٱلْجَبَلِ وَفَتَحُوا ٱلْمَدِينَةَ .

14

have you (sing. and plu.) written the letters ? — the boy
broke the dog's leg with a stone — they heard what the
governor said and returned to their homes — the kings
entered the land and conquered it — I opened the window
and a dog came in — the guardians of the cattle have
called for help ; did you hear them ? — the doctors
amputated the man's hand and foot — did you go into the
room ? — girls, did you play with the big dog ? — evil
men cut off the ears of the cattle — you two girls, have you
sent a present to your sister ?

LESSON 8

IMPERFECT INDICATIVE

Read Table 1. The inflection of the imperfect is by
prefixes and sometimes also by suffixes. The first radical
has no vowel.

The prefixes denote the person except in the third

feminine singular and dual where the *t* is feminine. Elsewhere *ya* stands for the third person, *ta* for the second, *ʔa* for the first singular (cf. اَنَا) and *na* for the first plural (cf. نَحْنُ).

a: is again the sign of the dual; *u:* of the masculine plural (except in the first person); *-na* of the feminine plural (cf. اَنْتُنَّ هُنَّ and كَتَبْنَ).

The imperfect has three forms يَفْعُلُ — يَفْعِلُ — يَفْعَلُ but the inflections are the same for all of them.

فَعُلَ has the imperfect يَفْعُلُ (no exceptions) كَرُمَ يَكْرُمُ

فَعِلَ has the imperfect يَفْعَلُ (perhaps five exceptions)

غَضِبَ يَغْضَبُ

فَعَلَ has any of the three forms but يَفْعَلُ usually occurs when one of the second or third radicals is a guttural consonant.

The word سَوْفَ or the particle سَ is prefixed to the imperfect when it is desired to show that it refers to the future.

It suffers no change when pronominal suffixes are added to it. It often denotes an act growing out of another.

'He came out and looked' may be translated خَرَجَ يَنْظُرُ or خَرَجَ وَيَنْظُرُ .

The imperfect suggests a close connection of the two acts ;

خَرَجَ وَنَظَرَ suggests two unconnected acts, Thus the imperfect often refers to past acts, as in the preceding example, when the whole sentence refers to the past.

An imperfect linked to the main sentence by ' and ' or a pronoun or by both indicates an attendant circumstance :

دَخَلَ وَهُوَ يَضْحَكُ he came in and he was laughing.

he came in laughing—while laughing.

Interrogative Adverbs

أَيْنَ where, whither ? أَيْنَ أَنْتَ where are you ?

أَيْنَ تَذْهَبُونَ where are you going ?

مِنْ أَيْنَ whence ; مِنْ أَيْنَ خَرَجُوا (from) where did they get out ?

كَيْفَ how ? كَيْفَ حَالُكَ how is your condition ? how are you ?

كَيْفَ فَعَلَ رَبُّكَ how did your Lord act ?

These words make no change in the form of the sentence.

كَمْ how much ? how many ?

When it asks a question, it is followed by a noun in the accusative singular :—

كَمْ حُجْرَةً فِي الْبَيْتِ

how many rooms are in the house ?

كَمْ إِنْسَانًا فِى ٱلْجَمَاعَةِ

how many persons are in the company?

بِكَمْ دِينَارًا ٱلثَّوْبُ

for how many dinars is the costume?

When exclamatory, it is followed by the genitive of a singular or of a broken plural; if there is a verb, it is in the perfect.

كَمْ كَأْسٍ شَرِبْتُ — كَمْ كُؤُوسٍ

what a lot of cups I have drunk!

In both usages, كَمْ may be followed by مِنْ with a genitive:—

كَمْ مِنْ حُجْرَةٍ فِى ٱلْبَيْتِ

how many rooms in the house?

Vocabulary 8

نَظَرَ u. نَظَرْ look at, see.	جَيْشٌ (b) army.
غَضِبَ be angry. غَضَبْ	بَلَدٌ (c) town.
فَعَلَ a. فَعْل do, act.	كَأْسٌ (b) (fem.) cup.
جَمَعَ a. جَمْع collect (trans.).	دِينَارٌ (دَنَانِيرُ) dinar, gold coin
سَبَحَ a. سِبَاحَة swim.	(Latin denarius).
عَدُوٌّ (a) enemy.	ثَوْبٌ (c) piece of cloth, clothing.
شِتَاءٌ winter.	كَرُمَ كَرَامَة be noble, generous.
صَفٌّ (b) row, rank.	ضَحِكَ ضَحْك laugh.

صَنَعَ a. صُنْع make, do.	صَيْف summer.
جَلَسَ i. جُلُوس sit.	خَشَب wood.
قَدِمَ قُدُوم advance, arrive.	(بُلْدَانٌ) بِلَادٌ country.
نَبَحَ a. نَبْح bark.	جَمَاعَة party, company.
طَبْل (b) drum.	

Exercise 15

دَخَلَ ٱلْأَوْلَادُ ٱلْبَحْرَ يَسْبَحُونَ ـ بَعَثَ ٱلنَّجَّارُ إِلَى

يَطْلُبُ خَشَبًا ـ جَلَسْنَا عِنْدَ ٱلْعَيْنِ نَشْرَبُ وَنَضْحَكُ ـ

خَرَجَ أَمِيرُ ٱلْجَيْشِ يَصْعَدُ فِى ٱلْجَبَلِ وَيَنْظُرُ إِلَى

صُفُوفِ ٱلْعَدُوّ ـ ذَهَبَ ٱلرُّفَقَاءُ مِنَ ٱلشَّامِ إِلَى ٱلْقُدْسِ

يَنْزِلُونَ كُلَّ لَيْلَةٍ فِى بَلَدٍ ـ إِنَّ ٱلنَّاسَ فِى ٱلصَّيْفِ

يَخْرُجُونَ مِنَ ٱلْبِلَادِ ٱلْحَارَّةِ وَيَنْزِلُونَ فِى بِلَادٍ

قَرِيبَةٍ مِنَ ٱلْبَحْرِ ـ قَدِمَ ٱلتَّاجِرُ مَدِينَةَ ٱلْمَلِكِ يَجْمَعُ

ٱلدَّنَانِيرَ مِنْ أَصْحَابِهِ ـ سَتَسْمَعُونَ صَوْتَ ٱلطُّبُولِ.

16

God will conquer the town by (on) the hand of his prophet
— the dogs came out barking — men wear heavy clothes
in winter — you sat down and listened to the words of the
poet — do the girls make their clothes ? — the king

strikes good dinars — the children went out to play —
the army advanced beating their drums — the carpenter
made cups of wood for us to drink from — we heard the
watchmen calling for help against the enemy — I looked
at him and he was angry at what I had said.

LESSON 9

DEMONSTRATIVE PRONOUNS

The letters *ð, h, l, k* have demonstrative force, the
pronouns are compounded from them. We have already
met *l* in the definite article and the emphatic *la*.

This. The simplest pronoun is *ða:* but more common is

the compound *ha:ða:* which is usually written هذَا or هَذَا.

	Singular.	Dual.	Plural.
masc.	هذَا هذَانِ هذَينِ		هَـأُولَاءِ *ha:Pula:Pi*
fem.	هذِى . هذِهِ هتَـانِ هتَينِ		

The inflections of ذَا can be found by cutting off the
prefix *ha:*.

That.

	Singular.	Dual.	Plural.
masc.	ذَاكَ ذَانِكَ ذَينِكَ		أُولَائِكَ *Pula:Pika*
fem.	تَاكَ تِيكَ تَانِكَ تَينِكَ		

More common in the singular are ذَلِكَ (masc.) تِلْكَ
(fem.).

A demonstrative pronoun precedes its noun and, as it is by nature definite, the noun must be definite also.

هٰذَا ٱلرَّسُولُ this messenger ; هٰذِهِ ٱلدَّابَّةُ this riding beast.

But if the noun has a pronominal suffix, the demonstrative follows it.

قُوتُكَ هٰذَا this your food = this food of yours.

If the noun is indefinite you have a sentence :—

هٰذَا قَلَمٌ this is a (reed) pen ; تِلْكَ أَمَةٌ that is a slave girl.

When the predicate of a sentence is definite, the pronoun of the third person is put between the demonstrative and the predicate.

ذٰلِكَ هُوَ ٱلْحَكِيمُ

that is the doctor (literally, wise man).

هٰذِهِ هِيَ ٱلضَّيْعَةُ this is the village (estate).

أُولٰئِكَ هُمْ أَصْحَابُ ٱلْحُكُومَةِ

those are the members of the government.

In sentences like these, the demonstrative is a nominative absolute and the real sentence is the personal pronoun plus the predicate. It is a mistake to say that the personal pronoun takes the place of the copula ' is ', ' are '.

Interrogative pronouns.

مَنْ ' who ? ' مَا ' what ? ' These are indeclinable.

مَا when combined with the preposition لِ is often

abbreviated لِمَا or لِمَ.

مَنِ ٱلْوَكِيلُ who is the agent?

مَنْ صَرَخَ who shouted for help?

مَنْ ذَكَرْتَ whom did you mention?

لِمَنِ ٱلْجَوْهَرُ whose is the jewel?

لِمَ نَظَرْتَ إِلَيْهَا for what (why) did you look at her?

مَنْ and مَا are also used as indefinite pronouns and
then they behave like conditional particles.

أَيٌّ أَيَّةٌ ' which of ' is always followed by a genitive
or a pronominal suffix.

أَيُّكُمْ صَعِدَ فِي رَأْسِ ٱلْمَنَارَةِ

which of you went up to the top of the minaret?

Vocabulary 9

مَشْهُورٌ well known, famous.

حُكُومَةٌ government.

فِرَاشٌ (d) bedding, furniture
(i.e. cushions and rugs).

ضَيْعَةٌ (c) estate, village.

قُوتٌ (a) food.

أَهْلٌ (أَهَالٍ) family.

أَمَةٌ (إِمَاءٌ) slave girl.

مَنَارَةٌ (مَنَاوِرُ) lighthouse, minaret.

دَابَّةٌ (دَوَابُّ) riding animal.

قَلَمٌ (a) reed pen.

حَكِيمٌ (حُكَمَاءُ) wise man.

ذَهَبٌ gold.

مَالٌ (a) wealth, property, money.

مَخْرَجٌ (مَخَارِجُ) exit.

وَرَقٌ (a) leaf, paper.

سَيْفٌ (b) sword.

دَقِيقٌ fine, thin (lit. powdered).

يَسِيرٌ few, easy.

وَكِيلٌ (وُكَلَاءُ) agent, man of business.

جَهْلٌ ignorance.

مَدْخَلٌ (مَدَاخِلُ) entrance.

فِضَّةٌ silver.

صِرَاطٌ path.

حَدِيدٌ sharp.

عَسِيرٌ difficult.

قَبِيلَةٌ (قَبَائِلُ) tribe.

قَوْلٌ (a) speech, word, what is said.

Exercise 17

هَذَانِ الرَّجُلَانِ هُمَا شَيْخَا الْقَبِيلَةِ ـ هَذِهِ هِيَ
الْأُمَّةُ الصَّادِقَةُ ـ ضَيْعَتِي هَذِهِ مَشْهُورَةٌ فِي الْبِلَادِ ـ
تَلْعَبُ هَذِهِ الْبَنَاتُ فِي صَحْنِ الْمَدْرَسَةِ ـ نَزَلَ أُولَائِكَ
الرِّجَالُ عِنْدَ مَدْخَلِ الْبَلَدِ ـ سَمِعْتُ كَلْبُكَ ذَلِكَ
يَنْبَحُ ـ هَذَا فِرَاشُكَ ـ لِمَنْ هَذِهِ الْجَوَاهِرُ ـ هِيَ
لِوَكِيلِ صَاحِبِ الضَّيْعَةِ هَذِهِ ـ أُولَائِكَ إِمَاءٌ مِنْ أَهْلِ

اَلشَّيْخِ ـ مَنْ صَنَعَ كُؤُوسَكَ وَصُحُونَكَ تِلْكَ ـ مَنْ بَعَثْتَ إِلَى ـ مِنْ قَوْلِ مَنْ هٰذَا .

18

short poems are the well-known ones — I am angry at what you have done — that agent has much silver and gold — whose is that estate ? — the watchman went up the minaret of that mosque and raised the alarm (cried for help) — the children will write on that paper with these pens — that poor friend of yours has gone away to look for food — this agent of yours has collected much wealth — the leaves of these trees are food for sheep — escape (exit) from his ignorance is hard for the ignorant — my wealth is my sword and my books.

LESSON 10

ADJECTIVES

Some of the common adjectival forms have already been mentioned.

فَعِيلٌ is often passive in meaning : قَتِيلٌ killed.

فَاعِلٌ the active participle is often used as an adjective

or noun : عَادِلٌ just ; شَاهِدٌ a witness, martyr.

مَفْعُولٌ the passive participle is used as an adjective :

مَشْهُورٌ famous.

فَعُوْلٌ is intensive. جَاهِلٌ ignorant; جَهُوْلٌ very ignorant; كَاذِبٌ untruthful كَذُوْبٌ a great liar; كَسُوْلٌ very lazy.

فَعْلَانٌ (without nunation) the feminine is فَعْلَى: تَعْبَانٌ – تَعْبَى angry; غَضْبَانٌ – غَضْبَى tired; كَسْلَانٌ – كَسْلَى lazy.

أَفْعَلُ has two meanings.

1. It denotes colours and bodily defects:—

	Masculine.	Feminine.	Plural
black	أَسْوَدُ	سَوْدَاءُ	سُوْدٌ
white	أَبْيَضُ	بَيْضَاءُ	بِيْضٌ
red	أَحْمَرُ	حَمْرَاءُ	حُمْرٌ

The dual of the feminine changes the final *ʔ* into *w*; سَوْدَاوَانِ two black (women).

2. The elative, the 'adjective of superiority'. Arabic has only one form which does duty for both our comparative and superlative, it denotes intensity, the quality of the simple adjective raised to a higher power. The form is :—

Masculine.	Feminine.	Plural.
أَفْعَلُ	فُعْلَى	فُعْل

Roughly, when this form is indefinite, it is comparative; when it is definite, it is superlative.

When indefinite or when defined by a following genitive or pronominal suffix, the masculine is used for both genders and all numbers. When defined by the article, it is inflected for both gender and number. Of course, it is always inflected for case.

'Than' is expressed by مِنْ .

big   كَبِيرٌ أَكْبَرُ كُبْرَى كُبَرٌ

اَلرَّجُلُ أَكْبَرُ مِنْ وَلَدِهِ

the man is bigger than his son.

دَارِى أَكْبَرُ مِنْ دَارِهِ

my house (fem.) is bigger than his.

شَوَارِعُ اَلْعَاصِمَةِ أَنْظَفُ مِنْ شَوَارِعِ اَلْقَرْيَةِ

the streets of the capital are cleaner than those of the village.

هُوَ اَلْأَطْوَلُ فِى أَهْلِهِ

he is the tallest in his family.

هُوَ أَطْوَلُ اَلْجَمَاعَةِ

he is the tallest of the party.

$$\text{هِىَ أَطْوَلُهُنَّ ذِرَاعًا}$$

she is the longest of them as to arm
= she has the longest arm of any.

$$\text{هِىَ الطُّولَى ذِرَاعًا}$$

she is the longest in arm.

When the second and third radicals are the same, the forms of the elative are :—

few	قَلِيلٌ	أَقَلُّ	قُلَّى	قَلَلٌ
strong	شَدِيدٌ	أَشَدُّ	شُدَّى	شَدَدٌ

To make the elative from adjectives denoting colours or bodily defects, an adjective meaning 'strong' in the elative is used with the noun denoting the colour. The noun is in the accusative.

$$\text{هٰذَا أَشَدُّ بَيَاضًا مِنْ ذٰلِكَ}$$

this is more white than that.

There are two irregular elatives.

خَيْرٌ as a noun means any sort of 'goodness' and, as an adjective, 'better,' 'best.'

شَرٌّ as a noun means any sort of 'badness' and, as an adjective, 'worse,' 'worst.'

Feminines of the form فَعْلَاءُ belong, of course, to the second declension with only two case endings and those of the form فُعْلَى are indeclinable (Lesson 5).

Vocabulary 10

لَوْنٌ (a) colour, course (at a meal).

زَهْرٌ (b) flower.

مُصِيبَةٌ (مَصَائِبُ) calamity.

صَلَاةٌ (صَلَوَاتٌ) prayer, the Muslim form of worship.

مَوْهِبَةٌ (مَوَاهِبُ) gift.

ذِرَاعٌ (e) forearm, arm, cubit.

تَمْرَةٌ dates, sing. تَمْرٌ

خُضْرَةٌ greenness, being a dark colour.

صُفْرَةٌ yellowness.

سَوَادٌ blackness.

أَزْرَقُ blue.

أَصْفَرُ yellow, pale.

نَوْمٌ sleep.

أَسْمَرُ brown.

نَخْلٌ palm tree. sing. نَخْلَةٌ

حُمْرَةٌ redness.

زُرْقَةٌ blueness.

بَيَاضٌ whiteness.

أَخْضَرُ green, dark coloured.

أَطْرَشُ deaf.

أَخْرَسُ dumb.

أَحْدَبُ hunch-backed.

حُلْوٌ sweet.

أَعْوَرُ one-eyed.

أَعْرَجُ lame.

مُرٌّ bitter, sour.

Exercise 19

كَلْبُكَ ذَلِكَ أَبْيَضُ ـ هَذَا الْفَرَسُ أَسْوَدُ ـ الْعَبْدُ الْأَسْوَدُ فِى الْحُجْرَةِ الْحَمْرَاءِ ـ هَذِهِ الشَّجَرَةُ خَضْرَاءُ فِى الصَّيْفِ ـ عَيْنَا الْبِنْتِ زَرْقَاوَانِ ـ الصِّرَاطُ أَحَدُّ مِنَ السَّيْفِ وَأَدَقُّ مِنَ الشَّعَرِ ـ لَوْنُ هَذَا الزَّهْرِ مَا

هُوَ ـ لَهُ لَوْنَانِ أَزْرَقُ وَأَصْفَرُ ـ إِنَّ أَوْرَاقَ الشَّجَرِ سَمْرَاءُ
وَحَمْرَاءُ فِى الْخَرِيفِ ـ الذَّهَبُ أَثْقَلُ مِنَ الْفِضَّةِ ـ
الصَّلَاةُ خَيْرٌ مِنَ النَّوْمِ ـ خَيْرُ الْمَوَاهِبِ الْعَقْلُ وَشَرُّ
الْمَصَائِبِ الْجَهْلُ ـ الْأُمَّةُ الْخَرْسَاءُ هِيَ الْحُسْنَى ـ
بِنْتِى أَطْوَلُ مِنِّي.

20

he has some deaf black slave-girls — our army is smaller
in number (fewer) than that of our enemies — the sheep
in the land of the Arabs are black — the food most dear to
the Arabs is the two blacks, meat and dates — the palm
is taller than the olive — your estate is smaller than mine —
this bird has a yellow breast and red wings — my friends
sent me many presents but (and) your present is the best
— God sent his prophet to all men, the black, the white,
and the red — your youngest (smallest) sister is the kindest
of them.

LESSON 11

IRREGULAR NOUNS

Three nouns are half way to having three radicals :—

أَبٌ (آبَاءٌ) ' father' : أَخٌ (إِخْوَةٌ ـ إِخْوَانٌ)
' brother ' : حَمٌ (أَحْمَاءٌ) ' husband's father '.

There is nothing peculiar about them when they have one of the articles :—

أَبٌ – أَيٍ – أَبَا – اَلْأَخُ – اَلْأَخَ – اَلْأَخِ :

Of course these forms are rare.

In the construct state the final vowel is lengthened :

أَبُو – أَبِى – أَبَا

and the dual is أَبَوَانِ ' two parents ' أَبَوَيْنِ .

The pronominal suffixes are added to the construct state :—

أَبُوكَ ' your father ' (nom.)   أَبَاهُ ' his father ' (acc.)

أَبِيهِ ' his father ' (gen.) but :   أَبِى ' my father ' (all cases)

أَبُو الْمُلُوكِ ' the father of kings ' :   أَبُو زَيْدٍ ' Zayd's father '.

When a man has a son, he is known not by his own name but as the father of his son.

ذُو ' possessor of ' occurs only in the construct state :—

	Sing.		Dual.		Plural.	
	Masc.	Fem.	Masc.	Fem.	Masc.	Fem.
nom.	ذُو	ذَاتُ	ذَوَا	ذَوَاتَا	أُولُو	ذَوَاتُ
acc.	ذَا ذَاتَ					
gen.	ذِى ذَاتِ	ذَوَىْ	ذَوَاتَىْ	ذَوِى	أُولِى	ذَوَاتِ

ذُو is never used with suffixes : it often takes the place of an adjective :—

ذُو عِلْمٍ ' learned ', ' a learned man '.

ذُو عَقْلٍ ' intelligent ' : ذَاتُ مَالٍ ' rich ', ' a rich woman '.

سَنَةٌ ' year ' has two plurals سَنَوَاتٌ and سِنُونَ ; the oblique case of the latter is سِنِينَ with assimilation.

فَمٌ ' mouth ' is regular but in the construct فَا — فُو فَاهُ — فُوهُ may also be used ; with suffixes : فِى — فِيهِ but فِىَّ ' my mouth ' (all cases).

A few nouns begin with liaison :—

اِبْنٌ (أَبْنَاءٌ) ' son ' : اِبْنَةٌ (بَنَاتٌ) ' daughter ' : اِسْمٌ (fem.) ' two ' : اِثْنَتَانِ (masc.) ' two ' : اِثْنَانِ ' name ' : اِمْرَأَةٌ نِسَاءٌ — نِسْوَةٌ) ' woman ' : (أَسْمَاءٌ) اِمْرُؤٌ ' man ' اِمْرَأً (acc.) اِمْرِئٍ (gen.).

اِمْرُؤٌ and اِمْرَأَةٌ drop the liaison after the definite

article and become اَلْمَرْءُ and اَلْمَرْأَةُ ; the other nouns

keep the liaison : اَلْاِبْنُ — اَلْاِبْنَةُ .

اِبْنٌ has a sound plural بَنُونَ — بَنِينَ which is used

in the names of tribes : بَنُو بَكْرٍ 'the tribe Bakr'.

Note the following spellings :—

بِسْمِ اللهِ 'in the name of God'.

زَيْدُ بْنُ مُحَمَّدٍ *Zaydubnu muḥammadin*
        Zayd, the son of Muhammad.

زَيْدُ ابْنُ مُحَمَّدٍ *Zaydunibnu muḥammadin*
        Zayd is the son of Muhammad.

In the last example the connecting vowel *i* is not
indicated in writing even in vocalized texts.

كِلَا ; fem. كِلْتَا 'both' is used only in the construct state. With a suffix it is inflected for case like any
dual, with a noun it is not.

Vocabulary 11

مَوْتٌ death.	جَدّ (a) grandfather.
جَمَالٌ beauty.	عَمّ (a) paternal uncle.
نَزَعَ i. نَزْعٌ take away.	عَمَّة paternal aunt.
عَرَفَ i. مَعْرِفَةٌ know.	مَطَرٌ rain.

هَوَاءٌ air.

شِمَالٌ north.

مَشْرِقٌ — شَرْقٌ east.

شَهْرٌ (b — e) month.

نَهَارٌ day, daylight.

جِدَارٌ (d) wall.

قَلْبٌ (b) heart.

نَجَحَ a. succeed.

تَبِعَ تَبَعَ and VIII follow.

جَدَّةٌ grandmother.

خَالٌ (a) maternal uncle.

خَالَةٌ maternal uncle.

نَوْءٌ (a) storm.

نَسِيمٌ (c) breeze.

جَنُوبٌ south.

مَغْرِبٌ — غَرْبٌ west.

(دَقَائِقُ) دَقِيقَةٌ minute.

ظَهْرٌ (b) back.

ظُهْرٌ noon.

Exercise 21

سَمِعَ أَبِى وَأَخُوكَ أَصْوَاتَ الدَّوَابِّ ـ طَلَبَتِ الْأَبْنَةُ
أَبَاهَا فِى السُّوقِ ـ جَمَعَ الشَّيْخُ أَبْنَاءَهُ عِنْدَ فِرَاشِهِ
قَبْلَ الْمَوْتِ ـ نَزَعَتِ ابْنَةُ الْبَقَّالِ الْأَوْرَاقَ الْبَيْضَاءَ
مِنْ يَدِ أَخِيهَا ـ دَخَلَتِ الْمَرْأَةُ مَعَ أَبْنَائِهَا بَيْنَ يَدَىِ
الْخَلِيفَةِ ـ يَا أَبْنَاءُ هَلْ تَعْرِفُونَ أَسْمَاءَ الزُّهُورِ ـ نَعَمْ
نَعْرِفُ اسْمَ كُلِّ زَهْرٍ فِى الْبُسْتَانِ ـ تَبِعْتُ أَخَاكَ
فِى الطَّرِيقِ أَكْتُبُ اسْمَهُ عَلَى جِدَارِ كُلِّ بَيْتٍ ـ

إِنَّ أَبَوَيْكَ يَفْرَحَانِ عَلَى نَجَاحِكَ ـ اَلْمَرْءُ بِأَصْغَرَيْهِ
قَلْبِهِ وَلِسَانِهِ ـ جَمَالُ الْمَرْءِ فِى لِسَانِهِ وَجَمَالُ
الْمَرْأَةِ فِى عَقْلِهَا.

22

do you and your brother understand what I have said? —
my two brothers and two sisters play with your brothers
and sisters — did your father send your brother to me? —
the woman sent her sons to seek wealth in distant lands
— what is your name? my name is well known, it is the
best known of the names of the Arabs — woman, have
you any children? — yes I have a son and two daughters
— this man has two fathers, the father of his body and the
father of his intelligence — did you stop at the house of
my friend's father? — the possessors of knowledge and
wealth are the fewest of men.

LESSON 12

IMPERATIVE. PARTICIPLES. INFINITIVE

The imperative (Table 1), being a command, is an
incomplete action and so connected with the imperfect.
It has no prefixes and the inflections are cut short. The
loss of the prefix makes a helping vowel necessary; this
is *u* when the characteristic is *u* and otherwise *i*.

أُكْتُبْ write; اِسْمَعْ hear; اِضْرِبْ hit.

The imperative is confined to the second person and is
affirmative only; a negative command is expressed
differently.

It can take the object suffixes.

The active participle is كَاتِبٌ ; فَعَلَةٌ and فُعَّالٌ are common forms for the plural.

When derived from a transitive verb, it can take an object and, being a noun, it takes its object in the genitive case :—

قَاتِلُ زَيْدٍ Zaid's murderer ;

طَالِبُو عِلْمٍ seekers after knowledge, scholars.

It is obvious that this participle easily passes into a noun or adjective.

The passive participle is مَكْتُوبٌ : the plural is مَفَاعِيلُ.

In themselves the participles contain no idea of time.

Infinitive.—There is no fixed form for the infinitive of the simple stem ; فَعْلٌ is common but the infinitive of each verb has to be learnt.

Many verbs of motion have the form فَعُولٌ :—

ذَهَابٌ but نُزُولٌ — دُخُولٌ — خُرُوجٌ.

فَعِلَ usually has فَعَلٌ :—

غَضِبَ be angry — فَرَحٌ — فَرِحَ rejoice غَضَبٌ.

As the infinitive is a noun, it can govern a genitive which may be either subject or object of the verbal idea.

قَتْلُ زَيْدٍ the killing of Zaid.

the killing by Zaid.

Therefore it is sometimes best translated as passive :—

إِنْ يُقْتَلُوا فَالْقَتْلُ أَكْرَمُ مِيتَةٍ

if they are killed, being killed is the noblest mode of death.

When both subject and object are mentioned, the subject is put in the genitive and the object in the accusative.

ضَرْبُ خَالِدٍ الْوَلِيدَ Khalid's hitting Waleed

بَعْثِى إِيَّاهُ my sending him.

The object can always be put in the accusative.

The object both of an infinitive or a participle is often introduced by لِ especially when the verbal noun is in the adverbial accusative.

قُمْتُ إِكْرَامًا لَهُ

I stood up to do him honour (Lesson 15).

The infinitive takes the place of the two English forms 'to write' and 'writing'.

It passes easily into an abstract noun and even into a concrete one.

وُجُودٌ existence (وَجَدَ 'find').

تَصْوِيرٌ picture (from a derived stem 'give shape to').

Vocabulary 12

طِفْل (a) infant.

عَظِيم glorious, great.

أَمْر (b) thing, affair.

سَهْل level, easy.

قَتَل u. قَتْل kill.

خَدَم i.u. خِدْمَة serve.

مَنْزِل — مَنْزِلَة (مَنَازِل) house, camp, stage (of a journey).

غُلَام (غِلْمَان) young man, servant, boy.

عذب II punish.

سَرَق i. سَرَق steal.

شَفَة lip.

أَنْف (b) nose.

جُبْن cheese.

سِر (a) secret.

أَمِين faithful.

أَمْر (أَوَامِر) command.

شَرَف honour, nobility.

كَتَم u. كِتْمَان hide (trans.).

ضَيْف (a) guest.

عَذَاب punishment.

خَد (b) cheek.

جِبْهَة (c) forehead.

جَفْن (b) eyelid.

جَوْز nut.

Exercise 23

يَا نِسَاءُ اسْمَعْنَ صَوْتَ أَطْفَالِكُنَّ ـ اَلدُّخُولُ فِي
هٰذَا اْلأَمْرِ أَسْهَلُ مِنَ اْلخُرُوجِ مِنْهُ ـ يَا خَادِمَةُ
اذْهَبِي إِلَى اْلسُّوقِ وَاطْلُبِي مِنَ اْلخَيَّاطَةِ ثِيَابِى
اْلجَدِيدَةَ ـ إِنَّ كَاتِمَ اْلسِّرِّ صَدِيقٌ أَمِينٌ ـ فَتْحُ نَفْسِكَ
هُوَ اْلفَتْحُ اْلعَظِيمُ ـ أَيُّهَا اْلأَمِيرُ انْزِلْ مِنْ فَرَسِكَ

وَادْخُلْ مَنْزِلِي وَهَذَا لِي شَرَفٌ عَظِيمٌ ـ الْمَطْلُوبُ

مِنْكَ الرُّجُوعُ مِنَ الْبِلَادِ الْبَعِيدَةِ إِلَى بَيْتِ

أَبَوَيْكَ ـ الْمَخْدُومُ عِنْدَكُمْ هُوَ خَادِمٌ كُلِّكُمْ ـ إِنَّا

لِلَّهِ وَإِنَّا إِلَيْهِ رَاجِعُونَ ـ خِدْمَةُ الرَّجُلِ أَخَاهُ شَرَفٌ.

24

my daughter, hear what I say — seek knowledge from all,
from men and women — entering into wealth is difficult
and the going out from it easy — knowledge of yourself
is the greatest knowledge and the most difficult — the
king rejoiced at the return of his army after its defeat of
his enemies — cutting off the hand is the punishment
of the thief — the generous man rejoices at the arrival of
guests — your keeping your tongue from evil is the fear
of God — the object of my sending this young man to you
is his entry into your service.

LESSON 13

MOODS

The perfect has only one form which serves for indicative,
conditional, and optative.

The imperfect has three besides the indicative (Table 1).

Subjunctive.—This is a suitable name for this mood
usually follows a subordinating conjunction. The *u* of
the indicative is changed to *a* ; the *ni* and *na* of the two
syllabled inflections are cut off ; while the feminine plurals
are not changed.

It is used after the conjunctions لِ and كَيْ ، in order

that ' and also after أَنْ when that follows a verb expressing
any sort of wish or purpose.

طَلَبَ مِنِّى أَنْ أَذْهَبَ إِلَى ٱلْقُدْسِ

he sought from me that I should go to Jerusalem.

أَنْ with the subjunctive can always be replaced by an
infinitive :—

طَلَبَ مِنِّى ٱلذَّهَابَ اِلى القدس

Jussive.—This is formed by dropping the inflection *u* of
the indicative ; in other places it is the same as the subjunctive.

It gets its name because it provides the imperative for
the first and third persons and the negative imperative for
the second :—

أُكْتُبْ write ;   لَا تَكْتُبْ do not write ;

لِيَكْتُبْ let him write ;   لَا يَكْتُبْ let him not write.

As a positive imperative the jussive always takes the
prefix لِ ; after وَ and فَ the لِ loses its vowel.

وَلْيَكْتُبْ and let him write.

The jussive has other uses which have nothing to do with
the imperative.

Energetic.—Roughly speaking, it is formed by adding
anna to the indicative ; but the individual forms must
be learnt.

With the emphatic لَ it is used in solemn statements, especially after oaths. It is also used to express commands and wishes.

قَدْ حَلَفَ لَيَقْتُلَنَّ he had sworn, he will kill.

Note.—Arabic has no strict rules for indirect speech as have English and Latin.

Conditional sentences.—The conjunction is إِنْ 'if'; either the perfect or the jussive may be used in both parts of the sentence.

إِنْ فَعَلْتَ هٰذَا هَلَكْتَ)
إِنْ تَفْعَلْ هٰذَا تَهْلِكْ) if you do this, you will perish.

إِنْ لَا 'if not' is often contracted to إِلَّا.

مَنْ and مَا, when indefinite pronouns, are often treated as conditional particles :—

مَنْ سَكَتَ سَلِمَ he who keeps silent is safe.

Vocabulary 13

حَلَفَ i. حَلَفَ swear.

مَسَحَ a. مَسَحَ measure.

شَهِدَ شُهُودٌ be present at.

نَدِمَ نَدَمٌ repent.

كَشَفَ i. كَشَفَ uncover, disclose.

مَزْرَعَةٌ (مَزَارِعُ) field.

مَرَضٌ (a) illness.

حَيَاةٌ life.

سَكَتَ u. سُكُوتٌ be quiet.

شُجَاعٌ bold.

سَمٌّ (b) poison.

سَقَطَ u. سُقُوطٌ fall.

بَدْوٌ bedouins, nomads.

هَلَكَ i. هَلَكٌ perish.

مَهْلَكٌ perish.

عَجِلَ عَجَلٌ hurry.

صَبَرَ i. صَبْرٌ be patient, endure.

كَرِهَ كُرْهٌ be unwilling, not like.

عَيْبٌ (b) fault, defect.

مَرِيضٌ (مَرْضَى) ill, sick.

فَرِيسَةٌ prey.

سَلِمَ سَلَامٌ be safe.

شَجَاعَةٌ bravery.

حَطَبٌ firewood.

ظَهَرَ a. ظُهُورٌ be manifest, conquer.

بَدَوِيٌّ a nomad.

Exercise 25

مَنْ يَعْجَلْ يَنْدَمْ ـ بَعَثَ الْحُكُومَةُ غِلْمَانَهَا لِيَمْسَحُوا
الْمَزَارِعَ ـ طَلَبَ مِنِّى الطَّبِيبُ أَنْ أَشْرَبَ لَبَنًا
كَثِيرًا ـ إِنْ شَهِدْتَ الْحَرْبَ عَرَفْتَ أَيُّ الْجَيْشَيْنِ
أَشْجَعُ ـ لِيَنْزِعْ مِنْ فَمِ الْأَسَدِ فَرِيسَتَهُ لِنَعْرِفَ قُوَّتَهُ
وَشَجَاعَتَهُ ـ أَكْرَهُ أَنْ تَنْظُرَ إِلَى عُيُوبِ جِيرَانِكَ ـ
كَتَبَ الْخَلِيفَةُ إِلَى أَمِيرِ جَيْشِهِ لَا تَقْتُلِ الشُّيُوخَ
وَالْأَطْفَالَ وَلَا تَقْطَعِ الْأَشْجَارَ ـ إِنْ تَخْرُجْ مِنْ

هَذَا ٱلْأَمْرِ تَفْرَحْ كُلَّ حَيَاتِكَ ـ مِنَ ٱلشَّجَاعَةِ
أَنْ تَصْبِرَ عَلَى ٱلْمَصَائِبِ وَٱلْمَكْرُوهِ ـ طَلَبَ
ٱلْأَبُ حَكِيمَيْنِ لِيَكْشِفَا عَنْ مَرَضِ ٱبْنِهِ.

26

do not play with that sharp sword — I shall certainly discover his secret — let the youth be silent before one who is older than he — let me go into your house that I may look at your carpets — they broke the cup that the posion in it might fall to the ground — send the servant to gather the dates fallen on the ground — the women of the tribe go out every day to collect firewood — be not angry with a friend — it is part of nobility to disapprove of defects in oneself.

LESSON 14

NEGATIVES

There are several negatives, each with its special uses. The negative stands at the beginning of the sentence, except when it denies a single word.

إِنَّكَ عِنْدِى كَلَا شَىْءٍ

in my opinion you were as nothing.

لَا is 'no' and also 'not'.

A nominal sentence may be denied by مَا :—

مَا قَوْمٌ كَقَوْمِى

a tribe is not like my tribe—no tribe is like my tribe.

مَا هُوَ مِنَ ٱلْكِتَابِ

it is not from the Book (Koran).

A general negation may be expressed by لَا 'which denies the class'; the noun loses nunation and is in the accusative :—

لَا رَجُلَ فِي ٱلدَّارِ   no man is in the house.

If there are two clauses, the nominative may be used in both :—

لَا خَوْفٌ عَلَيْهِمْ وَلَا فَزَعٌ

no fear is on them and no terror.

The defective verb لَيْسَ 'it is not' has no imperfect.

لَيْسُوا — لَسْتُمَا — لَيْسَا — لَسْتَ — لَيْسَتْ — لَيْسَ

— لَسْنَ, etc., is followed by a noun in the accusative or by ب with the genitive :—

لَسْتُ بِعَالِمٍ — لَسْتُ عَالِمًا   I am not learned.

Sometimes it is reduced in meaning to 'not' :—

لَسْتُ أَقْصِدُ ٱلْحَرْبَ   I do not intend war.

Verbal sentences.—The past is denied by مَا with the perfect or by لَمْ with the jussive :—

لَمْ يَكْتُبْ — مَا كَتَبَ he did not write.

The future is denied by لَنْ with the subjunctive; here the subjunctive stands in a main sentence.

لَنْ يَكْتُبَ he will not write — he will never write.

مَا with the imperfect denies the present :—

مَا يَكْتُبُ he is not writing (at the present moment).

لَا with the imperfect is a general negation and may refer to any time.

لَا يَكْتُبُ he does not write.

After another negative لَا may be used to continue a series of denials; the time is that of the first.

لَمْ يَدْخُلِ ٱلدَّارَ وَلَا نَظَرَ إِلَى شَيْءٍ فِيهَا

he did not enter the house and did not look at anything in it.

لَا with the perfect denies a wish :—

لَا رَحِمَهُ ٱللهُ may God not have mercy on him.

لَا after an oath denies the future :—

$$ وَٱللهِ لَا فَتَحْتُ هٰذَا ٱلْبَابَ $$

by God I will not open this door.

لَا with the jussive is a negative command as was said in the previous lesson.

لَمَّا with the jussive means 'not yet' :—

لَمَّا يَكْتُبْ he has not yet written (but still has time).

بَلْ introduces a correction :—

اِضْرِبْ زَيْدًا بَلْ زَيْنَبَ beat Zaid ; no, Zainab.

لَا تَضْرِبْ زَيْدًا بَلْ زَيْنَبَ do not beat Zaid but (beat) Zainab.

غَيْرٌ is a noun meaning 'change'; in the construct state it means first 'other' and then 'not' :—

ٱلْمُلُوكُ وَغَيْرُهُمْ the kings and others.

غَيْرُ ٱلْعَرَبِ non-Arabs.

وَجْهُهُ إِلَى غَيْرِ مِصْرَ his face was not towards Egypt.

Vocabulary 14

إِحْدَى fem. أَحَدٌ one.   شَيْءٌ (أَشْيَاءُ no nunation) thing.

وَقْتٌ (a) time.   قَوْمٌ (a) people, tribe, some.

كَفٌّ restraint.   فَزِعَ (فَزَعٌ) be afraid, seek refuge.

وَرَعٌ piety.   قَصَدَ i. قَصْدٌ aim at, purpose.

حَزِنَ حَزَنٌ be sorry.   هَرَبَ u. هَرَبٌ run away.

رَحْمَةٌ رَحِمَ have mercy on.   شُغْلٌ (a) work, labour.

خَوْفٌ fear.   حَدِيثٌ (أَحَادِيثُ) story, report.

خَبَرٌ (a) story, news.   عَلِمَ عِلْمٌ know.

قَنَاعَةٌ قَنِعَ be content, satisfied.   فَقْرٌ poverty.

بَلَاءٌ trial, misfortune.   حِرْصٌ greed.

شَرَهٌ greed.   أَسَدٌ (b) lion.

حَرٌّ heat.   حُسْنٌ goodness, beauty.

تَدْبِيرٌ management.   سَمَاءٌ (سَمَوَاتٌ) sky, heaven.

خُلُقٌ (a) nature, character.

Exercise 27

لَا تَضْرِبُوا أَوْلَادَكُمْ ـ لَمْ يَبْغَشِنِى أَبِى لِأَطْلُبَ كِتَابًا

لَكَ ـ لَنْ يَكْرُمَ مَنْ لَا يَكْتِمُ الْأَسْرَارَ ـ لَمْ نَسْمَعْ

مِثْلَ هَذَا الْحَدِيثِ ـ اللهُ أَحَدٌ لَيْسَ كَمِثْلِهِ شَيْءٌ ـ

لَا نَرْجِعُ مِنْ شُغْلِنَا فِى الْمَزَارِعِ وَالشَّمْسُ

فِى ٱلسَّمَاءِ ـ لَمْ نَفْرَحْ فِى هٰذَا ٱلْخَبَرِ وَلَا حَزِنَّا ـ
لَا فَقْرَ وَلَا بَلَاءَ كَٱلْحِرْصِ وَٱلشَّرَهِ وَلَا مَالَ
كَٱلْقَنَاعَةِ ـ لَا عَقْلَ كَٱلتَّدْبِيرِ وَلَا وَرَعَ كَٱلْكَفِّ
وَلَا حُسْنَ كَحُسْنِ ٱلْخُلُقِ ـ اَلْهَرَبُ فِى وَقْتِهِ خَيْرٌ مِنَ
ٱلصَّبْرِ فِى غَيْرِ وَقْتِهِ ـ اِثْنَانِ لَا يَشْبَعَانِ طَالِبُ عِلْمٍ
وَطَالِبُ مَالٍ.

28

our enemies, may God not have mercy on them, are many
— do not be afraid of work — the prophet never ate his
fill of meat in his life — be not satisfied with a little knowledge — the days which have gone will never return — I do
not seek gifts from the government to-day — do not take

refuge with (إِلَى) another than God — do not laugh,

my daughter, at the misfortune of the poor and be not angry
at the success of the rich — he is the possessor of wealth,
estates, and houses but (and) he is not yet content — you
are not the possessor of wisdom.

LESSON 15

MORE ABOUT CASES

Accusative.—This is the adverbial case, for true adverbs
are few.

Cognate accusative.—The infinitive, usually qualified in
some way, carries on the idea of the verb :—

ذَهَبَ ذَهَابًا سَرِيعًا

he went off a quick going (quickly).

أَخَذْنَاهُمْ أَخْذَ عَزِيزٍ

we laid hold on them the laying hold of a strong one = **we** took a good grip of them.

The infinitive may be left out :—

اُذْكُرُوا اللَّهَ كَثِيرًا remember God much (often).

Extensions of this construction are :—

ضَرَبْتُهُ مَرَّتَيْنِ I hit him twice.

ضَرَبْتُهُ سَوْطًا I hit him with a whip.

Accusative of reason or cause.—It is the infinitive of **a** verb of sensation or thought referring to the same time as the main verb :—

لَا تَقْتُلُوا أَوْلَادَكُمْ خَشْيَةَ إِمْلَاقٍ

do not kill your children from fear of poverty.

Accusative of extent in time or place.—All nouns **of** time may be used in this way :—

ذَهَبَ لَيْلًا he went away by night.

سَكَنَ فِي مَكَّةَ سِنِينَ [أَيَّامًا]

he dwelt some years (days) in Mecca.

For place only names of direction, measure, and general words can be used :—

ذَهَبَ مِيلًا he went away a mile.

نَظَرَ يَمِينًا وَيَسَارًا [شَمَالًا] he looked right and left.

جَلَسْتُ مَجْلِسَ زَيْدٍ ـ جَلَسْتُ مَكَانَ زَيْدٍ

I sat in Zaid's place.

but جَلَسْتُ فِي الْمَسْجِدِ I sat in the mosque.

Accusative of nearer definition.—This is used with weights, measures, verbs of filling and such like; it is always indefinite :—

هِيَ أَطْوَلُهُنَّ ذِرَاعًا she was the longest of them in arm.

رِطْلٌ عَسَلًا a *roll* of honey.

مَلَأَ الْكِيسَ ذَهَبًا he filled the purse with gold.

Accusative of accompanying circumstance.—It is indefinite and English would use the nominative :—

قَدِمَ الرَّجُلُ رَاكِبًا the man advanced riding.

أُدْخُلُوا رَجُلًا رَجُلًا come in, one by one.

The accusative may refer to any part of the sentence :—

نَظَرْتُ إِلَى زَيْدٍ جَالِسًا

I looked at Zaid as he was sitting.

دَخَلْتُ الْبُسْتَانَ زَاهِرًا

I went into the garden when it was in bloom.

ضَرَبْتُ زَيْدًا رَاكِبَيْنِ

I hit Zaid when we were both mounted.

Genitive.—This is used more freely than in English ; possession is only one of the ideas expressed by it. Examples will make the usage clear.

رِطْلُ عَسَلٍ a *rotl* of honey.

كُرْسِيٌّ خَشَبٍ a chair of wood.

سَمُّ سَاعَةٍ poison of a moment (instantaneous).

' My knowledge ' means ' what I know '.

عِلْمِى means ' what I know ' and ' what others know about me '.

In technical terms the English genitive is subjective, the Arabic may be subjective or objective.

فَخَرْتَ بِأَيَّامٍ لِغَيْرِكَ فَخْرُهَا

you boasted of days (battles) the boasting in which belonged to others.

We have just seen the genitive describing a noun; it can also describe an adjective :—

قَلِيلُ ٱلْعَقْلِ little of understanding, foolish.

In this construction the adjective, unlike the noun, can take the definite article :—

ٱلِٱبْنَةُ ٱلْحَسَنَةُ ٱلْوَجْهِ the girl, the pretty of face. the girl with the pretty face.

ٱلرَّجُلُ ٱلْكَثِيرُ ٱلْمَالِ the man the much of property. the rich man.

Vocabulary 15

مَرَّةٌ (c) time (repetition).

يَوْمٌ (أَيَّامٌ) day (24 hours).

لَيْلَةٌ one night.

مَكَانٌ (أَمْكِنَةٌ) place.

كِيسٌ (a) bag, purse.

سَاعَةٌ (سَاعَاتٌ) hour, moment.

سَكَنَ u. سُكُونٌ be quiet, dwell.

سَجَدَ u. سُجُودٌ bow down.

فَخَرَ u. فَخْرٌ boast.

مَكَثَ u. مَكْثٌ stay, remain.

غَرَسَ i. غَرْسٌ plant.

حَرِيرٌ silk.

جُبْنٌ cowardice.

سَوْطٌ (a) whip.

لَيْلٌ (لَيَالٍ) night.

خَشْيَةٌ fear.

كُرْسِيٌّ (كَرَاسِيُّ) chair.

ٱلْبَارِحُ yesterday.

رَكِبَ رُكُوبٌ ride.

زَهَرَ a. زُهُورٌ bloom, shine.

قَعَدَ u. قُعُودٌ sit, stay at home.

غَرَبَ u. غُرُوبٌ be, go far off set (star).

صُوفٌ wool.

Exercise 29

هُوَ أَصْفَرُ اللَّوْنِ ــ زَيْدٌ قَلِيلُ الْعَقْلِ وَعُمَرُ أَقَلُّ الْعَقْلِ

مِنْهُ ــ اَلرِّيحُ الْيَوْمَ أَشَدُّ مِنْهَا الْبَارِحَ ــ هَرَبَ مِنَ

الْبِلَادِ خَوْفًا مِنْ غَضَبِ السُّلْطَانِ ــ ذَهَبَ يَمِينًا

وَيَسَارًا يَطْلُبُ طَعَامًا ــ مَكَثُوا غَيْرَ طَوِيلٍ ــ قَعَدْتُ

عَنِ الْحَرْبِ جُبْنًا ــ غَرَسَ الْفَلَّاحُونَ مَزَارِعَهُمْ

شَعِيرًا ــ أَنَا أَشَدُّ مِنْهُ خَوْفًا مِنْهُ مِنِّي ــ قَصَدْتُ

خِدْمَةَ كَبِيرٍ مِنَ الْكِبَارِ طَلَبًا لِلْمَالِ ــ فَرِحْتُ

وَأَكْتُمُ مَا بِى حَزَنًا عَلَى الْمَرِيضِ ــ سَجَدْتُ لِلّٰهِ

فَرَحًا فِي بَعْثِهِ النَّبِيَّ .

30

she was much afraid — no one ran away as I did —
I lived in that town for many years — he has little money
but (and) is quite content in his poverty — the heat to-day
is greater than it was yesterday — he is as brave as a
lion — he is braver than a lion — he was silent for a long
time — I do not go to hot countries for fear of illness —
he wore garments of silk in his joy at having gathered much
wealth — he is strong in the arm and weak in the leg.

LESSON 16

WEAK—HOLLOW—VERBS

In these verbs (Tables 4—5) the middle radical is *w* or *y*. In the perfect the first radical has *a*: in an open syllable and *u* or *i* in a shut syllable according as the middle radical is *w* or *y*. Thus the perfect has only two syllables in place of the three of the strong verb.

In the imperfect the vowel after the first radical is long in an open and short in a shut syllable and is *u* or *i* as the middle radical is *w* or *y*.

In the jussive the forms with no final vowel have a shut syllable after the first radical, so the vowel in it is short.

The imperative is made as usual by cutting off the prefix of the jussive and what is left needs no helping vowel.

The active participle always has a glottal stop ; قَائِل may come from the root *qwl* or *qyl*.

The passive participle is مَقُول from *qwl* and مَقِيل from *qyl*.

The infinitive is often فَعْل, i.e. قَوْل and قَيْل, but there are many exceptions.

There is also a special intransitive form corresponding to فَعِل.

In this the long vowel of the perfect is *a*: and the short vowel always *i*. The vowel of the imperfect and its derivatives is *a*, long or short, as the syllable is open or closed.

The verb كَان – يَكُون ' become ' takes the place of the missing ' be ' when it is necessary to indicate past or future time :—

اَلرَّجُلُ فِي اَلدَّارِ the man is in the house.

كَانَ اَلرَّجُلُ فى الدار the man was in the house.

يَكُونُ اَلرَّجُلُ فى الدار the man will be in the house.

(A future particle is not needed, for the verb would not be used for the present.)

كَان is also an auxiliary verb; the perfect of it is used with another perfect to express the pluperfect; قَدْ is some-times added.

مَاتَ اَلرَّشِيدُ بِطُوسَ وَكَانَ خَرَجَ إِلَى خُرَاسَانَ

Rasheed died in Tus and (after) he had gone to Khurasan.

The perfect is also used with an imperfect to denote an act repeated in the past :—

كَانَ يَرْكَبُ فِي كُلِّ يَوْمٍ عِدَّةَ مِرَارٍ

he used to ride (rode) every day a number of times.

The imperfect with the perfect of another verb expresses the future perfect :—

يَكُونُ زَيْدٌ كَتَبَ Zaid will have written.

When it is an independent verb, the subject is in the nominative and the complement in the accusative :—

يَكُونُ اَلرَّسُولُ عَلَيْكُمْ شَهِيدًا

the apostle will be a witness against you.

كُونُوا حِجَارَةً أَوْ حَدِيدًا be stone or iron.

Peculiar is the construction—

مَا كَانَ لِ he is not the one to.

لَمْ يَكُنْ زَيْدٌ لِيَشْرَبَ خَمْرًا

Zaid was not the man to drink wine.

يَصِيرُ ــ صَارَ 'become' and other verbs also take the complement in the accusative.

قَدْ with the perfect shows that it has the sense of the English perfect or pluperfect :—

إِنَّ ابْنَتَكَ قَدْ مَاتَتْ

your daughter has died (is dead).

قَدْ أَمَرَتْ بِالْبُخْلِ أُمُّ مُحَمَّدٍ

Umm Muhammad (name of a woman) had given an order about stinginess ; had told me to be stingy.

قَدْ with the imperfect means 'sometimes' :—

قَدْ يَعْلَقُ الْقَلْبُ حُبًّا ثُمَّ يَتْرُكُهُ

the heart sometimes attaches itself to love, then leaves it.

The verb يَمُوتُ ــ مَاتَ 'die' is irregular ; in the perfect both مُتُّ and مِتُّ are possible.

Vocabulary 16

قَصُرَ قَصْرٌ be short.

قَالَ u. قَوْلٌ say.

قَالَ i. قَيْلٌ take a siesta.

عَلِقَ عُلُوقٌ be attached to.

صَارَ i. صَيْرٌ become.

قَامَ u. قِيَامٌ stand, stand up.

عَادَ u. عَوْدٌ return.

بَاعَ i. بَيْعٌ sell.

عِدَّةٌ number.

حَدِيدٌ iron.

حُبٌّ love.

حُجَّةٌ (حُجَجٌ) argument.

قَافِلَةٌ (قَوَافِلُ) caravan.

وَحْدَ (always with a suffix) alone.

طَالَ u. طُولٌ be long.

كَانَ u. كَوْنٌ become, be.

تَرَكَ u. تَرْكٌ leave.

مَاتَ u. مَوْتٌ die.

سَارَ i. سَيْرٌ go, travel.

خَافَ a. خَوْفٌ fear.

مَالَ i. مَيْلٌ incline.

غَلَبَ i. غَلْبٌ overcome.

بُخْلٌ avarice.

حَجَرٌ (a) stone.

لِصٌّ (b) thief, brigand.

حَبْلٌ (c) rope.

Exercise 31

مِنْ قَصُرَتْ حُجَّتُهُ طَالَ لِسَانُهُ ـ قُمْ يَا وَلَدِى وَسِرْ
إِلَى جَدِّكَ ـ كَانَ الأَوْلَادُ تَلْعَبُ فِى الشَّارِعِ ـ
خَافَتِ الْجَارِيَةُ مِنْ شِدَّةِ الرِّيحِ ـ عَادَتِ الْقَافِلَةُ
خَوْفًا مِنَ اللُّصُوصِ ـ لَا تَخَافِى يَا بِنْتِى لَا
تَسِيرِينَ عَلَى وَحْدِكِ ـ لِيَقُلْ مَا فِى قَلْبِهِ ـ كُنْتُ

اَبْنَ أَبِى ثُمَّ صِرْتُ أَبَا ابْنِى ـ إِنَّ لَوْنَ الْحَيَّةِ خُضْرَةٌ
تَمِيلُ إِلَى السَّوَادِ ـ كَانَ الْبَدْوُ يَبِيعُونَ جُلُودَ الْغَنَمِ
وَالْمَعْزِ مِنَ الْفَلَّاحِينَ ـ يَكُونُ الْجَيْشُ قَدْ غَلَبَ
عَلَى أَعْدَائِهِ قَبْلَ غُرُوبِ الشَّمْسِ .

32

he rose from his bed and the sun had inclined to its setting
— if a chief of our people dies, a chief arises — the caravan
will have travelled for many days — the whole company
had heard what I was saying — everybody takes a siesta
in the hot days of summer — many say other than what
they think — do not fear the unpleasantnesses of the road
— the woman had been making clothes for her children —
the guests will not have risen from their beds before your
departure — my grandmother, are you going with the
other women to Jerusalem ?

LESSON 17

STRONG VERB—DERIVED STEMS

The derived are formed from the simple stem (consult
Table 2) by additions of various sorts and express some
modification of the original verbal idea. It is the custom
in European grammars to number them, the simple stem
being I. They have each only one variety, unlike I, and

are made from فَعَلَ فَعِلَ فَعُلَ .

The inflections are the same as for the simple stem.
The derived stems fall into four groups determined by
the vowel sequence in the imperfect.

1.

II is formed by doubling the second radical: كَتَّبَ
impf. يُكَتِّبُ .

III by lengthening the first vowel: كَاتَبَ impf.
يُكَاتِبُ .

IV by prefixing *ʔa* and dropping the vowel of the first
radical: أَكْتَبَ impf. يُكْتِبُ .

The prefix of the imperfect has *u* and the characteristic
is *i*. Note that in the imperfect of IV the *ʔ* is dropped
though it reappears in the imperative, أَكْتِبُ .

2.

V is made by prefixing *ta* to stem II: تَكَتَّبَ impf.
يَتَكَتَّبُ .

VI by prefixing *ta* to III: تَكَاتَبَ impf. يَتَكَاتَبُ .

The imperfect has the vowel *a* throughout, except of
course in the final inflection.

3.

VII is made by prefixing *n* with liaison: إِنْكَتَبَ
impf. يَنْكَتِبُ .

VIII by inserting *t* after the first radical; the form

begins with liaison : اِكْتَتَبَ impf. يَكْتَتِبُ.

X by prefixing *sta* with liaison. This is really a form like VIII made from *saktaba* which does not occur in Arabic though it is found in other Semitic languages.

اِسْتَكْتَبَ impf. يَسْتَكْتِبُ

In this group the prefix of the imperfect has *a*, and the characteristic is *i*.

4.

IX and XI cannot be made from anything, which we should call a verb; they denote colours, and are best treated with the doubled verb.

Summary.—The perfects have *a* throughout, except of course in liaison.

If the imperfect has five syllables, the fourth has *a*.

Few verbs have all the nine stems.

In good Arabic VII is not made from roots beginning with *ʔ, w, y, r, l*, and *n*.

In VIII partial or total assimilation occurs when the root begins with *t, θ, ḍ, ð, z, s, ḍ t, ð*.

دَرَكَ	اِدَّرَكَ	overtake
ذخر	اِدَّخَرَ or اِذَّخَرَ	store up
زحم	اِزْدَحَمَ	crowd together
صنع	اِصْطَنَعَ	take into one's employment
ضرب	اِصْطَرَبَ	be confused

اِضْطَجَعَ or اِضْنَجَعَ   ضجع   lie down

اِطَّلَعَ   طلع   know (survey from
                                       above)

اِطَّلَمَ or اِظْلَمَ   ظلم   suffer wrong

Each stem has its own meaning or meanings.

II is

intensive : كَسَرَ break   كَسَّرَ smash

causative (this is an encroachment on IV) :

عَلِمَ know   عَلَّمَ teach

declarative : صَدَقَ speak truth   صَدَّقَ say that one
   speaks truth, believe

denominative : كَبَّرَ say, ' God is very great ' (اَللهُ أَكْبَرُ)

III is

conative : قَتَلَ kill   قَاتَلَ try to kill, fight

   نَزَعَ take away   نَازَعَ try to take away,
                                       quarrel

It takes as direct object the indirect object of I :—

كَتَبَ write   كَاتَبَ correspond with

رَكِبَ ride   رَاكَبَ ride with (a person)

It is always transitive.

IV is

causative : جَلَسَ sit down   أَجْلَسَ set down

V is the reflexive of II and then passive :

فَرَّقَ divide (trans.)   تَفَرَّقَ scatter (intrans.)

VI is

reciprocal : ضَرَبَ hit   تَضَارَبَ hit one another, have
a free fight

pretence : نَعَسَ sleep   تَنَاعَسَ pretend to sleep

VII is reflexive, then passive : اِنْكَسَرَ be broken

هَزَمَ defeat   اِنْهَزَمَ let oneself be defeated

VIII is
reflexive (sometimes passive) :

جَمَعَ collect (trans.)   اِجْتَمَعَ collect (intrans.)

X is to ask or think that the simple verbal idea should be
done.

حَسُنَ be good   اِسْتَحْسَنَ think good, approve

غَفَرَ pardon   اِسْتَغْفَرَ ask pardon from (trans.)

It is almost causative :

خرج go out   اِسْتَخْرَجَ extract from a mine, make
productive, till.

It takes considerable ingenuity to fit many verbs into this scheme ; thus كَلَّمَ speak to (trans.) تَكَلَّمَ speak (intrans.). Here are two sample roots :—

خَلَفَ u. خَلَفَ   سَلِمَ سَلَامٌ

I.   remain behind   be safe, well

II. خَلَّفَ leave behind   سَلَّمَ greet (denominative) make safe, protect, surrender (trans.)

III. خَالَفَ oppose   سَالَمَ make peace with, treat peaceably

IV. أَخْلَفَ break (promise)   أَسْلَمَ submit (make your word lag behind)   turn Muslim

V. تَخَلَّفَ hold back from   تَسَلَّمَ receive the surrender, turn Muslim

VI. تَخَالَفَ disagree with   تَسَالَمَ make peace together

VIII. اِخْتَلَفَ differ, be different   اِسْتَلَمَ kiss (the Black Stone)

X. اِسْتَخْلَفَ appoint a successor, take in exchange   اِسْتَسْلَمَ submit keep to the middle of the road

فَ ' and ' denotes a closer connection than وَ and may often be rendered ' so ', ' then '. In a conditional sentence it cannot be translated. Sometimes it denotes a change of subject.

Vocabulary 17

فَرَقَ u. i. فَرْقٌ separate.

غَفَرَ i. غُفْرَانٌ cover, pardon.

صَرَفَ i. صَرْفٌ turn (trans.).

نظر IV cause to wait.

قَبِلَ receive. قَبُولٌ

قبل III compare.

ضرب VIII be confused, in commotion.

زَحَمَ a. زَحْمٌ push.

ذَخَرَ a. ذُخْرٌ select.

دَرَسَ u. دَرْسٌ study.

ثَلْجٌ (b) snow.

عِيدٌ (a) festival.

علم II teach.

V learn.

هَزَمَ i. هَزْمٌ defeat.

بَلَغَ u. بُلُوغٌ arrive at.

VII turn away, go away.

VIII expect, wait for.

IV go forward.

نزع III try to take away, quarrel.

حصر III besiege.

VIII crowd.

VIII store up.

II teach.

حَاجَةٌ need, business, thing.

حِصْنٌ (b) fortress.

IV tell, make known.

غَابَ i. غُيُوبٌ be absent.

Exercise 33

كَلَّمْتُهُ وَلَمْ أَتَكَلَّمْ مَعَ غَيْرِهِ ـ أَطْعَمَ الْغَنِيُّ فُقَرَاءَ
كَثِيرَةً فَانْصَرَفُوا شَاكِرِينَ ـ لَا تُخَالِفُوا آبَاءَكُمْ يَا
أَيُّهَا الْأَوْلَادُ ـ كُنَّا نَتْبَعُ الْفَلَّاحَ وَانْفَرَدْنَا عَنْ
أَصْحَابِنَا ـ اِنْتَظِرْنِي فِي السُّوقِ وَلَا تَنْصَرِفْ ـ كَانَ

سُكَّانُ ٱلْبَلَدِ يَضْطَرِبُونَ عِنْدَ بُلُوغِ خَبَرِ ٱنْهِزَامِ
ٱلْجَيْشِ ـ كُلُّ شَيْءٍ تَسْتَحْسِنُهُ فِى ٱلْكَلْبِ فَاطْلُبْهُ فِى
ٱلْفَرَسِ ـ كَانَتِ ٱلنِّسَاءُ يَزْدَحِمْنَ عِنْدَ بَابِ ٱلْقَصْرِ
لِيَقْبِلْنَ تُحَفَ ٱلْمَلِكَةِ ـ غَلَبَ ٱللُّصُوصُ عَلَى ٱلْمَدِينَةِ
وَأَهْلَكُوا كُلَّ مَا فِيهَا ـ طَلَبْتُ مِنْ فَلَّاحِىَّ أَنْ
يَدَّخِرُوا ٱلثَّلْجَ فِى حُجَرٍ تَحْتَ ٱلْأَرْضِ ـ كَرِهْتُ أَنْ
تُقَابِلَ فَخْرِى بِفِعْلِهِى ـ سَلَّمَ ٱلرَّئِيسُ ٱلْحِصْنَ إِلَى
ٱلْمُحَاصِرِينَ .

34

I asked pardon of God and he pardoned me — let me wait
till the arrival of the guests that I may hear their news —
I shall expect you after sunset — brothers sometimes
quarrel with their sisters — I shall punish thieves and all
doers of evil — he tried to overcome me and I overcame
him — no child thinks its mother ugly — the company

differed about (فى) what they should do — the governor

appointed his son deputy during his absence — everyone
dresses his children in new clothes on the two great
festivals — does your father sometimes bring a poor
man into the house and give him food ?

LESSON 18

PASSIVE

The passive (Tables 3, etc.) is made by a change of vowels inside the verb. The inflections are the same as for the active except the vowel of the prefix of the imperfect. In stem I the perfect is *kutiba* and the imperfect *yuktabu*. The same scheme holds good for the derived stems; if there are more than three syllables, the extra one has *u* in the perfect and *a* in the imperfect.

a: in the perfect of III and VI becomes *u*: in the passive. The passive imperfect of IV is the same as that of I.

Hollow verb, stem I.—Some typical forms are put side by side to make the differences apparent.

w. active.	قَالَ	قُلْتُ	يَقُولُ	يَقُلْنَ	يَقُلْ
passive.	قِيلَ	قِلْتُ	يُقَالُ	يُقَلْنَ	يُقَلْ
y. active.	بَانَ	بِنْتُ	يَبِينُ	يَبِنَّ	يَبِنْ
passive.	بِينَ	بِنْتُ	يُبَانُ	يُبَنَّ	يُبَنْ

The passive can only be used when the agent is not mentioned.

' Zaid was killed ' قُتِلَ زَيْدٌ

' Zaid was killed by Muhammad ' cannot be translated into Arabic, which can only say: قَتَلَ مُحَمَّدٌ زَيْدًا

' Muhammad killed Zaid '.

If an active verb has two objects, the first becomes the subject of the passive and the second stays in the accusative.

وَعَدَنَا اللهُ الْحَيَاةَ الْأَبَدِيَّةَ God promised us eternal life.

وُعِدْنَا الْحَيَاةَ الْأَبَدِيَّةَ we were promised eternal life.

A verb may take two pronominal suffixes provided that they do not both refer to the same person or thing. When both are third person they cannot be of the same number and gender; indeed, it is better to make one of them independent by using *Piyya*:.

أَنْكَحَتَنِيهَا he gave her to me in marriage.

نُلْزِمُكُمُوهَا {(we make you stick to it).
{we compel you to take it.

أَسْكَنَهُمُوهُ he made them dwell in it.

Vocabulary 18

فَتَلَ i. فَتَل twist.

حَمَلَ i. حَمْل carry.

طَعَنَ u. طَعْن thrust, pierce, criticise.

حَرَمَ i. حَرِيم forbid.

نَشَدَ u. نَشْد seek, adjure.

صَامَ u. صَوْم fast.

الْأَسْتَانَة Stamboul.

مِيتَة mode of death.

عَنَايَة care.

فَرْسَخ parasang (about three miles).

مَشْكُوك doubted.

زُبْد butter.

خبر IV tell, report.

II put a burden on, load.

حَرُمَ حَرَام be unlawful, tabu.

نشد IV recite (poetry).

لَامَ u. لَوْم blame.

ضَاقَ i. ضِيق be narrow.

رِفْق kindness.

هَنْدَسَة engineering.

سِكَّة (سِكَك) coin, road.

نَسَب (a) pedigree, family honour.

تَمْر dates (coll.) تَمْرَة a date.

رَمَضَان ninth month of Muslim year.

Exercise 35

ضُرِبَتْ تِلْكَ السِّكَّةُ فِى ٱلْإِسْتَانَةِ ـ إِنَّ ٱلْإِنْسَانَ
يَعْرِفُ بِرِفْقَائِهِ ـ سِيَرَ مِيلَانَ ـ إِنْ تَقْتُلُوا فَالْقَتْلُ
أَكْرَمُ مِيتَةٍ ـ حَمَّلْتُ عَنَايَةَ إِخْوَانِى ٱلصَّغِيرَةِ
بَعْدَ مَوْتِ أَبِينَا ـ كَانَ مَشْكُوكًا فِى نَسَبِهِ
مَطْعُونًا عَلَيْهِ ـ مَنْ حُرِمَ ٱلرِّفْقَ حُرِمَ ٱلْخَيْرَ كُلَّهُ ـ
هٰذَا أَمْرٌ ٱخْتُلِفَ فِيهِ ـ صِيمَ رَمَضَانُ ـ مَاتَ
ٱلْخَلِيفَةُ وَٱسْتُخْلِفَ ٱبْنُ عَمِّهِ ٱلْأَصْغَرُ ـ ٱلدُّخُولُ
مَمْنُوعٌ ـ حُمِلَ عَلَى أَفْرَاسِ ٱلْحُكُومَةِ إِلَى
مِصْرَ ـ هَلْ تَعَلَّمْتُمْ عِلْمَ ٱلْهَنْدَسَةِ نَعَمْ عَلَّمَنَاهُ
ٱلْمُعَلِّمُ ـ زُرِعَ ٱلْمَزَارِعُ زُهُورًا .

36

his poetry is recited before the great ones of the land —
the fields were sown with wheat, barley, and millet —
entry to the mosques is forbidden — the leader was killed
and the army defeated — the earth was made a bed for
you — his face was turned from his goal — his boasting is
suspect — his father was killed, a man from Egypt killed
him — he goes forward like a laden camel — he was blamed
for his much fasting — his secret will be disclosed.

LESSON 19

THAT—CONJUNCTION

In the sentences :—
1. He said that he had done it.
2. That you are pleased pleases me.
3. The rain has been so heavy that the crops are good.
4. I sent him to school that he might not be spoiled at home.

In 1 ' that ' introduces indirect speech ; in 2 it introduces a sentence which takes the place of a noun and may be subject or object in a bigger sentence ; in 3 it denotes a consequence ; in 4 a purpose. Arabic does not distinguish sharply the first three types and only sometimes the fourth.

إِنَّ

We have seen that it is used to introduce an independent

nominal sentence and it cannot be translated. After قَال
' he said ' it is a conjunction.

قَالَ إِنَّ زَيْدًا مُسَافِرٌ   he said that Zaid was travelling.

أَنَّ

This is used after all other verbs or substitutes for verbs to introduce a nominal sentence.

أُخْبِرْتُ أَنَّ مَلِكًا مِنْ مُلُوكِ الْهِنْدِ كَانَ لَهُ زَوْجَةٌ

I was told that a king of India had a wife.
(Note how the impossibility of putting an indefinite noun before a definite genitive is evaded.)

وَفِى الْحَدِيثِ أَنَّ رَجُلًا قَالَ

and it is in the tradition that a man said.

زَعَمُوا أَنَّهَا أَخْبَرَتْ they claim that she related.

(This can also be expressed زَعَمُوهَا أَخْبَرت).

A verbal sentence can only follow أَنْ if it is separated from it by a pronoun of the third person which cannot be translated.

أَنَّهُ كَانَ فِى بَغْدَادَ تَاجِرٌ وَهُوَ ذُو مَالٍ وَافِرٍ

that there was in Baghdad a merchant possessed of abundant wealth.

It is also used after prepositions :—

شَهِدْتُ بِأَنَّ اللهَ حَقٌّ لِقَاءُهُ

I testify that God the meeting him is truth — that meeting God is a fact.

اَلدَّلَائِلُ عَلَى أَنَّهُ لَا يَعِيشُ إِلَّا اَلْأَنْسَبُ كَثِيرَةٌ

the proofs are many that only a man of the best family will live.

Or when a noun governs a sentence :—

مَا دَلِيلُ أَنَّكَ صَادِقٌ

what proof is there that you are truthful ?

(دليل loses nunation because it is in the construct state before a sentence.)

Note.—The pronoun, which cannot be translated, is also used after إِنْ:

يَا مُوسَى إِنَّهُ أَنَا اللهُ الْعَزِيزُ الْحَكِيمُ

O Moses, I am the mighty wise God.

أَنْ

It introduces direct speech :—

بَلَغَنِي أَنْ زَيْدٌ مُسَافِرٌ غَدًا

it has reached me (I have heard) that Zaid is travelling to-morrow.

سَمِعْتُ أَنْ زَيْدٌ عَالِمٌ I have heard that Zaid is learned.

When the main verb does not contain any wish or purpose, أَنْ may govern the perfect or the imperfect indicative :—

أَعْجَبَنِي أَنْ قُمْتَ it pleased me that you stood up.

أَعْلَمُ أَنْ يَنَامُ I know that he is asleep.

But these two sentences would be more often put :—

أَعْجَبَنِي أَنَّكَ قُمْتَ ـ أَعْلَمُ أَنَّهُ يَنَامُ

It is used with the subjunctive when the main verb contains any sort of wish or intention :—

أَمْ حَسِبْتُمْ أَنْ تَدْخُلُوا الْجَنَّةَ

do you reckon that you will enter the garden (paradise) ?

أَمَرَ أَنْ لَا يُولَدَ مَوْلُودٌ ذَكَرٌ إِلَّا ذَبَحَهُ

he gave orders that no male child should be born except one killed it.

أَبْلِغْ رَبِيعَةَ أَنْ يَغْضَبُوا

convey to Rabi'a that they should be angry.

The negative is أَنْ لَا or أَلَّا by assimilation.

إِنْ خِفْتُمْ أَلَّا يُقِيمَا حُدُودَ اللّٰهِ

if you fear that those two will not cause the limitations of God to stand (observe God's laws).

لَيْسَ عَلَيْكُمْ جُنَاحٌ أَلَّا تَكْتُبُوهَا

it is no sin for you that you do not write it.

حَتَّى

With the subjunctive it means ' so that ', ' until ' if any wish or purpose is intended.

لِكَيْ ـ كَيْ ـ لِأَنْ ـ لِ

These may mean ' in order that', but لِ and لِأَنْ may express consequence or even a substantival idea; they govern the subjunctive :—

قَدْ أُمِرَتْ لِأُقْتَلَ

she had given orders that I should be killed.

تُبْ لِيَغْفِرَ لَكَ اللّٰهُ

repent in order that God may pardon you.

تَعَلَّمُوا لِكَيْ تُعَلِّمُوا

learn in order that you may teach.

أُمِرْتُ لِأَنْ أَكُونَ أَوَّلَ الْمُسْلِمِينَ

I was commanded that I should become the first of those who submit (the Muslims).

لِأَنْ لَا – لِئَلَّ كَيْلَا is used as the negative of لِ ; and

لِكَيْلَا are usually written as one word.

Vocabulary 19

صَفَحَ u. صَفْح pardon.

عَقَدَ i. عَقْد tie, knot.

كَبِرَ كِبَر be big:

خَطَبَ u. خُطْبَة خِطَاب preach, ask
    a woman in marriage.

طَلَقَ u. طَلَاق be divorced.

عَتَبَ u. i. عَتْب blame.

كَفَرَ u. كُفْر be an unbeliever ;
    كُفْرَان be ungrateful.

دَمّ (دِمَاء) blood.

زَوْج (a) pair, husband.

حَقّ (b) truth, duty, right.

رَسُول (d) messenger, apostle.

شغل VIII work, be busy.

حَمَّ u. be hot.

حُمَّى fever.

فَاقَ u. فَوْق be superior to.

عقد VIII believe.

كبر V be proud, act proudly.

IV divorce.

III blame, speak contemptuously
    to.

رَبّ (a) lord.

زَوْجَة wife.

إِنَّمَا only (adv.).

خَلَطَ i. خَلْط mix.

حُمَّ (passive), suffer from fever.

حَمَّام bath (Turkish).

Exercise 37

هَلْ لَكَ أَنْ تَذْهَبَ – لَا يَكْرَهُ كَاتِبٌ أَنْ يَكْتُبَ –
اِنْزِلْ مِنَ الْجَنَّةِ فَمَا يَكُونُ لَكَ أَنْ تَتَكَبَّرَ

E*

فِيهَا ـ لَمْ نَشْتَغِلْ بِذِكْرِ ذَلِكَ كَيْلَا يَطُولَ ٱلْكِتَابُ ـ

مَا أَعْتَقِدُ أَنْ يَفُوقَ أَحَدٌ زَيْدًا فِى عِلْمٍ أَوْ أَدَبٍ ـ

إِنَّ ٱلصَّفْحَ ٱلْجَمِيلَ أَنَّكَ لَا تُعَاتِبُ مَنْ صَفَحْتَ

عَنْهُ ـ إِنَّ دِمَاءَكُمْ عَلَيْكُمْ حَرَامٌ إِلَى أَنْ تَقُومُوا

بَيْنَ يَدَىْ رَبِّكُمْ ـ خَطَبَ أَحَدٌ ٱمْرَأَةً فَقَالَتْ لَا

حَتَّى تُطَلِّقَ زَوْجَتَكَ ـ لَسْتُ أَخَافُ عَلَيْكَ أَنْ

تَخَافَ وَإِنَّمَا أَخَافُ عَلَيْكَ أَنْ لَا تَخَافَ ـ اَلطِّفْلُ

ثَقِيلٌ حَتَّى لَا تَحْمِلَهُ أُمُّهُ ـ سَمِعَ أَعْرَابِيٌّ رَجُلًا

يَقُولُ أَشْهَدُ أَنَّ مُحَمَّدًا رَسُولَ ٱللهِ فَقَالَ يَفْعَلُ

مَا ذَا .

38

his sermon was so long that the hearers went to sleep —
we believe that God is one and that he pardons the penitent
— the husband did not wish to divorce his elderly wife
out of pity for her — I listened attentively for fear that
anything of his speech should escape me (fall from me) —
what prevented you from prostrating yourself? (two
versions) — he sends his servants to bring down snow
from the mountains to preserve his food in the hot days —
we fear that the two parties will quarrel, one with the other
— tell him that I made this melody (voice) for him.

LESSON 20

ADVERBS

There are a few adverbs, mostly by-forms of prepositions; they are indeclinable.

مِنْ بَعْدُ after, after- ; بَعْدُ yet (in negative sentences);
wards; مِنْ قَبْلُ ـ قَبْلُ before (time); تَحْتُ ـ مِنْ تَحْتُ
below; فَوْقُ ـ مِنْ فَوْقُ above; حَيْثُ where;
مِنْ حَيْثُ whence.

لَمْ يَمُتْ بَعْدُ he is not yet dead.

لِلّهِ ٱلْأَمْرُ مِنْ قَبْلُ وَمِنْ بَعْدُ

God's is the command, before and after = the business is in
God's hands.

The infinitive takes the place of an adverb (Lesson 15).
Some English adverbs are replaced by verbs while the
English verb takes a subordinate place as imperfect or
participle.

Always.

زَالَ ـ يَزَالُ or بَرِحَ ـ يَبْرَحُ 'cease' with a negative :—

مَا زَالَ يَقُولُ ـ لَمْ يَزَلْ يَقُولُ

he did not cease talking = was always talking.

لَا يَزَالُ يَرْكَبُ he is always riding.

لَا تَزَلْ ذَاكِرَ الْمَوْتِ always remember death.

Almost.

يَكَادُ ـ كَادَ be on the point of doing (never used alone).

كَادَ يَقْتُلُهُ he almost killed him; كِدْتُ أَفْهَمُ I almost understood.

Scarcely.

يكاد ـ كاد with a negative :—

لَا يَكَادُ يَتَحَرَّكُ he scarcely moves.

وَجَدَ قَوْمًا لَا يَكَادُونَ يَفْقَهُونَ قَوْلًا

he found a people who scarcely understood speech.

ذَبَحُوهَا وَمَا كَادُوا يَفْعَلُونَ

they sacrificed it but were nearly not doing so.

Again.

يَزِيدُ ـ زَادَ ' increase '; يَعُودُ ـ عَادَ ' return ' :—

عَادَ يَضْرِبُهُ he hit him again.

زَادَ يَشْتِمُهُ he abused him again.

At once, immediately.

يَنْشَبُ ـ نَشِبَ ; 'remain' ; لَبِثَ 'stick to ' with a
negative :—

لَمْ يَلْبَثْ أَنْ قَالَ لَهَا   at once he said to her.

لَمْ يَنْشِبُوا أَنْ بَلَغَهُمُ ٱلْخَبَرُ بِذٰلِكَ

they did not stick that : immediately the news about this
came to them.

Soon, quickly.

أَوْشَكَ, IV of a verb first ' w ', more usually the

imperfect يُوشِكُ with أَنْ and the subjunctive ; rarely
the imperfect indicative. Three constructions are
possible :—

ـ يُوشِكُ أَنْ يَدْخُلَ زَيْدٌ ـ يُوشِكُ زَيْدٌ أَنْ يَدْخُلَ ـ

يُوشِكُ زَيْدٌ يَدْخُلُ

Zaid will soon come in.

The subordinate sentence أن يدخل زيد is the subject
of the verb.

Perhaps.

The defective verb عَسَى of which only the perfect
exists. Commonly the third masculine singular alone is
used.

عَسَى أَنْ تَكْرَهُوا شَيْئًا

perhaps you do not like something.

Less common is the construction :—

عَسَى ٱلْأَيَّامُ أَنْ يُرْجِعْنَ قَوْمًا

perhaps the days will bring a tribe back.

There is also the particle لَعَلَّ which is construed like أَنْ .

لَعَلَّ ٱللهَ غَافِرٌ perhaps God is a pardoner.

لَعَلَّهُ يُسَافِرُ perhaps he will go on a journey.

In the morning.

أَصْبَحَ IV do, be in the morning, become morning.

أَصْبَحَ زَيْدٌ مَرِيضًا in the morning Zaid was ill.

أَصْبَحْتُ أَحْزَنُ عَلَى مُعَاكَسَةِ ٱلْأَيَّامِ بِى

in the morning I was grieved by the contrariness of the days (fate) to me.

The verb may be followed by a noun or by a sentence with the imperfect; often it loses all sense of time and means no more than كَانَ or صَارَ ' become '.

أَمْسَى (IV of a verb third weak) ' do, be in the evening ' behaves just like أصبح .

In many other places the English adverb or adverbial expression becomes a verb in Arabic.

$$ \text{أَسْرَعَ الذَّهَابَ} $$

he made quick the going = he departed hurriedly.

$$ \text{أَبْعَدَ - النَّظَرَ} $$

he made distant the look = he looked into the distance.

A verbal sentence follows such phrases as :—

قَلِيلًا مَا ـ قَلَّ أَنْ ـ قَلَّ مَا seldom.

كَثِيرًا مَا ـ رُبَّمَا often.

طَالَ مَا it has lasted long.

قَلَّمَا رَأَيْتُ seldom have I seen.

قَلَّ مَا يَدُومُ وِصَالٌ seldom do (lovers') meetings last.

Vocabulary 20

حَرَّك II move (trans.).	ذَبَحَ a. ذَبْح cut the throat, sacrifice.
عَادَ u. عَوْد return, do again.	
شَتَمَ u. i. شَتْم abuse.	فَقِهَ فِقْه understand.
نَسِبَ نَسَب be attached to.	عَكَسَ i. عَكْس turn upside down.
سَرُعَ سُرْعَة be quick.	
بَعُدَ بُعْد be far, distant.	حَسُنَ حُسْن be good.

صُبْح (a) morning.

صبح II attack in the morning.

مَسَاء evening.

حَصَلَ u. حُصُول come to, befall (not of motion).

— II obtain.

رَزَقَ u. رِزْق provide.

سَفَر (a) journey.

نَصِيحَة advice, help.

حرك V move (intrans.).

هُهُنَا — هُنَا here.

ثَمَّ there.

زَاد i. زِيَادَة increase (trans and intrans.).

لَبِثَ لَبْث remain, stay.

سفر III journey, travel.

سرع IV make quick, go fast.

بعد II, IV make distant.

علج III treat (illness, etc.).

عكس III oppose.

حسن IV make good, do well.

صَبَاح morning.

صبح VIII drink in the morning.

غَد next day.

غَدًا to-morrow.

رِزْق (a) daily food, rations.

(إِسَا) أُسْوَة model.

هُنَالِكَ — هُنَاكَ there.

حِينَئِذٍ then.

Exercise 39

لَا يَلْبَثُ أَنْ يَرْجِعَ مِنْ سَفَرِهِ ـ لَا يَكَادُ الْمَرِيضُ
يَتَحَرَّكُ عَلَى فِرَاشِهِ ـ لَمْ تَزَلْ تَنْفَعُنِي بِنَصِيحَتِكَ
وَأُسْوَتِكَ ـ إِنْ حَدَّثْنَا أَحْسَنَ الْحَدِيثَ وَإِنْ حَدَّثْنَاهُ
أَحْسَنَ الِاسْتِمَاعَ ـ أَمِثْلُ هٰذَا يَقُولُ الشِّعْرَ أَوْ

يُحْسِنُ شِعْرًا ـ حَصَلْنَا عِدَّةُ لَيَالٍ لَا نَنَامُ مِنَ
الْبَرْدِ وَكِذْنَا نَهْلِكُ ـ أَصْبَحَ التَّاجِرُ وَالنَّاسُ
يَزْدَحِمُونَ قُدَّامَ دُكَّانِهِ ـ تَعَلَّمُوا الْعِلْمَ فَإِنْ تَكُونُوا
صِغَارَ قَوْمٍ فَعَسَى أَنْ تَكُونُوا كِبَارَ قَوْمٍ آخَرَ ـ
إِنْ أَنْكَحَكَهَا فَعَسَى أَنْ تُرْزَقَ وَلَدًا مِثْلِى ـ
أَكَادُ أَخَافُ مِنْ صَوْتِ الرِّيحِ.

40

I almost believed what he was saying — they fled quickly (two versions) — he went in without delay — perhaps they will come back to-morrow (two versions) — she scarcely blamed her son for swimming in the great river though (and) he did not swim well — the proud will soon repent of their pride — that young man almost turned the world upside down — they defeated us once and will not do so again — two men of great strength moved the stone but it scarcely moved — don't do this again.

LESSON 21

VERBS FIRST 'W' AND 'Y'

First ' w ' (Table 7).

Deviations from the strong verb occur in the imperfect of I and in VIII.

If the characteristic vowel of the imperfect of I is or ought to be ' i ', the ' w ' is omitted.

وَلَدَ produce young ; يَلِدُ imperfect ; لِدْ imperative.

In some verbs a final guttural has turned this ' i ' into ' a '
but the ' w ' is still omitted.

وَضَعَ	place	يَضَعُ	ضَعْ	وَضْعٌ
وَقَعَ	fall	يَقَعُ	قَعْ	وُقُوعٌ
وَدَعَ	leave	يَدَعُ	دَعْ	وَدْعٌ
وَزَعَ	restrain	يَزَعُ	زَعْ	وَزْعٌ

A few have ' i ' in the perfect and in the imperfect
contrary to rule.

وَرِثَ inherit   يَرِثُ   وَفِقَ find suitable   يَفِقُ

وَثِقَ trust   يَثِقُ   وَرِمَ be swollen   يَرِمُ

وَلِيَ be near   يَلِيَ (this is also third ' y ')

In the imperfect of IV the ' w ' combines with the preceding ' u ' to form a long vowel. From وَجَدَ find IV
means ' cause to be findable ' and then ' create ' : أَوْجَدَ

ـ إِيجَادٌ ـ أَوْجِدْ ـ يُوجِدُ ـ

There is no VII.

In VIII the 'w' is assimilated to the 't' :—

اِتَّهَمَ وهم   suspect ;   اِتَّفَقَ وفق   agree.

Verbs of the forms فَعُلَ فَعِلَ are regular in the imperfect of I :—

وَجِلَ be afraid ;   اِيجَلْ impf. يَوْجَلْ impv. but

وَبُلَ be unhealthy يَوْبُلْ   أُوبُلْ   فَوْبُلْ

Some nouns from these roots lose the first radical :—

جِهَّة direction   ثِقَّة reliability.

سَعَّة (width) wealth, ability.

Though only two radicals are visible, there is no doubt about the root. Feminine nouns from hollow roots have a long vowel in the middle : قَامَّة 'stature'; those from a third weak root have a long vowel after the second radical : زَكَاة 'act of sacrificing'. A few nouns from third weak roots are without the long vowel but they all have 'u' in the first syllable : لُغَة 'language'.

Verbs first 'y'.

There are only a few of these and the variations from the strong verb are few.

Two verbs have two imperfects in I :—

يَبِسَ be dry   يَيْبَسُ and   يَيْبِسُ

يَئِسَ despair   يَيْأَسُ   يَيْئِسُ

Note the imperative I : اِيسِرْ ـ يَيْسِرُ ـ يَسَرَ be easy.

The imperfect and participle IV : مُوسِرٌ يُوسِرُ become rich.

In VIII assimilation occurs : اتَّأَسَ despair.

Plurals, which can be deduced from the singular, are no longer put in the vocabulary.

Vocabulary 21

وجه II (turn the face) send.

وَجَدَ وُجُودُ find.

وَقَفَ وُقُوفُ stand.

وَسِعَ سَعَةُ a. be wide, include, be able.

وَجَبَ وُجُوبُ be necessary.

وَرِثَ i. وَرِثَ inherit.

وَدَعَ وَدْعُ a. leave.

وَكَلَ وَكْلُ entrust.

وهم VIII suspect.

صِفَةُ (صِفَاتُ) description, quality.

عَدْلٌ justice.

فَيْلَسُوفُ (فَلَاسِفَةُ) philosopher.

مَقْدَرَةُ strength.

سُوءُ evil, badness.

وجه V (send oneself) go.

وَصَلَ وُصُولُ reach, arrive at, give.

وَصَفَ وَصْفُ describe.

وسع VIII be wide.

وَرَدَ وُرُودُ go down.

وَضَعَ وَضْعُ put, put down.

ودع II say good-bye.

وكل II appoint as agent.

— VIII rely on.

وفق VIII agree.

حَالٌ f. (a) condition.

فِكْرٌ (a) thought, idea.

مَعْذِرَةٌ excuse.

مَفْجَرَةٌ sin (of any sort).

سَيِّءٌ bad.

Exercise 41

اَللهُ أَحَدٌ لَمْ يَلِدْ وَلَمْ يُولَدْ ـ هُوَ رَجُلٌ لَا يُوصَفُ
صِفَتُهُ ـ لَمْ يَدَعْ أَبْنَهُ ٱلصَّغِيرَ يَرِثُ مَعَ ٱلْكَبِيرِ ـ
دَعُوا ٱلْمَعَاذِرَ فَإِنَّ أَكْثَرَهَا مَفَاجِرُ ـ إِنَّ ٱللهَ
يَسَعُ عِلْمُهُ أَفْعَالَ عِبَادِهِ وَأَفْكَارَهُمْ ـ اَلْعَدْلُ أَنْ
تَضَعَ ٱلْأَشْيَاءَ فِى أَمْكِنَتِهَا ـ مَنْ أَسْوَأُ ٱلنَّاسِ
حَالًا قَالَ مَنِ ٱتَّسَعَتْ مَعْرِفَتُهُ وَضَاقَتْ مَقْدِرَتُهُ
وَبَعُدَتْ هِمَّتُهُ ـ اتَّهَمُوهُ بِٱلْكُفْرِ لِدَرْسِهِ كُتُبَ
ٱلْفَلَاسِفَةِ ـ يَجِبُ عَلَى ٱلْمُتَعَلِّمِ أَنْ يَطْلُبَ
ٱلْحَقَّ ـ انْتَظَرْتُ وُصُولَ ٱلْأَخْبَارِ وَلَمْ تَصِلْ بَعْدُ ـ
يُوشِكُ ٱلطَّبِيبَانِ أَنْ يَتَّفِقَا عَلَى عِلَاجِ ٱلْمَرِيضِ.

42

describe the conditions of your disease (symptoms) — fresh news was arriving every hour — the earth became narrow on him and it had been wide (his condition changed for the worse) — I sent him to you but he did not go — we heard you describing what you had done — we shall find them standing in the street — there is not found ingratitude like that of an ungrateful child — I heard his friends saying good-bye to him — was it necessary for you to entrust this business to someone else? — put your hand on the book of God and swear.

LESSON 22

RELATIVE CLAUSES

There is no relative pronoun in Arabic.

When the antecedent is indefinite, the relative clause is added without any connecting link.

$$ أَطْلُبُ رَجُلًا يَقُومُ عَلَى بُسْتَانِي $$

I am looking for a man who will stand over (look after) my garden.

When the antecedent is definite, اَلَّذِى is used as a link between the antecedent and the relative clause. It is inflected as follows :—

	sing.	dual, nom.	oblique	plural
masc.	اَلَّذِى	اَللَّذَانِ	اَللَّذَيْنِ	اَلَّذِينَ
fem.	اَلَّتِى	اَللَّتَانِ	اَللَّتَيْنِ	اَللَّوَاتِى

The link agrees in case with the antecedent; this is visible only in the dual.

When the English relative is in an oblique case, the link has to be supplemented by a personal pronoun in the relative clause. This pronoun is often omitted when it should be in the accusative.

اَلرَّجُلُ اَلَّذِى قَتَلَ أَبِى

the man who killed my father.

اَلرَّجُلُ اَلَّذِى قَتَلَهُ أَبِى

the man whom my father killed.

اَلْمَرْأَةُ اَلَّتِى كَانَ عِنْدَهَا اُبْنِى

the woman with whom my son was.

أَبْعَثُ إِلَيْكَ اَلْمَرْأَتَيْنِ اَللَّتَيْنِ تَطْلُبُ مِنْهُمَا خَبَرَ اَبْنَتِكَ

I am sending to you the two women from whom you can ask news of your daughter.

If the antecedent is first or second person, the pronoun in the relative clause may agree with it or be in the third person to agree with the link.

أَأَنْتِ اَلَّتِى اُسْتَوْدَعْتُكِ اَلسِّرَّ

are you she to whom I entrusted the secret?

كُنْ أَنْتَ اَلَّذِى تُكَلِّمُهَا

be you he who speaks to her.

نَحْنُ ٱلَّذِينَ بَايَعُوا مُحَمَّدًا

we are those who did homage to Muhammad.

' He who ' is rendered by الذى or مَنْ ; ' that which '

by مَا or الذى .

مِن may take the verb in the singular or plural ; مَا

always has a singular verb.

مَنْ أَشْعَرُ ٱلْعَرَبِ قَالَ ٱلَّذِى يَقُولُ ....

who is the most poetical of the Arabs ? he said, he who
says . . . .

يَا مَنْ لَا يَمُوتُ ٱرْحَمْ

O, he who dies not, have mercy = you who die not have
mercy.

عَرَفْتُ مَا عَرَفْتَه

I know what you know.

أَىُّ ' which of ' is always followed by a genitive,
either a noun or a pronominal suffix. It may be singular
or plural and may belong to the main sentence or the
relative clause.

سَلِّمْ عَلَى أَيِّهِمْ أَفْضَلُ

or

سَلِّمْ عَلَى أَيِّهِمْ أَفْضَلُ

greet those (him) of them who are most worthy.

Vocabulary 22

جَازَ u. جَوَازٌ	be allowable.	بَدَنٌ	(a) body.
طَرَحَ a. طَرْحٌ	throw down.	ذِهْنٌ	mind, intellect.
رسل III	write letters to.	جوز III	pass beyond.
زَعَمَ a. زَعْمٌ	think, claim.	قَسَمَ i. قَسْمٌ	divide.
رَغِبَ رَغْبٌ . فِي	like, be pleased with ؛ عَنْ dislike.	رسل IV	send.
زَرَعَ a. زَرْعٌ	sow.	وَجِعَ i. وَجَعٌ	feel pain.
		حَصَدَ u. حَصَادٌ	reap.
دَاءٌ	(a) disease.	دَوَاءٌ (أَدْوِيَةٌ)	medicine, remedy.
عِلْمٌ	(b) knowledge, science.	أَدَبٌ	(a) manners, arts.
سَرِيرٌ (أَسِرَّةٌ)	anything on which one can sit or lie.	صِحَّةٌ	health.
		ذَكَاءٌ	sharpness (metaphorical).
خَاتَمٌ (خَوَاتِمُ)	seal.	صَحِيحٌ	healthy, true.

Exercise 43

كَانَ لَهُ بَنُو عَمٍّ وَرِثُوهُ ـ مَا أَنْتُمُ ٱلَّذِينَ يَهْرُبُونَ
مِنَ ٱلْحَقِّ ـ ٱلَّذِى يَزْرَعُهُ ٱلْإِنْسَانُ ٱلْيَوْمَ يَحْصُدُهُ
غَدًا ـ نَزَلْتُ عَنِ ٱلسَّرِيرِ ٱلَّذِى كُنْتُ مَطْرُوحًا
عَلَيْهِ ـ كَانَ ذَلِكَ خَاتَمَ أَعْمَالِهِ ٱلْحَسَنَةِ ٱلَّتِى
تُجَاوِزُ ٱلْوَصْفَ ـ كَيْفَ لَا تَرْغَبُ فِى تَدْبِيرٍ يَجْمَعُ

لَكَ صِحَّةَ الْبَدَنِ وَذَكَاءَ الذِّهْنِ وَكَثْرَةَ الْمَالِ ـ

اَلْجَارِيَتَانِ اللَّتَانِ وَجَّهْتُهُمَا إِلَى مَدْرَسَةِ الْبَنَاتِ

قَدْ صَارَتَا ذَوَاتَىْ عِلْمٍ وَأَدَبٍ ـ كُنْ لَهُمْ كَالطَّبِيبِ

الَّذِى لَا يَعْجَلُ بِالدَّوَاءِ قَبْلَ مَعْرِفَةِ الدَّاءِ ـ هَلْ بِعْتِ

الْعَبْدَيْنِ الَّذَيْنِ تَرْغَبِيـنَ عَنْهُمَا ـ صِفِى لِى مَنْ

كَلَّمَكِ.

44

I appointed as my agent one in whom I trust — he asserts that what came down on him had never come down on another — he who does not know the disease does not know the remedy — they do not wish to sell the two books which they inherited from their uncle — we sowed the fields which we had found unsown — these are the two men who found the wounded man and carried him to my house — I came out by the same door as in I went — the duties, which were incumbent on me, were beyond my strength — I said good-bye to the work in which I took pleasure and turned to work in which I took no pleasure.

LESSON 23

DOUBLED VERBS

In these verbs (consult Tables 8 and 9) the second radical is the same as the third.

The variations from the strong verb can be summarized in three rules :—

1. When the third radical has a vowel, the second loses its vowel and the two consonants are written once with *shadda*.

2. When the third radical has no vowel, the second keeps its vowel and the two consonants are written separately.

3. In the imperfect, when Rule 1 applies, the vowel of the second radical is thrown back to the first.

Rule 2 applies, in the perfect, to the first and second persons and to the third feminine plural ; in the imperfect to the feminine plurals only.

(The word, contraction, is avoided for there is no reason to think that these verbs were originally strong.)

The jussive has two forms ; one is regular according to Rule 2, the other is short like the imperfect indicative. A final double consonant cannot be pronounced so a short vowel, usually ' a ', is added ; the result is that the jussive cannot be distinguished by form alone from the subjunctive. Both forms existed side by side.

The imperative may be formed from the short form of the jussive and then needs no liaison.

A long vowel between the second and third radicals prevents them from coalescing ; examples are the infinitives of stems II, VII, VIII, and X and the passive participle of I.

Stems IX and XI of the strong verb are only special forms of doubled verb and present no difficulties (Table 9).

The derived stems follow the same rules ; II is no exception, for the second radical is already doubled and no consonant can be tripled.

V is sometimes irregular, the third radical being changed into ' y ' and resembling a verb third weak. تَظَنَّنْتَ becomes تَظَنَّيْتَ you think.

Peculiar is the change from قَصَصْتَ to قَصَّيْتَ you cut.

Other forms behave like hollow verbs : ظَلَّتَ or ظَلِّتُ

from ظَلَّ remain أَحَسَّتُ for أَحْسَسْتُ I feel.

Nouns from these roots also follow the same rules.

مَحَلٌّ (مَحَالٌّ) 'place' come from theoretical *maḥlalun*

and *maḥa:lilu* ; حَلَالٌ (loosed) not taboo, lawful, per-
missible.

The connection of ideas is this :—

$$\text{حَلَّ u. حَلَّ}\quad \text{loose, untie.}$$

When the bedouin unties his baggage, he camps dwells so :—

$$\text{حُلُولٌ u. حَلَّ}\quad \text{.dwell.}$$

The antithesis of loosing and binding is familiar from the
Gospels :—

$$\text{صَاحِبُ ٱلْحَلِّ وَٱلْعَقْدِ}$$

the master of loosing and binding—holder of supreme power.

So حَلَّ i. حَلَّ be not taboo, be lawful, allowable.

The opposite of this is حَرَامٌ حَرُمَ be taboo, sacred,

unlawful. حَرِيمٌ حَرَّمَ i. or حَرَّمَ a. forbid, prevent.

The two senses appear in one sentence:—

$$\text{سَفَكُوا دَمَ ٱلْحَرَامِ فِى شَهْرِ ٱلْحَرَامِ فِى بِلَادِ ٱلْحَرَامِ}$$

they shed forbidden blood in the sacred month, in the holy place.

These verbs go back to a time before morality had been associated with religion.

In the last example a noun in the genitive case acts as an adjective:—

رِجَالُ ٱلسَّوْءِ evil men.

Vocabulary 23

سَرَّ u. سُرُورٌ please, delight.	حَيَّةٌ (حَيَّاتٌ) snake.
حَسَّ IV to perceive, know.	مُصْعَبٌ a man's name.
عَدَّ u. عَدٌّ count.	ظَنَّ u. ظَنٌّ have an opinion.
مَرَّ u. مُرُورٌ pass by.	فَرَّ i. فِرَارٌ run away.
مَدَّ u. مَدٌّ stretch.	عَدَّ IV prepare (trans.).
رَدَّ u. رَدٌّ come back, send back.	عَدَّ X prepare oneself.
خَفَّ i. خِفَّةٌ be light (weight).	مَرَّ X continue.
عَفَّ i. عِفَّةٌ be chaste, temperate.	مَدَّ IV help, reinforce.
قَصَّ u. قَصٌّ tell a story, cut.	مَدَّ X ask for help.
قَرَّ i. قَرَارٌ be firm, fixed.	خَفَّ X despise.
دَلَّ u. دَلٌّ guide.	حَبَّ IV love, like.
لِقَاءٌ (inf. of لَقِىَ) meeting.	مَلَّ a. مَلَلٌ be disgusted with.

قَرَّ u. قَرّ be cold.

— IV acknowledge, confirm.

ضَلَّ i. ضَلَال go astray.

(فَتَن) فِتْنَة temptation, civil war.

حَيَاء shame, modesty.

ٱلْبَصْرَة Basra.

Exercise 45

أُحِبُّهَا وَتُحِبُّنِى وَيُحِبُّ جَمَلِى نَاقَتَهَا ـ ظَنَنْتُ
أَنَّهُ يَسْتَعِدُّ لِلصُّعُودِ فِى ٱلْجِبَالِ ـ لَا تَظُنِّنِى
أُخَالِفُكَ ـ مَنْ عَفَّ خَفَّ عَلَى ٱلصَّدِيقِ لِقَاؤُهُ
وَأَخُو ٱلْحَوَائِجِ وَجْهُهُ مَمْلُولٌ ـ ذُكِرَ فِى أَمْرِ
مُصْعَبٍ وَعَزْلِ أَخِيهِ إِيَّاهُ عَنِ ٱلْبَصْرَةِ وَرَدِّهِ إِيَّاهُ
إِلَيْهَا غَيْرَ هَذِهِ ٱلْقِصَّةِ ـ أَسْرَعُ ٱلنَّاسِ إِلَى
ٱلْفِتْنَةِ أَقَلُّهُمْ حَيَاءً مِنَ ٱلْفِرَارِ ـ إِنِّى أَحْسَسْتُ
بِصَوْتِ مُرُورِ حَيَّةٍ أَلَمْ تُحِسَّ بِهِ ـ مُدَّ يَدَكَ
إِلَى حَبْلِ ٱللهِ وَيَمُدُّكَ ـ عُدُّوا ٱلْمَرْضَى وَأَعِدُّوا
ٱلْأَدْوِيَةَ لِعِلَاجِهِمْ ـ مَرَّ بِٱلْأَوْلَادِ يَقُصُّ عَلَيْهِمْ
قِصَصَ ٱلنَّبِىِّ .

guide me to what will delight me — I thought that you were guiding me aright and you have led me astray — the boy used to ask the teacher for help and he helped him — you want to become chief of the tribe ; then despise what folks may say — we thought that the women were fleeing in fear while (and) they were hurrying to meet their husbands — we do not know what to think — unbelievers are misled and mislead others — I saluted the company and they returned my salute — do you think they will acknowledge my rights ? — there is none to turn back what God does.

LESSON 24

HOLLOW VERBS—Continued (Table 6)

Stems II, III, V, and VI are like the strong verbs ; ' w ' verbs differ from ' y ' roots :—

زَوَّجَ give in marriage ; تَزَوَّجَ marry ;

بَيَّنَ distinguish, make plain ; تَبَيَّنَ make plain to oneself, be plain ;

بَايَعَ do, receive homage ; جَاوَبَ answer.

In the other stems there is no distinction between the two classes. A long vowel appears in place of the middle radical just as in I ; in the perfects that vowel is *a:* which is shortened where necessary to *a*.

In the imperfect of IV and X the vowel is *i:*, shortened where necessary to *i*.

In VII and VIII the imperfect unexpectedly has ' a '

long or short as is required. اِنْقَادَ obey (let himself be

led) ; اِخْتَارَ choose.

Indicative.	Jussive.	Imperative.	Infinitive.
يَنْقَادُ	يَنْقَدْ	اِنْقَدْ	اِنْقِيَادٌ
يَخْتَارُ	يَخْتَرْ	اِخْتَرْ	اِخْتِيَارٌ

Note the infinitive of IV and X ; the middle radical is
lost and the feminine ending ' at ' is added as compensation.

X. اِسْتِقَامَةٌ   IV إِقَامَةٌ

Some verbs have both strong and weak forms :—

rest. اِسْتَرَاحَ اِسْتَرْوَحَ give rest ; أَرَاحَ — أَرْوَحَ

A few of the type فَعِلَ have strong forms only :

سَوِدَ be black ; أَسْوَدَ blacken ;

but اِسْوَدَّ XI be black and سَوَّدَ II blacken are more
common.

Vocabulary 24

سوف II make future, postpone.   جوب III, IV answer.

صَادَ i. صَيْدٌ hunt, fish.   قَادَ i. lead.

رود IV wish, will.   خيّر II give a choice to.

نَقَدَ u. نَقْدٌ pay cash.

قَوم IV stay, set up.

قَيد VII obey.

وَعَدَ i. وَعْدٌ promise.

خير VIII choose.

طوع IV obey.

قوم X be straight.

طَوْعًا willingly.

وعد IV threaten.

عون IV help.

طوع X be able.

يَهُودِىٌّ Jews. يَهُودٌ (sing.).

وَعِيدٌ threat.

خُفَّاشٌ (خَفَافِيشُ) bat (animal).

عون X ask the help of.

بَالٌ mind.

نَصْرَانِىٌّ (نَصَارَى) Christian.

صوب II think right.

سَتَرَ u. سَتْرٌ hide.

حول VIII employ devices,
   tricks.

مَا بَالُ what about, what is the
   matter with ?

عَوْنٌ help.

صوب IV come upon, hit.

بيع VIII buy.

حِيلَةٌ (حِيَلٌ) trick, stratagem,
   device.

صيد VIII take by hunting.

حوج VIII need, be in want
   (always with إلى).

لَئِيمٌ (c) base, ignoble.

Exercise 47

وَعْدُ ٱلْكَرِيمِ نَقْدٌ وَوَعْدُ ٱللَّئِيمِ تَسْوِيفٌ ـ صِدْنَا
وَنَصْطَـــادُ ـ لَمْ تُرِدْ أُخْتِى أَنْ تُطِيعَ أَوَامِرَ
مُعَلِّمَتِهَا ـ لِمَا لَا تُرِيدِينَ أَنْ تَتْرُكِى شُغْلَكِ ـ

اَلْخَفَافِيشُ تَسْتَتِرُ بِالنَّهَارِ خَوْفَ أَنْ تُصْطَادَ

لِحُسْنِهَا ـ أَرَادَ أَبِى أَنْ يَبْتَاعَ مَا يَحْتَاجُ إِلَيْهِ

أَهْلُهُ ـ سَمِعَ أَحَدٌ رَجُلًا يَسْتَعِينُ اللهَ فِى أَمْرِ

أُمِّهِ فَقَالَ لَهُ مَا بَالُ أَبِيكَ قَالَ هُوَ رَجُلٌ

يَحْتَالُ لِنَفْسِهِ ـ أَخَيَّرَكَ أَبُوكَ فِى تَزَوُّجِكَ ـ لَا

اخْتَارَتْ أُمِّى زَوْجَةً لِى ـ سَمِعْنَا يَهُودِيًّا يُوعِدُ

غُلَامَهُ ـ يَجِبُ عَلَيْكُمْ أَنْ تُجِيبُوا طَلَبَ

الْحُكُومَةِ ـ قَادَ الشَّرَهُ تِلْكَ النِّسَاءَ أَنْ يَمِلْنَ

عَنْ طَرِيقِ الرِّفْقِ وَانْقَدْنَ .

48

he kept quiet and was quiet for a long time — avarice makes men incline from the Straight Path — we asked for his help and he helped us — he set up a great stone as a reminder of the evil which had befallen the people — the brigands frightened the inhabitants of out-of-the-way (distant) houses — care for my family and property is killing me — that Jew does what he likes and the Jews and Christians think him right — the wise man learns from the misfortunes of others — she needed help but found no helper — I used every device to get out of the fortress in which I was a captive but did not find a way out — my wife bought clothes of silk and wool.

LESSON 25

VERBS WITH THE GLOTTAL STOP

Verbs with the glottal stop (consult Tables 10–12) are regular in pronunciation, apart from a few freaks. There remains the difficulty of writing; the rule of thumb given in the chapter on the alphabet and the following notes will help to remove this.

FIRST HAMZA

When two hamzas should occur in one syllable, the second drops and the vowel is lengthened. Thus *PaꞦ* becomes *Pa:*, *PuꞦ* becomes *Pu:*, and *PiꞦ* becomes *Pi:*. *Pa:* is written with madda.

		Imperfect First Singular.	
		Active.	Passive.
أَمَلَ	hope	يَأْمُلُ آمُلُ	أُومَلُ

Imperative.

أمِل	hope	فَأْمُلْ but اُومُلْ
أَسَرَ	take captive	فَأْسِرْ اِيسِرْ يَأْسِرُ

Two drop the hamza always in the imperative :—

أَخَذَ take خُذْ ـ يَأْخُذُ ; eat أَكَلَ ـ يَأْكُلُ ـ كُلْ

أَمَرَ drops hamza when the imperative stands alone but

retains it after و and ف : مُرْ command but وَأْمُرْ.

Stem III

أُوكِلَ perf. pass. آكَلَ impv. يُوَاكِلُ impf. آكَلَ eat with

Stem IV

آكِلَ impv. أُوكِلُ 1 per. يُؤكِلُ impf. آكَلَ feed. إِيكَالٌ infin.

There is no VII.

Stem VIII

فَأْتَزَرَ but اِيتَزَرَ wear a loin cloth

يَأْتَزِرُ impf. اِيتَزِرْ impv. but فَأْتَزِرْ .

Passive

أُوتُمِنَ was given authority; اَلَّذِى أُوتُمِنَ he who was given authority.

أخَذَ assimilates ? to t: اِتَّخَذَ .

MIDDLE HAMZA

The spelling is often not rigid: يَسْئَلُ — يَسْأَلُ .

The passive perfect I is سُئِلَ ; this spelling seems to be derived from a dialect which used the form si:la.

سَأَلَ has also an irregular imperative سَلْ, jussive

يَسَلْ .

The active participle I is like that of the hollow verb so

سُئِرَ   be left over

يَسِيرُ ـ سَارَ   go   سَائِرٌ

يَسُورُ ـ سَارَ   jump

THIRD HAMZA

Some of the spellings are not rigid :—

3 masc. dual perfect   قَرَأَا ـ قَرَآ

2 fem. sing. impf.   تَقْرَأَيْنَ ـ تَقْرَئِينَ

3 masc. plu. impf.   يَقْرَأُونَ ـ يَقْرَؤُونَ

Vocabulary 25

أدب II educate.

أَمِنَ أَمَانٌ be safe from.

أَجَرَ u.i. أَجْرٌ hire out.

أثر II make a mark on,
   influence.

أثر IV prefer.

سَأَلَ a. سُؤَالٌ ask, beg.

نبأ IV tell.

كفأ III reward.

أَنِسَ أُنْسٌ be friendly.

قِرَاءَةٌ a. قَرَأَ read, repeat.   الف II compose (a book), unite

(أُسْرَى) أَسِيرٌ prisoner.   (men), win over.

دِينٌ (a) religion.   هنأ II congratulate.

حَسَدَ u.i. envy.   انس III treat kindly.

إِذْنٌ أَذِنَ permit.   اخر II make late.

بَدَأَ a. and VIII begin.   — V be late.

امن IV believe.   (مَلَائِكَةٌ) مَلَكٌ ـ مَلْأَكٌ angel.

اجر X hire, rent.   جِسْمٌ (a) body.

اثر V receive a mark, be   آخِرٌ last.

influenced.   نَصِيبٌ share.

لجأ VIII take refuge.

Exercise 49

مَنْ أَدَّبَ وَلَدَهُ صَغِيرًا سَرَّ بِهِ كَبِيرًا ـ آمَنْتُ بِٱللهِ

وَبِمَلَائِكَتِهِ وَبِرُسُلِهِ وَبِكُتُبِهِ وَبِٱلْيَوْمِ ٱلْآخِرِ ـ

هَلْ يَأْذَنُ لِى ٱلْقَائِدُ بِسُؤَالِ ٱلْأَسْرَى ـ كُنْتُ

أَسْتَأْجِرُ مَنْزِلِى مِنْ تَاجِرٍ وَأَدْفَعُ أَجْرَهُ لَهُ كُلَّ

شَهْرٍ ـ اِبْتَدَأَ ٱلْعِيدَ بِقِرَاءَةِ ٱلْقُرْآنِ ٱلْكَرِيمِ ثُمَّ

خَاطَبَتِ امْرَأَةٌ مِنَ ٱلنِّسَاءِ تُنْبِئُ نَبَأَ ٱلرَّسُولِ ـ

كَانَ ٱلشَّيْخُ يُؤَانِسُ ٱلسَّائِلِينَ وَٱلْمُلْتَجِئِينَ ـ

اِكْتَسَبَ مُكَافَأَةً عَظِيمَةً بِتَأْلِيفِهِ كِتَابًا يُدَافِعُ
عَنْ دِينِ النَّصَارَى ـ كَانَ النَّاسُ يَهْنِئُونَهُ بِرُجُوعِهِ
سَالِمًا عَنِ الْحَرْبِ ـ اِقْرَأُوا عَلَيْهِ السَّلَامَ وَأَنْبِئُوهُ
بِوُصُولِى إِلَيْهِ غَدًا ـ مَا كُنْتُ لِأُوثِرَ بِنَصِيبِى مِنْكَ
أَحَدًا ـ أَأَمِنَ أَحَدٌ الْمُصِيبَةَ.

50

give this beggar food and tell him to go away — he was not
safe from the devices of the envious — have you hired
men to harvest your fields ? — I treated these people with
friendliness and they rewarded me richly — your friends
will eat and drink with me — I shall feed it on bread and
dates — then the poets will ask the governor's permission
to begin the recitation of their poems — the sun left its
mark on the face of the peasant but the strength of his
body was not affected — the caravan is late ; rain has
delayed it.

LESSON 26

VERBS—THIRD WEAK (Tables 13–16)

These verbs have 'w' or 'y' as third radical.

فَعَلَ . The third masculine singular of the perfect and
the short forms of the imperfect have only two syllables
instead of the three of the strong verb. In the simple stem
of verbs third 'w' the third masculine singular of the

perfect is written with *alif*, in those third ' y ' and in all the derived stems of both classes it is written with ' y '. This probably points to an original difference in pronunciation but this has long been ignored. When the inflections of the perfect begin with a consonant, the forms are like those of the strong verb except that the weak radical forms a diphthong with the characteristic vowel. Elsewhere there is contraction for which no rules can be given. The third masculine dual cannot be contracted for the inflection is already long.

Most verbs with ' w ' have ' u ' in the imperfect and most with ' y ' have ' i '. The radical combines with the characteristic to form a long vowel. When a back vowel is followed by a front vowel, the weak consonant reappears to separate them, as in the dual. When two back vowels come together, one is lost ; the survivor is the vowel of the inflection for, if that were lost, the significant form would be destroyed. Thus تَدْعِينَ (root *dʕw*) second feminine singular ; if the ' u ' had survived, the resulting word would be تَدْعُونَ which is second masculine plural.

Again, يَرْمُونَ (root *rmy*) third masculine plural ; if the ' i ' had been kept, the result would be يَرْمِينَ which is third feminine plural.

The subjunctive explains itself.

The short forms of the jussive lose the letter of prolongation and with it all trace of the third radical.

The emphatic can only be learnt.

The imperative, of course, has liaison.

فَعِلَ . In verbs third ' w ' there is partial assimilation of ' w ' to ' y ' so there is only one form for both classes.

Perfect. The characteristic ' i ' is separated from ' a '

of the inflection by the third radical and is lost before *u:*.
When the inflection begins with a consonant, ' y ' coalesces
with the characteristic to form *i:*.

Imperfect. As in the transitive the short forms have only
two syllables, the vowel of the second being *a:*. Before a
back vowel, this is shortened and forms a diphthong.
Before a consonant, it is resolved into the diphthong *ay*.
Before *a:* (in the dual) it is resolved into ' a ' and ' y ' which
begins the next syllable.

Passive. What has been said about the intransitive
applies to the passive also.

Derived stems. Both classes become third ' y '.

Active participle. Contraction takes place in the
nominative and genitive ; the third radical and the case
ending drop and nunation is given to the second radical :—

رَامٍ ' a shooter ' (nom. and gen.) but رَامِيًا (acc.)

اَلرَّامِى ' the shooter' (nom. and gen.) but اَلرَّامِىَ (acc.)

This applies to all active participles of the derived stems
and to all nouns from these roots with ' i ' before the weak
radical.

Something similar happens in some plurals :—

فَاعِلَةٌ has for plural فَوَاعِلُ .

So جَارِيَةٌ should have جَوَارِىُ but *iyu* is contracted
to ' i ' and nunation is added to indicate the contraction.

جَوَارٍ (nom. and gen.)   جَوَارِىَ (acc.)

اَلْجَوَارِى (nom. and gen.)   اَلْجَوَارِىَ (acc.)

Passive participle. In stem I verbs final ' w ' have forms

like مَدْعُوٌّ and final ' y ' like مَرْمِىٌّ with assimilation because the resulting word cannot be confused with any other part of the verb.

When a noun from these roots has ' a ' after the second radical, contraction occurs; the case ending is dropped and nunation put over the second radical. *Alif* is written in the ' w ' roots and ' y ' in those with ' y '.

اَلْفَتَى (فِتْيَانْ) فَتًى   a man in the prime of life

اَلْعَصَا (عِصِىٌّ) عَصًا   stick

These nouns are indeclinable. All passive participles of the derived stems are of this form. مُصْطَفَى ـ مُلْقَى ـ مُسْتَلْقَى .

Infinitive. Stem II shortens the *i:* and adds *at* for compensation. تَسْلِيَة .

Stem III. In the form مُفَاعَلَة contraction occurs مُلَاقَاة ; the dotted ' h ' shows that it cannot be a feminine plural.

Stems V and VI. The ' u ' is assimilated to the ' y ' and contraction occurs.

V تَلَقٍّ   VI تَرَاضٍ

When the second radical has *a:*, the final radical becomes *ʾ* :—

(أَرْدِيَة) رِدَاءٌ cloak (final ' y ').

(أَكْسِيَة) كِسَاءٌ covering, dress (final ' w ').

Stems III, IV, VII, VIII, and X form their infinitives in this way.

اِسْتِلْقَاءٌ ـ اِبْتِلاءٌ ـ إِلْقَاءٌ ـ لِقَاءٌ

أَفْعَلُ. The elative, like the imperfect, has only two syllables :—

عُلَّى   عُلْيَا   أَعْلَى   higher, etc.

In the feminine the radical ' w ' is usually changed to ' y ', so the *a:* is indicated by *alif* to avoid the repetition of ' y '.

Similarly عُمْيٌ ـ عَمْيَاءُ أَعْمَى blind.

غِنِيٌّ ـ قَوِيٌّ becomes فَعِيلٌ.

فَعُولٌ by assimilation becomes مُضِيٌّ infinitive of

يَمْضِي مَضَى.

Further assimilation occurs occasionally :—

قِسِيٌّ plural of عَصًا is the form فَعُولٌ as is عِصِيٌّ

the irregular plural of قَوْسٌ bow (weapon).

مُفْعَلٌ . Place nouns always have 'a' in the second syllable :—

اَلْمَنَاجِى - مَنَاج place of safety, refuge. Plural مَنْجًى

Note.—The elative أَعْلَى has probably been influenced by the IV stem. The passive participles are inflected for number as follows :—

dual	مُصْطَفَيَانِ	مُصْطَفَيَيْنِ
plural	مُصْطَفَوْنَ	مُصْطَفَيْنِ

Vocabulary 26

أَخَذَ u. أَخْذٌ take.

نَسِيَ نِسْيَانٌ forget.

جَنَى i. جَنًى gather, جِنَايَةٌ commit a crime.

هَجَا u. هِجَاءٌ lampoon.

غنى IV make rich, self-sufficient.

لَهَا u. لَهْوٌ play.

غَزَا u. غَزْوٌ raid, go to war.

بَكَى i. بُكَاءٌ weep.

نَهَى a. نَهْىٌ forbid.

وَلِىَ i. وَلِىَ be near.

— IV do a kindness.

حوط IV surround.

فقر IV make poor.

بغض IV hate, dislike.

حق X deserve.

قَلَّ i. قِلٌّ be little.

—X think little, be independent.

سَيِّدٌ (سَادَاتٌ سَادَةٌ) prince, chief.

اخذ VIII make, choose.

عِمَامَةٌ (عَمَائِمُ) turban.

قِلَادَةٌ (قَلَائِدُ) necklace.

عَصَبَ i. عَصْبٌ fold, tie.

حصى IV count.

غنى X be self-sufficient. | ولى II make one governor.

لهو IV distract attention. | فقر VIII be poor, in need.

كَنَى i. كِفَايَة be sufficient for. | جَاءَ i. جِيءَ come.

شرى VIII buy. | رَكَضَ u. رَكْض run.

بَقِىَ بَقَاء remain. | مَعْرُوف known, kind act.

نهى VIII let oneself be for- | قَلَّ IV make little, support.
bidden, desist. | مُعَمَّم wearing a turban.

Exercise 51

إِذَا اتَّخَذْتُمْ عِنْدَ رَجُلٍ يَدًا فَانْسَوْهَا ـ لَا خَيْرَ فِى

الْمَعْرُوفِ إِذَا أُحْصِىَ ـ سَتَرَ رَجُلٌ مَا أَوْلَى وَنَشَرَ

مَا أَوْلَى ـ الْعَرَبُ تَقُولُ سَيِّدٌ مُعَمَّمٌ يُرِيدُونَ أَنَّ

كُلَّ جِنَايَةٍ يَجْنِيهَا أَحَدٌ مِنْ قَوْمِهِ مَعْصُوبَةٌ بِرَأْسِهِ ـ

لِمَا لَا تُطِيلُ الْهِجَاءَ قَالَ يَكْفِيكَ مِنَ الْقِلَادَةِ

مَا أَحَاطَ بِالْعُنُقِ ـ الَّذِى أَرْضَاهُ لَا يَحِيشِنِى

وَالَّذِى يَحِيشِنِى لَا أَرْضَاهُ ـ أَغْنِنِى بِالِافْتِقَارِ إِلَيْكَ

وَلَا تُفْقِرْنِى بِالِاسْتِغْنَاءِ عَنْكَ ـ إِنَّ مَا قَلَّ وَكَفَى

خَيْرٌ مِمَّا كَثُرَ وَأَلْهَى ـ مَا لَكَ لَا تَغْزُو فَقَالَ

لَأُبْغِضُ الْمَوْتَ عَلَى فِرَاشِى فَكَيْفَ أَمُرُّ إِلَيْهِ

رَكْضًا ـ اِشْتَرِ التَّمْرَ مِنَ الْمَوْصِلِ وَاحْمِلْهُ إِلَى

الْبَصْرَةِ فَإِنَّكَ تُهْلِكُ مَالَكَ .

52

I will square (be sufficient for) him for you — whatever I forget, I shall not forget your friendliness — did you buy what you needed ? — daughter, take what I give you and buy what you like — the women wept for the slain — those who weep now shall laugh — I think they will remain in (on) their present condition — let no play distract you from your studies — I forbade her and she stopped (let herself be forbidden) — their (masc. and fem.) attention was diverted from what they were making — the caliph, may God preserve him, does not forget to reward those who deserve it.

LESSON 27

VERBS DOUBLY WEAK

These verbs are regular according to both the classes to which they belong, except for occasional aberrations. The pronunciation is easy though the writing may cause difficulty. Here follow a few typical verbs.

Hollow and Hamza

Root اول ' return '

آلَ   أُلْتَ   يَؤُولُ   يَؤُلْ   أُلْ

Root جيء ' come '

جِيءَ   يَجِيءُ   يَجِيءُ   جِئْتَ   جَاءَ

The active participle is جَاءٍ   اَلْجَائِي

Hamza and third ' y '

أَتَى ' come ': the perfect is regular.

Imperfect يَأْتِي jussive يَأْتِ imperative اِيتِ and

فَأْتِ .

رَأَى ' see ': the perfect is regular.

In the imperfect the hamza is dropped :—

يَرَيْنَ   تَرَيْنَ   يَرَيَانِ   يَرَوْنَ   يَرَيْنَ   يَرَى

As in رَضِيَ the second feminine singular has the same
form as the second feminine plural.

In IV the hamza is also dropped :—

perfect	أَرَيْتَ	أَرَتْ	أَرَى
imperfect	يُرُونَ	تُرِينَ	يُرَى
jussive	يُرِ	imperative	أَرِ

The active participle I رَاءٍ and IV مُرٍ

Infinitive I إِرَاءَةٌ ; IV رَأْيٌ or رُؤْيَةٌ .

In verbs third weak with ' w ' or ' y ' as second radical the second is usually treated as a strong consonant.

حَيِىَ ' live ' is irregular in places.

I may be treated as a doubled verb حَيَّ .

II. The infinitive is like that of a doubled verb with the feminine ending as compensation تَحِيَّةٌ .

X, when it means ' be ashamed ', may be shortened :—

perfect اِسْتَحْيَتْ – اِسْتَحَى

imperfect يَسْتَحُونَ – يَسْتَحِى

First ' w ' and third ' y '

وَفَى ' accomplish, fulfil '; the perfect is regular :—

imperfect يَفِينَ يَفُونَ يَفِيَانِ تَفِينَ يَفِى

imperative فِينَ فُوا فِى فِ

active participle أَلْوَافِى – وَافٍ   infinitive وَفَاءٌ

A weak form can only be identified by grammar and common sense.

يدعو must be singular and must come from دعا.

يَدَعُوا is plural and may be يَدْعُوا from دعا or يدعوا

from ودع.

يجد may come from وجد and be any form of the

imperfect; it may be يَجِدْ or يُجِدْ jussive I or IV from

يَجُودُ جَادَ ; and it may be يَجْدِ or يَجْدِ jussive of

جدى or جدا.

فِيهِ may mean ' in it ', ' of his mouth ' or ' accomplish

it ', imperative singular feminine of وفى.

Vocabulary 27

وصى IV make a will, give a
dying charge.

شاء a. مَشِيئَة wish, will.

عَيِيَ a. عَيَّ be weary.

وَقَى i. وِقَايَة guard.

عَفَا u. عَفْوٌ pardon, refrain; be
abundant.

نَجَزَ u. نَجْزَ finish off, fulfil.

وَدَعَ a. وَدْعَ leave.

حيى II greet.

كرم IV honour.

حِلْمٌ statecraft, clemency, kindness.

قَدْرُ amount, measure.

وَدع IV deposit. | (وَصَايَا) وَصِيَّة will, testament.
نَفَع a. be useful to. | تُهْمَة suspicion.
وهم VIII suspect. | وَعَى i. وَعَى contain, understand.
(حُلِيّ) حَلْي jewels. | عيى IV fatigue, distress.
أَبَدًا (with a negative) never. | وقى VIII be on one's guard, fear, be pious.
سَهْم (c) arrow, share. | وَدع II say good-bye.
(سِنْگَة sing.) سَمَك fish.

Exercise 53

قَالَ دَعْنِى أُوصِى فَقَالَ أَوْصِ ـ رَأَوْا أَرَآءَ

ٱلْفَلَاسِفَةِ ـ أَمَا تَسْتَحِى أَنْ يَكُونَ هٰذَا قَدْرَ حِلْمِكَ

عَنِ ٱبْنِكَ ـ إِذَا لَمْ تَسْتَحِ فَٱصْنَعْ مَا شِئْتَ ـ مَا

لَـكُمْ تَسْمَعُونَ وَلَا تَعُونَ ـ أَغْنَوْهُ وَكَانَ قَلِيلَ ٱلْوَفَاءِ

لَهُمْ ـ أَرَاكَ ٱللهُ فِى بَنِيكَ مَا أَرَى أَبَاكَ فِيكَ

وَأَرَى ٱللهُ بَنِيكَ فِيكَ مَا أَرَاكَ فِى أَبِيكَ ـ كَانَ

إِذَا وَعَدَ ٱلْخَيْرَ وَفَى وَإِذَا أَوْعَدَ أَخْلَفَ وَعَفَا ـ آثِرْ

مَا تَلْقَاهُ غَدًا عَلَى مَا لَا تَرَاهُ أَبَدًا ـ كُنْتُ أَجِدُ

مَنْ يَعِدُ وَيَنْجُزُ فَقَدْ أَعْيَانِى مَنْ يَعِدُ وَلَا يَنْجُزُ ـ

اِسْتَحْيَيْتُ مِنْهُ وَبَعَثْتُ إِلَيْهِ بِالْحُلِيِّ ـ حَاجَتُكَ
عِنْدَنَا فَأْتِ مَنْزِلَكَ فَإِنَّهَا سَتَأْتِيكَ ـ لِيَقِ أَحَدُكُمْ
وَجْهَهُ النَّارَ ـ يُوَلِّى الْخَلِيفَةُ مَنْ يَشَاءُ.

54

he told them to bring their books — what do you think
of Egypt ? — these women, will they perform what they
have promised ? — be on your guard against suspicion —
they greeted us politely — show me how that will benefit
me — ask the keeper to show you what the boxes contain
— fear God and honour the king — I prefer that men
should fear me than that they should fear God — bring
me my share of the food and I will eat it by the river —
did you not all see what your aunt wrote ? — much study
wearies the young.

LESSON 28

CONDITIONAL AND EXCEPTIVE SENTENCES

The two main types of conditional sentences have been
mentioned in Lesson 13. There are, however, many
irregularities. Besides إِنْ the following words follow the
same rules :—

مَنْ he who ; مَا that which ; أَيَّ which of ; أَيْنَ ـ حَيْثُ
where ; مَتَى when ; كَيْفَ how ; كُلَّمَا whenever ;
إِذَا when.

مَا أَنْسَ لَا أَنْسَ

whatever I forget, I shall not forget . . .

كَيْفَ قَضَيْتَ فَعِنْدَهُ أَخْطَأْتَ

however you decide, in his opinion you will be wrong.

The apodosis must be introduced by فَ when it is :—

1. A nominal sentence.

إِنْ قُلْتَ هٰذَا فَأَنْتَ مِنَ الْكَافِرِينَ

if you say this you are of the infidels.

2. A sentence beginning with an incomplete verb, such

as قَدْ ـ سَوْفَ ـ سَ or عَسَى، one of the particles لَيْسَ

or one of the negatives لَنْ ـ مَا.

إِنْ تَسْتَغْفِرْ لَهُمْ فَلَنْ يَغْفِرَ اللهُ لَهُمْ

if you ask pardon for them, God will never pardon them

3. A verbal sentence expressing a wish or command.

أَيَّهُمَا شِئْتُمْ فَبَايِعُوا

do homage to which of the two you will.

4. When a perfect in the apodosis has to keep its
meaning as a past tense.

إِنْ كَانَ قَمِيصُهُ قُدَّ مِنْ قُبُلٍ فَصَدَقَتْ

if his shirt is torn in front she has told the truth.

A condition may also be expressed by an imperative and a jussive :—

$$ قِفِى أُخْبِرْكِ $$

stand, let me tell you = if you wait I will tell you.

$$ قُمْنَ عَنْهُ يَقُلْ بِحَاجَتِهِ $$

stand away from him, he will speak of his need = if you stand back he will say what he wants.

إِمَّا follows the same rules as إِنْ but is often followed by the energetic.

وَإِنْ often means ' even if '.

If the condition is improbable, لَوْ is used in place of

إِنْ ; the same rules apply for tenses but the use of the simple imperfect is more common.

$$ سَيَذْكُرُونَنِى لَوْ قَدْ جَرَّبُوا ٱلْعُمَّالَ بَعْدِى $$

they will remember me should they have experience of governors after me.

لَوْ is also used to express an impossible wish :—

$$ لَوْ كَانَ يَنْفَعُ ٱلْإِنْظَارُ $$

if only postponement were of some use.

إِلَّا ' if not ' is often used elliptically ; an example is the best explanation :—

$$ \text{إِنْ قَبِلْتَ رَأْيِى وَإِلَّا خُبْتَ} $$

if you accept my opinion (all will go right), but if (you do)
not, you will be disappointed.

لَوْلَا is also used elliptically:

$$ \text{لَوْلَا ٱلشَّمْسُ بَرَدَتِ ٱلْأَرْضُ} $$

but for the sun the earth would grow cold.

A sentence following لولا is usually introduced by
أَنَّ or أَنْ .

Exceptions.

The most common word for these is إِلَّا . When the

main sentence is affirmative, the noun after إِلَّا is accusative unless, of course, it is governed by a preposition.

جَاءَ ٱلْقَوْمُ إِلَّا زَيْدًا the tribe came except Zaid.

$$ \text{فَرَضَ لِأَبْنَاءِ ٱلْبَدْرِيِّينَ ٱلْفَيْنِ ٱلْفَيْنِ إِلَّا حَسَنًا} $$
$$ \text{وَحُسَيْنًا} $$

he allotted to the sons of those who fought at Badr
(Lesson 31) two thousand apiece except Hasan and Husain.

When the exception comes before the main noun the
accusative is used.

لَمْ يَكُنْ إِلَّا غَالِبًا مَيِّتٌ يَقْرِى

no dead man except Ghalib gave hospitality.

When the sentence is negative, actually or virtually, the exception is in the same case as the main noun.

مَا مَرَرْتُ بِأَحَدٍ إِلَّا زَيْدٍ

I passed by no one except Zaid.

When the sentence is negative and the main noun left out, the exception is in the case the main noun should have.

مَا جَاءَ إِلَّا امْرَأَتُهُ only his wife came.

مَا مررت الَّا بِزَيْدٍ I passed only Zaid.

مَا يَخْدَعُونَ إِلَّا أَنْفُسَهُمْ

they deceive only themselves.

مَا كَانَ إِبْرَاهِيمُ إِلَّا يَهُودِيًّا

Ibrahim (Abraham) was only a Jew.

When the exception is of a different sort from the main noun, the accusative is used. One feels sometimes that this is a desperate attempt to bring the facts of language under rule.

مَا لَهُمْ بِهِ مِنْ عِلْمٍ إِلَّا اتِّبَاعَ الظَّنِّ

they have no knowledge of it but the following of fancy.

إِلَّا is often used loosely.

$$ قَدْ أَدْرَكَنِي ٱلْمَوْتُ إِلَّا قَلِيلاً $$

death almost overtook me.

$$ لَا يَبْقَى حَيٌّ إِلَّا مَاتَ $$

no living one remains without dying.

$$ مَا شَعَرْتُ بِهِ إِلَّا وَقَدِ ٱحْتَمَلَنِي $$

I did not perceive him except he had picked me up = the next thing I knew was that he had carried me.

'Only.' As we have just seen, this is often expressed by إِلَّا with a negative. It can also be expressed by إِنَّمَا; the word excepted is put at the end of the sentence.

$$ إِنَّمَا عَلِيٌّ شُجَاعٌ $$

Ali is only brave (has no other good qualities).

$$ إِنَّمَا شُجَاعٌ عَلِيٌّ $$ the only brave man is Ali.

Note.—The addition of مَا to أَنَّ makes no difference to its meaning.

Vocabulary 28

بَقَى X preserve, keep alive.

تَابَ u. تَوْبَةٌ repent.

سَلَكَ u. سُلُوكٌ go.

فوض III be partners, discuss.

صَلَحَ u. صَلاحٌ be good, service-
able.

— IV repair, restore.

كَدَّ u. كَدٌّ work hard, persevere.

يَسَرَ i. يُسْرٌ be easy, easy-going.

— IV become rich.

قَمِيصٌ (قُمْصَانٌ) shirt.

حَرِيصٌ eager, greedy

خَطِئَ خَطَأ sin.

يَقِظَ IV wake up (trans.).

شَبِهَ III resemble.

X ask to repent.

جَلَسَ III sit with.

نِكَاحٌ i.a. نَكَحَ marry.

III make peace with.

عَبَأَ a. عَبْأَ (with negative) ignore.

عَمَّ u. be general, concern many

بِرٌّ goodness, filial piety.

II make easy.

فَضْلٌ excellence, superiority.

بَيْتٌ (a) verse of poetry.

بَطُؤَ IV make slow, do slowly.

IV make a mistake.

X wake up (intrans.).

Exercise 55

إِنْ لَمْ تَقْتُلْهُ لَأَتَزَوَّجَنَّهُ فَيَكُونُ قَدْ قَتَلَ أَبَاكَ وَنَكَحَ
أُمَّكَ فَقْتُلْهُ ـ لَوْ كَانَ الْبُخْلُ قَمِيصًا مَا لَبِسْتُهُ وَلَوْ
كَانَ طَرِيقًا مَا سَلَكْتُهُ ـ إِنْ كَانَ رِزْقِي فِى السَّمَاءِ
فَأَنْزِلْهُ وَإِنْ كَانَ فِى الْأَرْضِ فَأَخْرِجْهُ وَإِنْ كَانَ

بَعِيدًا فَقَرِّبْهُ وَإِنْ كَانَ قَرِيبًا فَيَسِّرْهُ ـ إِذَا جَالَسْتَ

اَلْعُلَمَاءَ فَكُنْ عَلَى أَنْ تَسْمَعَ أَحْرَصَ مِنْكَ عَلَى

أَنْ تَقُولَ ـ لَوْلَا أَنَّ أَفْعَالَهُ لَا تُوجِبُ اَلْعَفْوَ عَنْهُ

لَكَانَ حَقِيقًا بِالْاِسْتِبْقَاءِ لِهَذَا اَلْفَضْلِ ـ مَا اَلْعِزُّ

إِلَّا تَحْتَ ثَوْبِ اَلْكَدِّ ـ لِمَ لَا تُطِيلُ اَلْهِجَاءَ قَالَ

لَمْ أَجِدِ اَلشِّعْرَ اَلسَّائِرَ إِلَّا بَيْتًا وَاحِدًا ـ أَوْدَعَ

ذَلِكَ اَلْمَالَ رِجَالًا بِهِ إِلَّا يَهُودِيًّا ـ مَا

جِئْتُ إِلَّا فِى أَمْرٍ يَخُصُّ اَلْوَزِيرَ وَيَخُصُّنِى لَمْ تَصْلُحْ

مُفَاوَضَتُهُ فِيهِ إِلَّا عَلَى خَلْوَةٍ شَدِيدَةٍ ـ لِكُلِّ دَاءٍ

دَوَاءٌ إِلَّا اَلْمَوْتَ ـ مَا أَنْتَ بِشَيْءٍ إِلَّا شَيْءٌ لَا يُعْبَأُ

بِهِ ـ هُمْ كُفَّارٌ يُسْتَتَابُونَ فَإِنْ تَابُوا وَإِلَّا ضُرِبَتْ

أَعْنَاقُهُمْ.

56

he who has never made a mistake has never made anything
— all the inhabitants came except your father — if you
think that he is right, follow his example — if you find that

I have come on business which concerns myself alone and does not concern the whole people, send me away — it was only the sun's heat on my back which awakened me — wherever you live you will meet friends — none of the children resemble their father except Muhammad — if you believe in what he says, you ought to act according to it — he did not leave any act of filial piety without doing it — if you eat slowly, you will prolong your life — if he dies, his heirs will fight over the inheritance — but for him the army had perished.

LESSON 29

TEMPORAL CONJUNCTIONS

لَمَّا with the perfect denotes a definite event in the past and means ' when ' or ' after '.

$$ لَمَّا أَنْبَأَهُمْ بِأَسْمَائِهِمْ قَالَ $$

when he had told them their names he said . . .

لَمَّا with the jussive means ' not yet ' (Lesson 14).

مَتَى ' when ' is first an interrogative adverb.

$$ مَتَى تُسَافِرُ $$ when will you travel ?

As a conjunction it is treated as a conditional particle.

إِذْ ' when ' may be followed by the perfect or imperfect and usually refers to the past but often passes into ' because '.

لَوْ شَهِدْتُكَ إِذْ تَدْعُو تَمِيمًا

would that I had been with you when you summoned
Tamim (a tribe).

قَدْ ظَلَمْتُمْ إِذْ حَبَسْتُمُوهُمْ

you did wrong when (because) you put them in prison.

It may be followed by a nominal sentence.

إِذَا ‘ when ’ refers to the future though the perfect is
used with it ; it is often treated as a conditional particle.

إِذَا رَأَيْتَهُمْ تُعْجِبُكَ أَجْسَامُهُمْ

when you see them their bodies will please you.

Both إِذْ and إِذَا are used to introduce a fact which is
not the direct consequence of what has gone before ; hence
they often suggest the sudden or unexpected. إِذْ takes a

verbal sentence after it and إِذَا (usually فَإِذَا or وَإِذَا)
takes a nominal sentence :—

بَيْنَمَا الْعُسْرُ إِذْ دَارَتِ الْمَيَاسِيرُ

while distress (is present suddenly) easy times come round.

نَظَرْتُ إِلَى الْمَقْتُولِ فَإِذَا هُوَ زَيْدٌ

I looked at the murdered man ; lo and behold, it was Zaid.

إِذَا may be construed with بِ; two forms are possible :—

$$ شَقَقْتُ الْعَصَا وَإِذَا بِدَنَانِيرِى $$

$$ شققت العصا وَإِذَا أَنَا بِدَنَانِيرِى $$

I split the stick and there were my dinars (and there was I with).

There is no real difference in meaning.

حَتَّى ' until ' when temporal is used with the perfect or the imperfect indicative :—

$$ زُرْتُكِ حَتَّى قِيلَ لَيْسَ لَهُ صَبْرٌ $$

I visited you until it was said, ' he has no patience ' (self-control).

For حَتَّى ' so that ' see Lesson 19.

It is also used to co-ordinate two statements and means ' then, later on '; an example is the best explanation :—

$$ زَرَعْتُهُ حَتَّى اشْتَرَيْتُ مِنْهُ بَقَرًا $$

I sowed it and then bought from it cattle.

I sowed and reaped the field and did this till I had gathered enough money to buy cattle.

بَيْنَا ـ بَيْنَمَا ' while ' take either a verbal or a nominal sentence :—

بَيْنَا نَحْنُ نَرْقُبُهُ أَتَانَا

بينا نرقبه أتانا

while we were on the look out for him he came.

Often combined with إِذْ.

بَيْنَا أَنَا فِى الْحَدِيثِ إِذْ قَدِمَ زَيْدٌ

while I was in talk, Zaid came.

مَا is used with the perfect but refers to the present with the sense ' as long as ' :—

لَسْتَ ضَائِرَهَا مَا أَطَّتِ الْإِبِلُ

you cannot hurt it as long as camels grunt.

مَا دَامَ حَيًّا as long as he continues alive.

كَمَا ، ' as ' ; اِفْعَلْ كَمَا يَفْعَلُ النَّاسُ do as others do ; كَمَا it passes easily to a sense of time :—

سَلِّمْ كَمَا تَدْخُلُ salute as (soon as) you enter.

Note. كَمَا أَنْتَ stop where you are.

Many prepositions can be turned into conjunctions by combining them with أَنْ or مَا; أَنْ governs the subjunctive. قَبْلَ مَا after; بَعْدَ أَنْ until; إِلَى أَنْ before, etc.

Vocabulary 29

ثَارَ u. ثَوْرٌ be stirred up.	IV stir up.
شرك IV associate with (trans.).	VIII be associated with.
لَزِمَ لُزُومٌ and VIII be attached to, be necessary.	أَلِمَ أَلَمٌ suffer pain.
دَفَنَ i. دَفْنٌ bury.	قلد II put a necklace on, invest with.
دَعَا دُعَاءٌ and X call, summon.	سرّ III whisper to.
دَنَا دُنُوٌّ be near.	وفى III arrive.
مَضَى مُضِيٌّ go, be past.	IV execute (order, etc.).
عَدَا عَدْوٌ go, go against.	طَرَدَ u. طَرْدٌ drive, drive away, round up.
عَقَبَ u. عَقْبٌ come after.	III wager.
رَهَنَ a. رَهْنٌ give a pledge to.	عَاقِبَةٌ consequence.
رَبِحَ رِبْحٌ make a profit, be profitable.	نَوْعٌ (a) kind, sort.
عَادَةٌ (عَادَاتٌ) custom.	جَنَازَةٌ — جِنَازَةٌ (جَنَائِزُ) funeral.
وَزِيرٌ (وُزَرَاءُ) minister of state.	وِزَارَةٌ ministry.

Exercise 57

عَلِمَ أَنَّهُ مَتَى رَدَّهُمْ ثَارَتْ فِتْنَةٌ لَا يَأْمَنُ عَوَاقِبَهَا

وَأَنَّ الرَّأْىَ يُوجِبُ الرِّفْقَ بِهِمْ ـ بَيْنَا نَحْنُ نَدْفِنُهُ إِذْ

حُمِلَتْ جَنَازَةٌ أُخْرَى ـ أَلِمْتُ أَلَمًا شَدِيدًا فَلَمَّا كَانَ

فِى اللَّيْلِ سَكَنَ الْأَلَمُ وَنِمْتُ ـ لَمَّا أَخْطَأَ آبَاؤُكَ

لَمْ يُصِبْ إِلَّا أَنْتَ ـ لَمَّا اشْتَدَّ الْمَرَضُ عَلَيْهِ لَزِمَ

فِرَاشَهُ ـ مَا مَضَى عَلَى هٰذَا إِلَّا دُونَ شَهْرٍ حَتَّى

اُسْتُدْعَى الْخَلِيفَةُ ابْنَ أَخِيهِ وَقَلَّدَهُ الْوِزَارَةَ ـ إِنِّى

أُكَلِّمُهُ فَإِذَا بِفِتْيَانٍ فَاسْتَدْنَى الْأَكْبَرَ مِنْهُمْ فَسَارَّهُ

بِشَيْءٍ دُونِى وَدُونَ أَصْحَابِهِ ـ عَدَا مَعَهُ حَتَّى وَافَيَا

الْبَيْتَ كَفَرَسَىِ الرِّهَانِ ـ لَمْ يَشْعُرْ صَاحِبَاهُ وَقَدْ

سَاءَ ظَنُّهُمْ وَتَخَوَّفَا عَلَيْهِ حَتَّى إِذَا هُمَا بِهِ يَطْرُدُ

الْإِبِلَ فَطَرَدَاهَا مَعَهُ ـ بَقِىَ فِى الْمَدِينَةِ حَتَّى إِذَا

أَعْيَاهُ حَرَارَةُ الصَّيْفِ خَرَجَ إِلَى ضَيْعَتِهِ .

58

after they had shared in the work they shared in the profit
— I have not yet received my share of the pay — when did
you see anyone resembling him in face ? — he associated
me with himself in his request to the government — when
you go to a foreign country, adopt its customs — I asked
the shopkeeper for fish and he had several kinds — when
they gave me my share, I was not satisfied with it —
poverty befell him and then his friends stood by him —
when she saw that forbidding was useless, she wept — he
was busy writing till, when he had written many pages,
the whiteness of the paper tired his eyes — a promise, when
fulfilment which makes it true does not accompany it, is
like words with no meaning.

LESSON 30

NUMERALS

The numerals are the nightmare of a bankrupt financier.

1   أَحَدٌ fem. إِحْدَى is a pronoun.

     وَاحِدٌ fem. وَاحِدَةٌ is an adjective.

Both these agree in gender with the noun to which they
refer.

2   اِثْنَانِ const. اِثْنَا construct fem. اِثْنَتَانِ const. اِثْنَتَا

oblique   اِثْنَيْنِ const. اِثْنَى construct fem. اِثْنَتَيْنِ const. اِثْنَتَى

This is a noun which agrees in gender with the noun

numbered. Usually the dual takes its place but it is used in apposition for emphasis.

لَا تَتَّخِذُوا إِلَاهَيْنِ اثْنَيْنِ do not choose two gods.

3-10. Used with the masculine :   with the feminine :

3	ثَلَاثَةٌ	ثَلَاثٌ
4	أَرْبَعَةٌ	أَرْبَعٌ
5	خَمْسَةٌ	خَمْسٌ
6	سِتَّةٌ	سِتٌّ
7	سَبْعَةٌ	سَبْعٌ
8	ثَمَانِيَةٌ	acc. ثَمَانِيًا ثَمَانٍ
9	تِسْعَةٌ	تِسْعٌ
10	عَشَرَةٌ	عَشْرٌ

These numerals are fully declined nouns, disagree in gender with the singular of the noun numbered, and put that noun in the genitive plural, if possible, a plural of paucity. (See below.)

ثَلَاثُ نِسَاءٍ three women; ثَلَاثَةُ رِجَالٍ three men.

When the thing numbered is definite, two constructions are possible :—

اَلرِّجَالُ الثَّلَاثَةُ or ثَلَاثَةُ الرِّجَالِ the three men.

Note.—The construct state of ثَمَانٍ is ثَمَانِى nom. and gen. ثَمَانِىَ acc.

Note.—ثَمَانِيهِنَّ the eight of them = the eight women.

11-12.

	Masc.	Fem.
11	أَحَدَ عَشَرَ	إِحْدَى عَشْرَةَ
12	اِثْنَا عَشَرَ	(ثِنْتَا) اِثْنَتَا عَشْرَةَ
oblique	اِثْنَىْ عَشَرَ	اِثْنَتَىْ عَشْرَةَ

These numerals are not declined—except the part اِثْنَا and its variants. The noun is in the accusative singular. Both parts of the numeral agree in gender with the noun which is in the accusative singular.

Note the variations in the words for ‘ten’.

13-19.

	With masculine :	With feminine :
13	ثَلَاثَةَ عَشَرَ	ثَلَاثَ عَشْرَةَ
14	أَرْبَعَةَ عَشَرَ	أَرْبَعَ عَشْرَةَ

15	خَمْسَةَ عَشَرَ	خَمْسَ عَشْرَةَ
16	سِتَّةَ عَشَرَ	سِتَّ عَشْرَةَ
17	سَبْعَةَ عَشَرَ	سَبْعَ عَشْرَةَ
18	ثَمَانِيَةَ عَشَرَ	ثَمَانِىَ عَشْرَةَ
19	تِسْعَةَ عَشَرَ	تِسْعَ عَشْرَةَ

These are indeclinable and govern the noun in the accusative singular. The unit disagrees in gender with its noun and with the ten.

20–30.

20	عِشْرُونَ	50	خَمْسُونَ	80	ثَمَانُونَ
30	ثَلَاثُونَ	60	سِتُّونَ	90	تِسْعُونَ
40	أَرْبَعُونَ	70	سَبْعُونَ		

These are ordinary external plurals and have the two cases ; they take the thing numbered in the accusative singular.

In compound numbers between 21 and 99 the unit comes first.

100 مِائَةٌ (anomalous spelling) *miʔatun*. 200 is

مِائَتَانِ ; 300 ثَلَاثُ مِائَةٍ (sometimes written ثَلَاثمِائَة)

with the hundred in the singular. مِائَة puts its noun in the genitive singular.

1000 أَلْفٌ . Note أَرْبَعَةُ آلَافٍ . The noun numbered
is in the genitive singular.

Order of the numerals :—

3822. ثَلَاثَةُ آلَافٍ وَثَمَانِى مِائَةٍ وَاثْنَانِ وَعِشْرُونَ

Ordinal Numbers.

	M.	F.		M.	F.
first	أَوَّلُ	أُولَى	sixth	سَادِسٌ	سَادِسَةٌ
second	ثَانٍ	ثَانِيَةٌ	seventh	سَابِعٌ	سَابِعَةٌ
third	ثَالِثٌ	ثَالِثَةٌ	eighth	ثَامِنٌ	ثَامِنَةٌ
fourth	رَابِعٌ	رَابِعَةٌ	ninth	تَاسِعٌ	تَاسِعَةٌ
fifth	خَامِسٌ	خَامِسَةٌ	tenth	عَاشِرٌ	عَاشِرَةٌ

These are ordinary adjectives and offer no peculiarities.
11–19. These are indeclinable.

	M.	F.
11th	حَادِىَ عَشَرَ	حَادِيَةَ عَشْرَةَ
12th	ثَانِىَ عَشَرَ	ثَانِيَةَ عَشْرَةَ
13th	ثَالِثَ عَشَرَ	ثَالِثَةَ عَشْرَةَ

etc.

For higher numbers the cardinal forms are used.

Note the compounds with ' first ' :—

nom.   حَادٍ وَعِشْرُونَ   اَلْحَادِى وَالْعِشْرُونَ

gen.   حادٍ وَعِشْرِينَ   اَلْحَادِى وَالْعِشْرِينَ

acc.   حَادِيًا وَعِشْرِينَ   الحادِىَ والعشرين

حَادِيَةٌ وَعِشْرُونَ   etc.

etc.

Four of the broken plural forms أَفْعَالٌ ـ أَفْعُلٌ ـ فِعْلَةٌ ـ أَفْعِلَةٌ are sometimes plurals of paucity, i.e. indicate a number less than ten. If a noun has two or more plurals and one of them is one of these four forms, it is used for numbers below ten.

بَقِىَ فِى السِّجْنِ شُهُورًا

he stayed in prison many months.

بقى فى السجن أَشْهُرًا

he stayed in prison a few months.

An undefined number between 3 and 10 is expressed by the noun بِضْعٌ (part): بِضْعُ رِجَالٍ a few men; بِضْعُ نِسَاءٍ a few women.

With larger numbers نَيِّفٌ is used: نَيِّفٌ وَعِشْرُونَ twenty odd.

Fractions.

½. نِصْفٌ

⅓. ⅓ to ⅒ are expressed by فُعْلٌ (أَفْعَالٌ), e.g. ثُلُثٌ

Some fractions can be expressed by combinations of these words: 3/32. ثُمْنُ رُبُعٍ

Others can only be expressed in words :—

1/29 {
سَهْمٌ مِنْ تِسْعَةٍ وَعِشْرِينَ سَهْمًا

قِطْعَةٌ مِنْ تِسْعٍ وَعِشْرِينَ قِطْعَةً
}

Distributives.

These may be expressed by repeating the numeral :—

فَرَضَ عَلَيْهِمُ الْفَيْنِ الْفَيْنِ he allotted them 2,000 apiece.

Time.

The day begins at sunset so the Arabs often count by nights : صُمْتُ عَشْرًا I fasted 10 nights (days).

عَشْرًا as لَيْلَةٌ is feminine.

Note.—عُمْرُهُ أَرْبَعُ سِنِينَ or هُوَ ابْنُ أَرْبَعٍ he is four years old.

Vocabulary 30

عجل II hasten, do quickly.	(فَتَيَاتٌ) فَتَاةٌ young woman.
تَمَّ i. تَمّ be complete, perfect.	II, IV complete.
حَدَثَ u. حُدُوثٌ be new, happen.	شَكَّ u. شَكّ doubt.
— IV make new, produce.	صغر II make little.
شَمِلَ u. شَمْلَ and شَمِلَ be common	حدث II tell.
to, concern; VIII surround,	حدث V, VI talk, converse.
consist of (عَلَى).	زَلْزَلَةٌ earthquake.
عَمَدَ i. عَمْدٌ support, direct oneself	(دَجَاجَاتٌ) دَجَاجٌ fowls, hens.
towards.	(بَضَائِعُ) بِضَاعَةٌ goods, merchan-
شِرْكٌ polytheism.	dise.
دِيكٌ (b) cock.	عَنَايَةٌ عَنَى mean.
عُمْرٌ (a) life, age.	فَتْوَى counsel's opinion.
خَفِيَ خَفَاءٌ be hidden.	مَعْنًى meaning, idea.
فتى IV give counsel's opinion.	شَكَا شَكْوَى complain.

Exercise 59

بَقِيتُ فِى بِلَادِ الشِّرْكِ أَرْبَعَةَ أَشْهُرٍ وَأَحَدَ عَشَرَ

يَوْمًا ـ اِشْتَرَتْ دِيكًا وَاحِدًا وَخَمْسَ دَجَاجَاتٍ ـ

اِشْتَمَلَ قَافِلَتُهُ عَلَى مِائَةِ إِبِلٍ وَخَمْسَةٍ وَعِشْرِينَ

حِمَارًا ـ وُلِدَ فِى سَنَةِ أَلْفٍ وَتِسْعِمِائَةٍ وَاثْنَتَيْنِ

وَثَلَاثِينَ ـ دَامَتِ الْحَرْبُ سِتِّينَ وَنِصْفَ سَنَةٍ ـ يَأْخُذُ
الْحُكُومَةُ الْعُشْرَ مِنْ كُلِّ بَضَائِعِ التُّجَّارِ الَّذِينَ
يَدْخُلُونَ بِلَادَهَا مِنَ الْخَارِجِ ـ مَا أَكَلْتُ مُنْذُ
ثَلَاثٍ شَيْئًا فَأُرِيدُ أَنْ تُقِيمَ عِنْدِى لِنَأْكُلَ وَنَتَحَدَّثَ ـ
كَانَ مَوْتُهُ قَبْلَ الزَّلْزَلَةِ الْكَبِيرَةِ بِسِتَّيْنِ ـ هُوَ ابْنُ
خَمْسٍ وَسِتِّينَ سَنَةً ـ لَا يَتِمُّ الْمَعْرُوفُ إِلَّا بِثَلَاثٍ
تَعْجِيلِهِ وَتَصْغِيرِهِ وَسَتْرِهِ .

60

there are 72 kinds of dates — she is 17 years old — that
chief was the father of his tribe, he had 16 sons and 12
daughters — she cut the meat into 12 shares — the guests
went away by twos — he travelled for 19 days,
crossing 3 rivers and climbing 7 mountains — forgive him
70 times — my messenger arrived three hours after me —
his daughter inherited one-sixteenth of his property —
he is the seventh son of a seventh son.

LESSON 31
NOUN FORMS

Every word form has its special meaning, sometimes
more than one.

فَعِيل is commonly an adjective but it is also an
infinitive and a broken plural.

فَعْلَةٌ as an infinitive denotes the doing of the action once, whatever form the ordinary infinitive may have :—

نَصَرَهُ اللهُ نَصْرَةً God helped him (gave him victory) once

infinitive نَصْرٌ

فَرَّ فَرَّةً he ran away once   infinitive فِرَارٌ

فِعْلَةٌ as an infinitive denotes the doing of the act in a certain manner :—

هُوَ حَسَنُ الْكِتْبَةِ he is good in (his style of) writing

infinitive كِتَابَةٌ

قُتِلَ قِتْلَةَ سَوْءٍ he was killed horribly   infinitive قَتْلٌ

مَشَى مِشْيَةَ الْمَرِيضِ he walked like a sick man

infinitive مَشْيٌ

فَعَّالٌ denotes one who follows a trade or does something habitually. Examples have been given in Lesson 4. It is also used as an emphatic :—

كَذَّابٌ a great liar.

Noun of place or time.

مَفْعِل ـ مَفْعَل When the characteristic of the imperfect is ' u ' or ' a ' the noun is مَفْعَل . مَطْبَخ kitchen; مَخْرَج exit.

There are a few exceptions ; the commonest are—

مَسْكِن dwelling house ; مَسْجِد mosque.

مَفْعِل is used when the characteristic of the imperfect is ' i ' :—

مَقْصِد goal ; مَنْزِل house, stage (of a journey) ;

مَوْضِع place.

Note.—The ' a ' in the imperfect is due solely to the guttural.

Roots middle ' w ' have forms like مَقَام place.

Those middle ' y ' have forms like مَقِيل place of the siesta.

Roots first ' w ' have also a variant : مَوْلِد ـ مِيلَاد birthday ; مِيقَات ـ مِيعَاد appointed time.

Roots third weak have always ' a ' in the second syllable (Lesson 26).

In the derived stems of all verbs the passive participle is used as the noun of place : مُسْتَشْفَى hospital.

مَفْعَل may also be used as a noun of action (practically an infinitive) and as a concrete noun :—

مَقْدَم arrival ; مَطْلَب object, thing looked for ;

مَرْكَب carriage, ship, riding beast.

Noun of instrument.

مِفْعَل ـ مِفْعَال ـ مِفْعَلَة may express this :—

مِبْرَد file (tool) ; مِفْتَاح key مِكْنَسَة broom ;

مِيزَان scales ; مِقْرَاض ـ مِقَصّ scissors.

Diminutive.

فُعَيْل ـ كُلَيْب a little dog, puppy. It is often used as a form of endearment ; very common is بُنَىّ my little son.

Relative adjectives.

Adjectives can be made from most nouns by adding *iyyun* feminine *iyyatun* to the noun. If the noun has the feminine ending *at* it is dropped and a long second syllable is shortened. There are many irregularities.

بَلَد town, village , رَجُل بَلَدِيّ a country bumpkin

مِصْرُ Egypt ; مِصْرِىُّ an Egyptian

مَدِينَةُ town اَلْمَدِينَةُ al-Medina ; مَدَنِىُّ a townsman,
a man from al-Medina

مَكَّةُ Mecca ; مَكِّىُّ a man from Mecca

قُرَيْشُ Quraish (Muhammad's tribe) ; قُرَشِىُّ a man
of the tribe.

These adjectives are very common in modern Arabic.

أَصْلُ (أُصُولُ) root, principle. فَرْعُ (فُرُوعُ) branch.

مَسْأَلَةُ أَصْلِيَّةُ a problem involving first principles.

مَسْأَلَةُ فَرْعِيَّةُ a question of detail.

The feminine is used as an abstract noun :—

كَيْفَ how ? كَيْفِيَّةُ quality : كَمْ how much ? كَمِّيَّةُ
quantity.

Broken plurals.

فَعَلَةُ ـ فِعَالُ ـ فُعَّلُ are common as plurals of the
active participle of Stem I.

فُعَلَةُ is plural of the active participle of Stem I of verbs
third weak : قَاضٍ judge قُضَاةُ .

فِعْلَى (p. 147). فَعْلَى and فَعْلَى ـ فَعْلَاءُ is plural of فَعَالٍ

فَتَاوٍ a legal opinion فَتْوَى : عَذَارٍ virgin عَذْرَاءُ .

فَعَالَى is plural of the same three forms and of

فَعْلَانُ :ـ

كَسْلَانُ ـ كَسَالَى : حَيْرَانُ perplexed حَيَارَى ;

and of فَعِيلَة from verbs third weak :ـ

مَطِيَّة riding مَنِيَّة fate مَنَايَا : مَطِيَّة gift هَدِيَّة : هَدَايَا مَنَايَا

مَطَايَا animal .

Other plurals are فُعْلٌ ـ فِعَلَةٌ ـ فُعْلَةٌ ـ فِعْلَانُ

ـ فُعْلَانُ ـ فَعْلَى .

مَفَاعِلَةٌ sometimes becomes مَفَاعِيلُ .

Second declension.

The grammarians give many rules for finding whether a noun belongs to this declension or not ; it is simpler to trust to memory. To it belong :—

Some forms of the broken plural ;

All proper names which are feminine in form or belong to **women** (few exceptions) ;

Most foreign names of men, إِبْرَاهِيم Abraham;

Some native names, especially those which resemble verbs, يَزِيد Yazid;

All proper names with a suffixed *a:n*, نُعْمَان Nuʕma:n;

The adjectives أَفْعَل and فَعْلَان;

All nouns ending in *a:u*, صَحْرَاء desert.

Secondary roots.

These commonly have the radical ' t '.

اِتَّهَم تُهْمَة ' suspicion ' from وهم through

اِتَّقَى تَقْوَى ' piety ' from وقى through

تَلِيد ' born in the house, ancestral ' from ولد

Vocabulary 31

خَرَق u. خَرْق tear rend.	مِعْبَر ferry.
جرب II test.	مَخَاض ford.
بَرَد u. بَرْد file.	مَسْمَع place from which is heard,
عَبَر u. عُبُور pass over, cross.	ear.
تَعِب تَعَب be tired.	مَأْمَنَة place of safety.
تَعْبَان tired.	مَبْعَث time of sending, mission.

مُنْخُل sieve.	مَشْرِق east, sunrise.
مَسْأَلَة question, problem.	قَطُّ (with negative) ever.
غَسَلَ i. wash.	شَيْطان devil.
مَأْسَدَة place where lions are	دَقَّ u. hit, pound.
plentiful.	شهر VIII be well known.
مَغْرِب west, sunset.	زول IV remove.
جَمِيع (collected) together,	سَهَرَ سَهَر be wakeful at night.
all.	أرخ II date.
نظف II clean.	تَأْرِيخ history.

Exercise 61

جَلَسَ جِلْسَةَ الثَّعْبانِ ـ أَسَمِعْتَ مِثْلَ هذَا قَطُّ قَالَ لَا مَا

خَرَقَ مَسَامِعِي قَطُّ مِثْلُهُ ـ ضَرَبَ مُوسَى الْحَجَرَ ضَرْبَةً

وَيَخْرُجُ مَاءٌ يَكْفِى الْقَوْمَ جَمِيعًا ـ أَخْرَجَتْ صَاحِبَةُ

الْبَيْتِ اللِّصَّ تَضْرِبُهُ بِالْمِكْنَسَةِ ـ أَسْمِعُوهُمْ كَلَامَ

اللهِ وَأَبْلِغُوهُمْ مَأْمَنْتَهُمْ ـ سَافَرْنَا مَنَازِلَ وَبَلَغْنَا

مَأْسَدَةً نَخَافُ فِيهَا عَلَى خَيْلِنَا ـ فَلْنَذْكُرِ الْآنَ

التَّأْرِيخَ مِنْ مَوْلِدِ رَسُولِ اللهِ إِلَى مَبْعَثِهِ ـ جَرَّبُونِى

بِمَسَائِلَ لَمْ أَفْهَمْ مِنْهَا شَيْئًا ـ عَبَرْنَا النَّهْرَ بَعْضُنَا
فِى مِعْبَرٍ وَبَعْضُنَا بِمَخَاضَةٍ ـ كَانَ أَحْفَظَ النَّاسِ
لِمَا سَمِعَ وَأَقَلَّهُمْ نَوْمًا وَأَصْبَرَهُمْ عَلَى السَّهَرِ .

62

his name is famous in the east and the west — the thief
came in like a lion and went out like a sheep — all his
children swim like fish — as long as life remains I shall
not leave the battle field — the child cut off his finger
with the tailor's scissors — he washes his dog twice daily —
reason is to a man a file with which he files the roughness
of the heart, a broom with which he removes evil deeds,
a mallet with which he bruises the head of the devil, and
a sieve with which he cleans his thoughts — the Syrian
boasts of the snow and fruits of his mountains and the
Egyptian of the water of his river — the carpenter must
not be ignorant of the qualities of the different kinds of
wood.

LESSON 32

SOME VERBS

Quadriliteral roots.

Verbs from these roots have two stems like II and V of
the strong verb but with two different instead of the middle
radical doubled. A common type is a group of two consonants reduplicated.

perfect. imperfect. imperative. infinitive.

دُحْرَجَةٌ ـ دِحْرَاجٌ   دَحْرِجْ   يُدَحْرِجُ   دَحْرَجَ

roll (trans.)

تَدَحْرُجٌ   تَدَحْرَجْ   يَتَدَحْرَجُ   تَدَحْرَجَ

(intrans.)

There is nothing peculiar about weak verbs :—

دِهْدَاءٌ or دَهْدَاةٌ ـ دَهْدِ ـ يُدَهْدِى ـ دَهْدَى

Impersonal expressions.

The passive cannot be used absolutely, it must be qualified by a prepositional phrase :—

سِيرَ إِلَى الْعِرَاقِ there has been a going to Irak.

The result is that there seem to be a lot of superfluous prepositions and pronouns.

اُخْتُلِفَ فِيهِ there has been a difference about it.

الْمَسْأَلَةُ الْمُخْتَلَفُ فِيهَا the question under discussion.

الْمَرْغُوبُ فِيهِ the thing liked;

الْمَرْغُوبُ عَنْهُ the thing disliked.

غُشِىَ عَلَيْهِ it was covered upon him = he fainted.

غُشِىَ عَلَيْهَا she fainted.

اَلْمُغْشِيُّ عَلَيْهِ the man who fainted.

اَلْمُغْشِيُّ عَلَيْهَا the woman who fainted.

سَقَطَ فِى يَدِهِ it was fallen into his hand = he repented.

هُوَ مَسْقُوطٌ فِى يَدِهِ he is repenting.

اَلشَّجَرَةُ الْمَنْهِيُّ عَنْهَا the forbidden tree (nom.)

(gen.) اَلشَّجَرَةِ الْمَنْهِيِّ عَنْهَا   اَلشَّجَرَةَ الْمَنْهِيَّ عَنْهَا (acc.)

Auxiliary verbs.

Several verbs, of which the commonest are جَعَلَ ‑ أَخَذَ

a. جَعَلَ 'make', are used with a following imperfect in the sense of 'begin':

جَعَلَ يَتَكَلَّمُ he began to talk.

Verbs of thought and feeling.

These may govern two accusatives; the causative may even govern three:—

أَرَاكَ أَفْعَالَكَ خَبِيثَةً

he showed you that your deeds were evil.

They may be used parenthetically; so you can say both

أَظُنُّ الْحُسَيْنَ شُجَاعًا ‑ أَظُنُّ الْحُسَيْنَ شُجَاعٌ

I think Husain is brave.

With a verbal sentence following three constructions are possible :—

أَظُنُّ أَنَّ عُمَرَ يَبْنِى بَيْتًا

أَظُنُّ يَبْنِى عُمَرُ بَيْتًا ـ أَظُنُّ عُمَرَ يَبْنِى بَيْتًا

I think that Umar is building a house.

' Can.'

The imperfect alone may be used.

اِنْتَهَى ٱلْأَمْرُ إِلَى وَقْتِهِ ٱلْمَحْدُودِ ٱلَّذِى لَا يَدْفَعُهُ دَافِعٌ

the affair went on to its allotted time which no pusher can push back (postpone).

قَدَرَ ' be strong, able ' may be used or قَدِرَ u.i.

يَقْدِرُ أَنْ يَمْشِىَ ـ يَقْدِرُ عَلَى ٱلْمَشْىِ

he can walk.

لَنْ نَقْدَرَ عَلَيْهِ ٱلْعُقُوبَةَ we can never punish him.

اِسْتَطَاعَ X of طوع .

أَمَا تَسْتَطِيعُ أَنْ تَكْفِيَنَا هٰذَا

can you not arrange this for us ?

لَنْ يَسْتَطِيعَ مَعِى صَبْرًا

he will never be able to have patience with me.

مكن IV. The action is the subject and the agent the object :—

لَا يُمْكِنُهُ النُّهُوضُ he cannot get up.

(نهض ' stand up ' as a preliminary to action.)

طوق IV and وسع can also be used :

لَمْ يُطِقْ مِنَ الْوَجَعِ أَنْ يَرْكَبَ بَعِيرًا وَلَا دَابَّةً

he could ride neither camel nor horse because of the pain.

هٰذَا كَذَّابٌ أَوْ جَهُولٌ لَا يَسَعُنِي قَبُولُهُ

he is a liar or grossly ignorant, I cannot accept him.

' Must.'

لَا بُدَّ مِنْ there is no separation from (for loss of nuna-tion see Lesson 14).

أَخْبَرَهُ بِحُضُورِ قَوْمٍ لَا بُدَّ مِنْ وُصُولِهِمْ

he told him of the presence of people, there was no escape from their arriving (were on the doorstep and must be admitted).

This phrase may be followed by a sentence introduced by أَنْ ; the مِنْ may be omitted :—

لَا بُدَّ [مِنْ] أَنْ تُحَدِّثَنِي بِمَا يَيْنَكُمَا

you must tell me what is between you two.

وجب ' be necessary ' and لزم ' stick to ' also have the meaning ' must '. The subject of both verbs may be a noun or a sentence with أَنْ :—

وَجَبَ عَلَيْهِ النُّهُوضُ he had to stand up ;

لَزِمَهُ أَنْ يَصْحَبَنِى he had to accompany me ;

يَلْزَمُهُ الْاِسْتِفْهَامُ

he must ask questions (ask to understand).

Vocabulary 32

قَضَاءٌ قَضَى judge, settle, finish.	زَمَنٌ زَمِنَ be paralysed.
بَرْءٌ بَرُؤَ بَرِىَ be cured.	II cure, acquit.
قرض IV lend.	X ask a loan.
خُلُوصٌ u. خَلَصَ be pure.	II make pure, save.
قلب II turn (trans.).	جُوعٌ u. جَاعَ be hungry.
هُدًى هَدَى lead aright.	لُطْفٌ u. لَطَفَ be kind.
شَدَّةٌ u. شَدَّ attack, tie.	نقم VIII punish.
عسر IV be poor.	طَأْطَأَ bow (the head).
وَلْوَلَ wail.	هَمٌّ (b) care, anxiety.
ثَعْلَبٌ fox.	حَرَكَةٌ movement, vowel.
طَبِيعَةٌ nature.	مَحْكَمَةٌ law court.
جَنْبٌ (b) side.	بَطِّيخٌ water melon.
وَثَاقٌ bonds.	حَىٌّ alive.
مَيِّتٌ dead.	زَلْزَلَ shake (trans.).

Exercise 63

قَضَى ٱلْقَاضِى عَلَى ٱلْمُدَّعِى وَبَرَّأَ ٱلْمُدَّعَى عَلَيْهِمْ ـ
أَخَذَ يَسْتَقْرِضُ مِنِّى وَأَقْرَضْتُهُ خَمْسَمِائَةِ دِينَارٍ لَا تَخْلُصُ
مِنْهُ ـ رَأَى ثَعْلَبًا ضَعِيفًا لَا يَسْتَطِيعُ ٱلْحَرَكَةَ فَقَالَ
إِنَّ هٰذَا ٱلثَّعْلَبَ لَا بُدَّ أَنْ يَمُوتَ جُوعًا ـ اِهْدِنَا
ٱلصِّرَاطَ ٱلْمُسْتَقِيمَ صِرَاطَ ٱلَّذِينَ أَنْعَمْتَ عَلَيْهِمْ غَيْرِ
ٱلْمَغْضُوبِ عَلَيْهِمْ وَلَا ٱلضَّالِّينَ ـ يُرِيدُ ٱلْإِنْسَانُ
طَبِيعَةَ ٱلْأَشْيَاءِ ٱلْمَنْهِىِّ عَنْهَا ـ تَنَازَعَ قَوْمٌ وَطَلَبُوا
مَارًّا يَقْضِى بَيْنَهُمْ وَلَمَّا سَأَلَ فِى أَمْرِ ٱلْأِخْتِلَافِ
لَمْ يَصِفُوا لَهُ ٱلْمُخْتَلَفَ فِيهِ ـ ثُمَّ يُطَأْطِئُ ٱلْكَافِرُونَ
رُؤُوسَهُمْ خَوْفَ مَا يَرَوْنَ وَيَوْلُولُونَ ـ لَا يُمْكِنُكُمُ
ٱلدِّفَاعُ عَنْ نُفُوسِكُمْ فَيَلْزَمُكُمُ ٱلتَّسْلِيمُ ـ ٱلْمَصَائِبُ
حَالَةٌ لَا بُدَّ مِنْهَا فَمِنْهَا مَا يَكُونُ رَحْمَةً مِنَ ٱللّٰهِ
وَلُطْفًا بِعَبْدِهِ وَمِنْهَا مَا يَكُونُ ٱنْتِقَامًا ـ كُنْ مُوسِرًا
إِنْ شِئْتَ أَوْ مُعْسِرًا لَا بُدَّ فِى ٱلدُّنْيَا مِنَ ٱلْهَمِّ .

64

carry the boy who has fainted to the hospital — the
defendant is in court but where is the plaintiff? — a
girl was paralysed for about 15 years; she could not turn
from side to side nor could anyone else turn her — I did
not think that he could have mentioned me when there
was a summons for me — as long as you had the price of
this melon on you you could not hold back your desire
(soul) from it — I am left with my bonds fast on me —
we had to pay that to him — my own perceptions are
enough for me — how is your husband? she said, not alive
that he could be hoped for and not dead that he could be
forgotten — you cannot give what you have not.

LESSON 33

SOME NOUNS

Accusative as vocative.

A noun in the vocative when qualified by a genitive or a
prepositional phrase is put in the accusative :—

يَا عَبْدَاللهِ { Abdullah ! (a common name).
servant of God.

يَا سَاعِدًا فِى الْجِبَالِ climber of mountains.

Note that أَيُّهَا cannot be used before a construct state
because it must be followed by the definite article.

Construct state before a sentence.

A noun may govern a sentence in the genitive; usually
it is a noun of time in the adverbial accusative.

$$شَهَادَةُ أَنْ لَا إِلٰهَ إِلَّا اللّٰهُ$$

the confession that there is no god but God.

$$هٰذَا يَوْمٌ يَنْفَعُ الصَّادِقِينَ صِدْقُهُمْ$$

this is the day when the truthful will profit by their truthfulness.

$$وُلِدْتُ لَيْلَةَ قُبِضَ النَّبِيُّ$$

I was born the night the prophet was taken (died).

$$فَرَّ خَوْفَ أَنْ يُعَذِّبَهُ الْعَامِلُ$$

he fled for fear the governor would punish him.

خوفَ is the accusative of cause.

كَأَنْ .

This is a compound of أَنْ and follows the same rules, meaning ' as if '.

$$كَانَ النَّاسُ كَأَنَّهُمْ يُكَذِّبُونَنِي$$

the people were as if they did not believe me (seemed not to).

It may be a complete sentence in itself, when it must be translated ' it is as if ' :—

$$كَأَنِّي أَنْظُرُ إِلَى الدِّمَاءِ بَيْنَ الْعَمَائِمِ$$

it is as if I were looking at the blood (pl.) between the turbans (and necks).

Note the expressions :—

$$كَأَنِّى بِكَ تُخَادِعنِى$$

it seems to me that you are deceiving me.

$$كَأَنِّى بِكَ قَتِيلًا$$ I think I see you slain.

(قَتِيلًا accusative of accompanying circumstance.)

Attraction.

This occurs in a kind of relative clause. To understand the construction, it helps to think of two separate sentences of which the second consists of a noun and adjective with a pronoun referring back to the noun in the first. Instead of using a relative link, the order of the second sentence is inverted and the adjective made to agree in case with the noun of the first sentence.

$$رَأَيْتُ رَجُلًا ـ أَبُوهُ حَسَنٌ$$

I saw a man ; his father is handsome.

The combined sentence becomes :—

$$رَأَيْتُ رَجُلًا حَسَنًا أَبُوهُ$$

I saw a man whose father is handsome.

The adjective agrees in gender with its own noun and in case with the principal noun.

$$مَرَرْتُ بِامْرَأَةٍ حَسَنٍ أَبُوهَا$$

I passed a woman whose father is handsome.

$$سَافَرْتُ مَعَ رَجُلٍ حَسَنَةٍ أَخْلَاقُهُ$$

I travelled with a man whose character was good.

Is the principal noun definite, the adjective is definite also :—

$$ نَظَرْتُ إِلَى الرَّجُلِ الْحَسَنِ أَبُوهُ $$

I looked at the man whose father is handsome.

$$ فِى الْحُلَلِ الْمُضَاعَفِ نَسْجُهَا $$

in the garments which are double woven.

When the predicate of the subordinate sentence is a noun, inversion happens only exceptionally.

$$ مَرَرْتُ بِحَيَّةٍ ذِرَاعٌ طُولُهَا $$

I passed a snake the length of which was a cubit.

$$ لَقِيتُ رَجُلًا سَوَاءٌ عَلَيْهِ الْخَيْرُ وَالشَّرُّ $$

I met a man to whom good and evil are alike.

'Enough.'

This may be expressed by the verb كَفَى or by the noun حَسْبُ which usually has a pronominal suffix :—

$$ حَسْبُكَ مِنْ عَيْبٍ أَبُوكَ $$

your father is disgrace enough for you.

$$ حَسْبُكَ جُودًا أَنْ يَكُونَ كَحَاتِمٍ $$

it is generosity enough for you that he should be like Hatim.

It may be used absolutely and means 'only'.

إِنَّمَا كَانَ ٱلرِّيَاسَةُ لَهُ بِبَيْتِ ٱلْمَقْدِسِ حَسْبُ لَا
غَيْرَ ذَلِكَ

authority was his in Jerusalem alone and nowhere else.

Vocabulary 33

سَبَقَ u. سَبَقَ precede, come in first.

III race.

ظَلَمَ i. ظُلْمٌ do wrong.

صلو II say the ritual prayers.

IV be dark.

قَسَا قَسْوٌ be hard.

III find hard, oppressive.

هم VIII pay attention to, think important.

بيض II whiten.

جَلَبَ u. جَلْبٌ come, bring, drive.

عَظُمَ عِظَمٌ be big.

II honour.

حَقَرَ i. حَقْرٌ and VIII despise.

بَرَكَةٌ blessing.

برك III (with على) bless.

هَدِيَّةٌ (هَدَايَا) gift.

زِرَاعَةٌ agriculture.

قُطْنٌ cotton.

زَمَانٌ (أَزْمِنَةٌ) time, period.

عَارٌ defect, disgrace.

دُعَاءٌ (أَدْعِيَةٌ) prayer, petition.

عِشَاءٌ evening.

فَجْرٌ dawn.

عشو V eat the evening meal.

غدو V eat the morning meal.

فَطَرَ u.i. فَطْرٌ break one's fast.

Exercise 65

رَأَيْتُ الْفَقِيرَ مُحْتَقَرَةً حِكْمَتُهُ ـ سَأَغْسِلُ عَنِّى الْعَارَ
بِالسَّيْفِ جَالِبًا عَلَىَّ قَضَاءُ اللهِ مَا كَانَ جَالِبًا ـ
قَدْ عَلِمْتُ لَأَمْرُ رَسُولِ اللهِ أَعْظَمُ بَرَكَةً مِنْ أَمْرِى ـ
كَأَنَّكَ بِالْحُسَيْنِ مُقْبِلًا ـ خَافَ الْجَيْشُ مِنَ الْمَوْتِ
حَتَّى كَأَنَّ قُلُوبَ أَكْثَرِهِمْ هَوَاءٌ ـ تَقُولُ قَوْلَ الَّذِى
لَيْسَ الْوَفَاءُ لَهُ خُلْقًا ـ لَقَدْ صَغُرَ عَبْدُ الرَّحْمَانِ فِى
عَيْنَى عِظَمُ الدُّنْيَا فِى عَيْنِهِ وَكَأَنَّهُ يَرَى السَّائِلَ إِذَا
أَتَاهُ مَلَاكَ الْمَوْتِ ـ لَمْ يَكُنْ هَدَايَا السُّلْطَانِ
إِلَّا لِلْفُقَرَاءِ وَالْمُؤَلَّفَةِ قُلُوبُهُمْ ـ أَخْرِجْنَا مِنْ هٰذِهِ
الْبِلَادِ الظَّالِمِ أَهْلُهَا ـ كَأَنِّى بِكَ تَتَجَاهَلُ ـ كُنْتُ
أُقَاسِى الزَّمَانَ طُولَ عُمْرِى حَتَّى لَا أَرْجُو الْيُسْرَ ـ
يَهْتَمُّ مَلِكُ مِصْرَ بِإِصْلَاحِ الزِّرَاعَةِ لَا سِيَّمَا الْقُطْنِ.

66

the worst man was born the night the best man died —
you seem not to like me — if you do it again, we shall
again make a lampoon on you the words of which travel

200 TEACH YOURSELF ARABIC

— hearer of prayer! deliver me from what my enemies devise against me — it seems to me that you are betting on a horse which will not come in first in the race — the dressmaker showed us dresses of various colours — he who teaches an old man is as if he were making a black man white — I have not seen one of the caliphs to whom bloodshed was more distasteful than Hishām — he took an evening meal and no morning meal and this was enough for him for the space of forty years.

LESSON 34

EXCLAMATIONS

Admiration and its opposite are expressed by two defective verbs نِعْمَ ' how good ' (نَعَمَ u. نِعْمَةٌ be well off) and بِئْسَ ' how bad ' (بُؤْسٌ بَؤُسَ be badly off). The thing approved is the subject of the verb.

1. It must be definite or a sentence.

نِعْمَ ٱلرَّجُلُ عَمْرُو   what a fine chap Amr is.

بِئْسَ مَا صَنَعَ عُمَرُ   what a shocking thing Umar did.

2. The subject may be accompanied by an accusative of nearer definition.

نِعْمَ ٱلْحَسَنُ رَجُلًا   how good is al-Hasan as a man.

Less general ideas are expressed by two forms of Stem IV

أَفْعِلْ بِ and مَا أَفْعَلَ .

مَا أَكْرَمَ عَلِيًّا how generous Ali is.

أَعْظِمْ بِالْحَارِثِ قَدَرًا how strong al-Harith is.

When IV cannot be made from the ideas wanted, words
like أَشَدّ are used as with adjectives of defects and colours.
Thus the sentence

تَسْتَقْبِحُ النُّفُوسُ الْكَرِيمَةُ الظُّلْمَ

noble souls abhor wrongdoing

becomes

مَا أَشَدَّ مَا تَسْتَقْبِحُ النفوس الكريمة الظلم

how violently the noble souls abhor wrongdoing.

The second مَا with its verb is equivalent to أَنْ with
the subjunctive and both can be replaced by an infinitive
with the same meaning.

ما أشدّ اسْتِقْبَاحَ النفوسِ الكريمةِ الظلمَ

Admiration is also expressed by the phrase دَرُّ لِلَّهِ with
a pronoun.

دَرُّ is the flow of milk from the udder and the words imply that the man and his flocks are under the special protection of God. Then the use was generalized. Two constructions are possible :—

لِلّٰهِ دَرُّهُ فَارِسًا what a fine horseman he is.

لله دره مِنْ خَطِيبٍ what a fine speaker he is.

' Beware.'

إِيَّا كُمْ وَالْكَلْبَ beware of the dog.

ايا كم وقتله beware of killing him.

و here is the و of accompaniment which takes the accusative, as in :

مَشَيْتُ وَالنِّيلَ I walked beside the Nile.

Prepositions used idiomatically.

هَلْ لَكَ فِى الْمَاءِ الْبَارِدِ would you like some cold water.

دُونَكَ الدَّرَاهِمَ take the dirhams ; دُونَكَهُ take it.

عَلَيْكَ حَارِثَةَ seize Haritha (a man's name).

عَلَىَّ بِهِ bring him to me.

لَا عَلَيْكَ أَنْ تَفْعَلَ

there is no (harm) to you that you do = do as you like.

بِٱللهِ عَلَيْكَ I implore you by God.

Oaths.

With nouns وَ is the commonest particle; it takes the genitive :—

وَٱللهِ by God ; وَرَبِّ ٱلْكَعْبَةِ by the lord of the Kaaba ;

وَحَيَاتِكَ by your life.

لَ is used with the nominative of عَمْرُ (note the vocalization) :

لَعَمْرُكَ by your life ; لَعَمْرُ ٱللهِ by the life of God.

When a verb is present, بِ is usual :

أَقْسَمْتُ بِٱللهِ I swear by God ; but

نَشَدْتُكَ ٱللهَ I adjure you by God.

When the oath confirms a statement of fact it usually makes no change in the sentence.

When the oath confirms an intention, various things may happen.

If the intention is positive the energetic is used with لَ :

$$ وَاللهِ لَأَسِيرَنَّ $$ by God, I will go.

If negative, لَا with the perfect is used :

$$ والله لَا عَصَيْتَ رَبِّى $$

by God you shall not disobey my lord.

The negative may be omitted and then the imperfect is used :

$$ قُلْتُ يَمِينَ اللهِ أَبْرَحُ قَاعِدًا $$

I said, the oath of God, I shall not cease sitting.

إِلَّا with the perfect may be used in an affirmative sense :

$$ أَقْسَمْتُ عَلَيْكَ إِلَّا لَبِسْتَ دِرْعِى $$

I adjure you, put on my coat of mail.

$$ سَأَلَهُ بِالصُّحْبَةِ إِلَّا حَدَّثَهُ $$

he besought by (their good) fellowship, tell him.

This construction may be explained from the Old Testament oath : The Lord do so to me and more also if I do not = I will do.

Verbs of fear, hindrance, etc.

When these verbs are followed by أَنْ with the subjunctive, لَا may be inserted after أَنْ without changing the sense :—

$$\left.\begin{array}{r} مَا مَنَعَكَ أَنْ تَسْجُدَ \\ مَا مَنَعَكَ أَنْ لَا [أَلَّا] تَسْجُدَ \end{array}\right\}$$ what prevented you from bowing down.

Vocabulary 34

كَسَبَ i. كَسْبٌ and VIII earn, earn a living.

عَجَزَ i. عَجْزٌ be weak, unable.

عَجِبَ and V wonder. عَجَبٌ

فَرَغَ u.a. فُرُوغٌ فَرِغَ be empty.

عَدِمَ be without, not to have. عَدَمٌ

بين II explain.

رَوِيَ رَوَى be satisfied with drink.

عَذَرَ i. عُذْرٌ excuse, accept an excuse.

نَصِيرٌ helper.

عَطْشَانُ thirsty.

رَائِحَةٌ scent.

غُرْيَانُ naked.

حُمْقٌ folly.

عَطِشَ عَطَشٌ thirst.

IV weaken, incapacitate.

IV please.

II empty.

غَفَلَ u. غُفُولٌ neglect.

شَمَّ u. شَمٌّ smell.

امر VIII consult together.

حُرٌّ freeborn.

VIII excuse oneself.

مَوْلًى master, servant, freedman, cousin.

غَلِيظٌ rough, difficult.

أَحْمَقُ foolish.

فُرْصَةٌ opportunity.

Exercise 67

إِيَّاكُمْ وَمَسْأَلَةَ ٱلنَّاسِ فَإِنَّهَا آخِرُ كَسْبِ ٱلرَّجُلِ ـ

مَا أَشَدَّ مَا يَغْتَسِلُ ـ نَسْأَلُكَ بِٱللهِ إِلَّا حَفِظْتَ فِينَا

وَصِيَّةَ رَسُولِ ٱللهِ ـ بِئْسَ مَا ٱثَّمَرُوا ـ ٱعْلَمُوا أَنَّ

ٱللهَ مَوْلَاكُمْ نِعْمَ ٱلْمَوْلَى وَنِعْمَ ٱلنَّصِيرُ ـ يَا مُصْعَبَ

ٱلْخَيْرِ ٱلْكَرِيمَ جُدُودُهُ ـ مَا أَغْفَلَهَا عَمَّا يَخُصُّ

نَفْسَهَا وَمَا أَشْغَلَهَا بِمَا يَخُصُّ غَيْرَهَا ـ مَا أَعْطَشَ

ٱلْوَلَدَ عَجَزْتُ عَنْ إِرْوَائِهِ ـ إِيَّاكُمْ وَٱلَّذِينَ يَعْتَذِرُونَ ـ

أَقْسَمْتُ أَيْمَانًا غَلِيظَةً لَا عَطِشَ مَا دُمْتُ حَيًّا ـ

أَعْجَزَنِى عَنْ إِعَانَتِهِ أَنِّى عَدِمْتُ ٱلْمَالَ وَٱلْفُرْصَةَ .

68

what a fine swimmer that boy is — what a liar he is! and
the wonder is that every one believes him — how thirsty
the child is! I filled three cups of milk for him and he
emptied the lot — how quickly the enemy come upon
us — when the waters were cut off from them they said,
you have destroyed us. He said, you have reached the
water, how near you are to it — you are a bad husband
for a freeborn woman — by him in whose hand is my

soul, he shall sleep naked in the snow — by the lord of the Kaaba, explain to me your letter — by God, the slayer of a Muslim shall not smell the scent of paradise — I must let you know that you are the fool not I.

LESSON 35

CIRCUMSTANTIAL CLAUSES, ETC.

An attendant circumstance may be expressed by one word in the accusative (Lesson 15) or by a clause (Lesson 8). This clause may refer to any part of the main sentence; the noun to which it refers is usually definite. The clause may be linked up by a pronoun, by ' and ', or by both.

نَهَضَ مَحْمُودٌ لِلسَّفَرِ وَالْمَطَرُ وَاقِعٌ

Mahmud stood up (started) on the journey while rain was falling.

رَأَيْتُ خَالِدًا عَصَاهُ فِى يَدِهِ

I saw Khalid with his stick in his hand.

خَرَجُوا مِنْ دِيَارِهِمْ وَهُمْ أُلُوفٌ

They came out of their tents in their thousands.

Attraction can occur:

صَعِدَ مَسْلَمَةُ فِى السَّطْحِ بَاكِيًا أَبُوهُ

Maslama went up to the roof while his father was crying.

Indirect speech.

There is little indirect speech as there are no tenses. Pronouns and verbs may be put in the third person, but there is often a mixture of direct and indirect speech.

أَمَرَهُ أَنِ ابْنِ جِسْرًا

امره أَنْ يَبْنِيَ جِسْرًا

he told him to build a bridge.

كَتَبَ إِلَى عُمَرَ أَنَّ سَعْدًا اسْتَعْمَلَهُ عَلَى جِبَايَةِ
الْخَرَاجِ وَقَدْ أَحْبَبْتُ الْجِهَادَ

he wrote to Umar that Saad had appointed him (the writer) to collect the tribute but I wanted to go to the front.

There is no change in an indirect question.

أَسَائِلُكُمْ هَلْ يَقْتُلُ الرَّجُلَ الْحُبُّ

I ask you if love kills a man.

Alternative sentences.

أَوْ or. Used in statements and question; it need not be repeated.

إِمَّا ـ إِمَّا either — or. Used in statement or question. The clauses may be treated as parts of conditional sentences.

أَمْ or. Used only in questions preceded by أَ or هَلْ.

أَخَدِيجَةُ عِنْدَكِ أَمْ فَاطِمَةُ

is Khadija with you or Fatima ?

The answer to the question must be one of the two names.

Words construed like إِنَّ.

(لِئَنَّ) لِأَنَّ ـ فَإِنَّ for, because.

لَكِنَّ but. The shortened form لَكِنْ makes no change in the following sentence.

لَيْتَ would that. Common is لَيْتَ شِعْرِى would that I knew.

Genitive.

رُبَّ many a . . . is followed by an indefinite noun in the genitive singular and may be continued by any sort of sentence.

رُبَّ اُمْرَأَةٍ عَارِيَةٍ فِى اُلدُّنْيَا كَاسِيَةٌ فِى اُلْآخِرَةِ

many a woman naked in this world is clothed in the next.

Note that an active participle is sometimes used where a passive would be expected.

وَ with the genitive is used in the same way.

Emphasis.

أَمَّا . أَمَّا . . . . فَ is followed by a nominative

absolute and the sentence is introduced by فَ . It may be
translated ' as for '.

أَمَّا ٱلسَّفِينَةُ فَكَانَتْ لِمَسَاكِينَ يَعْمَلُونَ فِى ٱلْبَحْرِ

as for the ship, it belonged to poor men who worked on the
sea.

Subjunctive.

When the main clause says that an event may happen,
a subordinate clause describing a consequence of it is

introduced by فَ or وَ with the subjunctive.

لَيْتَ لِى مَالًا فَأَتَصَدَّقَ بِهِ

would that I had money so that I might give it in alms.

أَوْ ' unless,' ' until ' is followed by the subjunctive.

مَا .

This can be added to a number of words without
changing their meaning, e.g. أَيْنَمَا ; بَيْنَمَا while ;
wherever.

أَنَّمَا does not govern the accusative.

It can also be added to nouns in any case to make them
more indefinite.

مِنْ لَوْنٍ مَا of some colour or other.

Vocabulary 35

عَمِلَ عَمِلَ do, make, be a governor.

X appoint, use.

بَدَّلَ u. تَبَدَّلَ change, exchange.

عَمَلٌ (a) work, list.

قَصَرَ u. قُصُورٌ be inadequate.

مِنْشَفَةٌ towel.

خَلَا i خَلَاءٌ be empty, pass away.

هَضَمَ i هَضْمٌ ـ هَضَمَ digest.

شَكَلَ u. and IV be involved, difficult.

II make empty, leave.

فَضَلَ u. فَضْلٌ be in excess.

مَلَكَ i مُلْكٌ possess, be king.

حَدَاثَةٌ newness, youth.

نشف II make dry.

عَهْدٌ (b) agreement, treaty, time, period.

فَضِلَ u. be excellent.

دَهْرٌ epoch, age, time, fate.

نُورٌ (a) light.

صَحْرَاءٌ (صَحَارٍ) desert.

ذَخِيرَةٌ stores, treasure.

عَامِلٌ workman, governor.

خَلْوَةٌ private place, privacy.

قَدَرٌ God's decree, providence.

Exercise 69

لَا أَدْخُلُ وَلَا أَنْصَرِفُ أَوْ تَرْكَبَ إِلَى الْمَسْجِدِ ـ إِمَّا
أَنَا أَسِيرُ إِلَى الشَّامِ فَمَا أَكْرَهُهُ وَإِمَّا أَنْ أُقِيمَ فَلِى
فِيهِ أَجْرٌ ـ نَزْعُمُ أَنَّ تَفَاضُلَ النَّاسِ فِيمَا بَيْنَهُمْ لَيْسَ
بِآبَائِهِمْ وَلَكِنَّهُ بِأَفْعَالِهِمْ وَأَخْلَاقِهِمْ وَشَرَفِ نُفُوسِهِمْ

وَبَعْدِ هِمَمِهِمْ ـ تَقُولُ الْعَرَبُ لِمَنْ سُئِلَ وَهُوَ لَا يَقْدِرُ

فَرَدَّ بَيْتِي يَبْخَلُ لَا أَنَا ـ خَلَوْتُ بِهَا وَالْقَمَرُ يُرِينِهَا

فَلَمَّا غَابَ أَرَتْنِيهِ ـ لَا تَقُلْ فِيمَا لَا تَعْلَمُ فَتُتَّهَمَ فِيمَا

تَعْلَمُ ـ لَا تِبْنَه عَنْ خُلُقٍ وَتَأْتِيَ مِثْلَهُ ـ لَا تَرْضَى

الْعَرَبُ أَنْ يَسْتَعْمِلُوكَ وَأَنْتَ مِنْ غَيْرِهِمْ ـ هٰذَا الشِّعْرُ

شَيْءٌ كَانَ فِى الْحَدَاثَةِ قُلْتُهُ فِى زَوْجَتِى وَ كُنْتُ إِلَيْهَا

مَائِلًا وَ كَانَتْ لِى مَمْلُوكَةً وَلِقَلْبِى مَالِكَةً فَأَمَّا

الْآنَ فَلَا عَهْدَ لِى بِمِثْلِهِ مُنْذُ سِنِينَ وَلَا عَمِلْتُ شِعْرًا

مُنْذُ دَهْرٍ طَوِيلٍ .

70

would that my mother had not borne me and I had not seen the light of day — I was in hiding in her house and she came up to me every day to ask me what I wanted — he swore that he would not change this shirt unless he had finished the business of the man who had abused him — letters came to Mahmud when he was governor of Syria to collect us in the mosque and we should stop there till he had satisfied us — many who eat gratefully have a greater reward than those who fast — he told the girl to wash the clothes and dry them thoroughly — many a desert have I crossed, many a treasure discovered, and many a difficulty solved — he asked me how old I was — would that you could go in, salute the prince, and tell him the truth of the affair so that his anger against us might cease — eat slowly so that you may digest the food thoroughly.

LESSON 36

PREPOSITIONS ; CALENDAR

مِنْ (originally a noun ' part ') from, of, than.

بَاعَ مِنْهُ he sold to him ; قَالَ مِنْهُمْ some of them said.

عَنْ from (often in the realm of ideas).

اَلْهَرَبُ عَنْ قَضَاءِ اللهِ flight from God's decree.

قَالَ مَاقَالَ عَنْ حَسَدٍ he said what he said out of envy.

سَأَلَ عَنْهُ he asked about it.

إِلَى to, towards.

حَتَّى to, even. It cannot take suffixes.

أَكَلْتُ السَّمَكَةَ حَتَّى رَأْسِهَا

I ate the fish up to the head.

اكلت السمكة حتى رأسها

I ate the fish, even the head (it has no governing power).

لِ to, for, belonging to.

فِى in, concerning.

قُتِلَ كُلَيْبٌ فِى نَاقَةٍ Kulaib was killed for a she-camel.

ثَلَاثَةٌ فِى خَمْسَةٍ three multiplied by five.

بِ by, at, in, with (instrumental).

جَاءَ بِهِ he brought it.

اَلْمَعْرُوفُ بِأَبِى الْحَسَنِ the man known as Abu l-Hasan.

أَرَغِبْتَ بِى عَنْهَا

do you take pleasure in me from her = do you think me
too good for her ?

مَعَ with (accompaniment).

عَلَى upon, on account of, in spite of, against. (In
Arabic you are always on a condition.)

عَلَى ٱلْفَقْرِ in poverty.

عَلَى ٱلرِّيقِ on the spittle = on an empty stomach.

لِى عَلَيْهِ دَيْنٌ to me on him a debt = he owes me money.

مُنْذُ since, for (time). It takes the nominative, genitive, or a sentence.

مُنْذُ يَوْمَانِ ـ منذ يومين for two days.

منذ يَوْمُ ٱلْجُمْعَةِ ـ منذ يَوْمِ الجمعة since Friday.

مُنْذُ خُلِقَ since he was created (born).

The following are really nouns in the accusative ; many can be combined with مِنْ and are put in the genitive, unlike the corresponding adverbs.

نَحْوَ towards, according, about (not of place).

نَحْوَ قَوْلِهِ according to his saying (or, his ideas).

نَحْوَ عِشْرِينَ about twenty.

عِنْدَ beside, in the opinion of.

بَيْنَ between (usually repeated)

بَيْنِي وَبَيْنَه between me and him.

اِقْتَتَلُوا فِيمَا بَيْنَهُمْ they fought each other.

تَحْتَ under.

فَوْقَ over, above.

دُونَ below, between (as being an obstacle to the meeting of two things).

دُونَ ٱلْجَبَلِ at the foot of the mountain.

قَاتَلَ دُونَهُمْ he fought in defence of them.

هٰذَا دُونَ ذٰلِكَ this is less than that.

هٰذَا لِى دُونَكَ this is mine not yours.

قَبْلَ before (time). قُبَيْلَ a little before.

بَعْدَ after (time).

قُدَّامَ ـ أَمَامَ before (place).

وَرَاءِ behind (place).

حَوَالَى ـ حَوْلَ around (place).

قِبَلَ (usually مِنْ قِبَلِ) in possession of.

عَامِلٌ مِنْ قِبَلِ الْخَلِيفَةِ

a governor representing the caliph.

مَنْ مِنْ قِبَلِكَ your subordinates.

Many prepositions can be turned into conjunctions by joining them to أَنْ; e.g. الى ان until.

Calendar.

Days of the week.

يَوْمُ الْأَحَدِ Sunday		يَوْمُ الْخَمِيسِ Thursday
يَوْمُ الِاثْنَيْنِ Monday		يَوْمُ الْجُمْعَةِ Friday
يَوْمُ الثَّلَاثَاءِ Tuesday		يَوْمُ السَّبْتِ Saturday
يَوْمُ الْأَرْبَعَاءِ Wednesday		

Syrian Christian months.

كَانُونُ ٱلثَّانِى	January	تَمُّوزُ	July
شُبَاطُ	February	آبُ	August
أَذَارُ	March	أَيْلُولُ	September
نِيسَانُ	April	تِشْرِينُ ٱلْأَوَّلُ	October
أَيَّارُ	May	تِشْرِينُ ٱلثَّانِى	November
حَزِيرَانُ	June	كَانُونُ ٱلْأَوَّلُ	December

The Muslim year is lunar and has twelve months of alternately 29 and 30 days. The era begins from A.D. 621, the year of the prophet's removal from Mecca — ٱلْهِجْرَةُ.

Names of the months.

مُحَرَّمُ	1	جُمَادَى ٱلْأُولَى	5	رَمَضَانُ	9
صَفَرُ	2	جُمَادَى ٱلْآخِرَةُ	6	شَوَّالُ	10
رَبِيعُ ٱلْأَوَّلُ	3	رَجَبُ	7	ذُو ٱلْقَعْدَةِ	11
رَبِيعُ ٱلْآخِرُ	4	شَعْبَانُ	8	ذُو ٱلْحِجَّةِ	12

The usual way of dating within the month is by counting the first half from the beginning and the second half from the end. Rajab has 30 days :—

on the 1st.

غُرَّةَ رَجَبٍ ـ لِغُرَّةِ رَجَبٍ ـ لِأَوَّلِ لَيْلَةٍ مِنْ رَجَبٍ ـ

لِلَيْلَةٍ خَلَتْ [مَضَتْ] مِنْ رَجَبٍ ـ لِمُسْتَهَلِّ رَجَبٍ

on the 2nd.

لِلَيْلَتَيْنِ خَلَتَا مِنْ رَجَبٍ

on the 3rd.

لِثَلَاثٍ خَلَوْنَ [لِثَلَاثِ لَيَالٍ مَضَيْنَ] مِنْ رَجَبٍ

on the 20th.

لِعَشْرٍ بَقِينَ مِنْ رَجَبٍ

on the 30th.

لِسَلْخِ رَجَبٍ ـ لِآخِرِ لَيْلَةٍ مِنْ رَجَبٍ

Note.—غُرَّةٌ blaze on a horse's forehead.

مُسْتَهَلٌ from هِلَالٌ new moon.

سَلْخٌ skin.

Vocabulary 36

حِسَابٌ u. حَسَبَ count

حُضُورٌ u. حَضَرَ be present.

جَرَيَانٌ i. جَرَى run, flow.

زُهْدٌ زَهِدَ leave, be content with little, be ascetic.

شَهْوَةٌ شَهَا and VIII desire.

نَجَاةٌ نَجَا be safe, escape.

غنى IV make rich and independent, enable one to dispense with; (with negative) be useless in the face of.

عِصْيَانٌ عَصَى disobey.

نَفَقَةٌ expenditure.

صِنَاعَةٌ handicraft, skill.

خَلَقٌ old, worn out.

صِنْفٌ (a) equal.

(دَوَاوِينُ) دِيوَانٌ ministry of state, register, collected works of a poet.

دَخْلٌ revenue.

حِسْبَانٌ i. حَسِبَ think.

جُودَةٌ u. جَادَ be generous.

حَذَرٌ حَذِرَ be on one's guard, be cautious.

قدر II estimate, imagine.

عزو II console, condole.

نُقْصَانٌ u. نَقَصَ be diminished, imperfect.

جَوَادٌ liberal ; swift horse.

حَلِيفٌ ally.

قِدْرٌ (fem.) (b) cooking pot.

مَحَبَّةٌ love.

خَرْجٌ expenditure.

Exercise 71

إِنِّى أُحِبُّكَ لِنَفْسِكَ فَوْقَ مَحَبَّتِى إِيَّاكَ لِنَفْسِى ـ
كَيْفَ تَجِدُكَ قَالَ تَجِدُنِى أَجِدُ مَا لَا أَشْتَهِى وَأَشْتَهِى
مَا لَا أَجِدُ لَقَدْ أَصْبَحْتُ فِى شَرِّ زَمَانٍ وَشَرِّ نَاسٍ

مَنْ جَادَ لَمْ يَجِدْ وَمَنْ وَجَدَ لَمْ يَجُدْ ـ قَدْ أَغْنَاكَ

اللهُ بِالْعُذْرِ مِنَّا عَنِ الِاعْتِذَارِ وَأَغْنَانَا اللهُ بِالْمَحَبَّةِ

لَكَ عَنْ سُوءِ الظَّنِّ بِكَ ـ إِلَى مَنْ أَوْصَى بِكَ أَبُوكَ

قَالَ أَوْصَى إِلَيَّ وَلَمْ يُوصِ بِى ـ يَا جَوَادَ اللِّسَانِ

مِنْ غَيْرِ فِعْلٍ لَيْتَ جُودَ اللِّسَانِ فِى يَدَيْكَ ـ لٰكِنَّ

اللهَ نَجَّانِى بِكَ وَمَا عَزَّانِى أَحَدٌ بِأَنْفَعَ مِنْ

تَعْزِيَتِكَ ـ أَرْضِ أَخِى وَحَلِيفِى الَّذِينِ اشْتَرَكَا فِى

أَسْرِ الْأَسِيرِ ـ أَرَادَ سُلْطَانٌ بِنَاءَ قَصْرٍ وَقَدَّرَ لِذٰلِكَ

أُلُوفَ أُلُوفٍ دِرْهَمٍ وَزَادَتِ النَّفَقَةُ عَلَى التَّقْدِيرِ

أَضْعَافًا وَكَانَ يُطَالِبُ وَزِيرَهُ بِتَوْجِيهِ الْأَمْوَالِ

لِذٰلِكَ مَعَ قُصُورِ الدَّخْلِ مِنَ الْخَرْجِ ـ كَانَ يَعْمِدُ

إِلَى مَنْ يَبِيعُ فِى الْأَسْوَاقِ مِثْلَ قِدْرٍ وَقَمِيصٍ خَلَقٍ

وَمَا يَغْلِبُ عَلَى الظَّنِّ أَنَّ مِثْلَهُ لَا يُبَاعُ إِلَّا مِنْ

ضُرٍّ شَدِيدٍ وَإِلَى امْرَأَةٍ تَبِيعُ غَزْلَهَا عَجُوزٍ فَيُعْطِيهِمْ

أَضْعَافَ ثَمَنِهِ وَيَدَعُهُ عَلَيْهِمْ .

72

I do not know a value for these pieces of cloth and have
never seen the like of them ; had I not actually seen them
I should not have believed that their like existed ; were
I to say that the price of each one is 100,000 dinars I should
not fear being far wrong — by God, it was not in me to
give her except 200 dirhams but God sent to her by my
hand 200 dinars and I shall not go back on this ; give her —
the minister despised the head of the ministry of finance
(tribute), and when he wanted some statement or account
from the ministry, he neglected the head, summoned the
clerks and asked their advice in the head's presence ;
when he wanted a statement which, he knew, the head's
skill was not equal to, and about which he could not speak,
he discussed it with him in the presence of others to make
his insufficiency plain — the prophet said of women,
consult them and oppose them (do the opposite). I dis-
obeyed him and obeyed my wife ; I bought a slave and
he became a thief — caution is useless in face of (does not
dispense with) providence — what is asceticism in the
world ? he said that what is forbidden does not overcome
your patience and what is allowed your thankfulness —
teach my sons swimming before writing ; for they can
find one to write for them and cannot find one to swim
for them.

CONCLUSION

It is important to remember that Arabic is essentially
simple however complicated it may be on the surface.
When the meaning of a passage is not obvious at the first
glance, make a literal translation giving each word its
simplest meaning ; then this crude English will usually
suggest the right sense.   A chronicler writes :—

$$\text{ثُمَّ دَخَلَتْ سَنَةَ ٢٤٦ وَلَمْ يَجْرِ فِيهَا شَىْءٌ يُكْتَبُ}$$

then came in the year 246 and a thing which is written
did not run in it ; this explains itself.

Some phrases have exact parallels in English ; ' he came out against the government ' is quite general while ' he came out in '45 ' is particular.

For further study Wright's grammar (two vols.) is indispensable. That is the only definite recommendation which can be made at present ; the good books are out of print and too expensive or come from abroad and cannot be got. There is no satisfactory dictionary ; an old copy of Hava's Arabic-English can be recommended but not one of the newer reprints which are smudged.[1] Apart from this, the two volumes by Elias, Arabic-English and English-Arabic, are the most useful. The price of each volume to-day is probably over one pound. There is a smaller edition of the Arabic-English but the type is small.

Nicholson's series of readers (Cambridge University Press) is the best introduction to classical Arabic and each of the three books has a vocabulary. In spite of its name, it is probably better to begin with the second reader. The history entitled *al-Fakhri* is a fairly easy book, but the first chapter on politics should be left to the last. There is a French translation. The beginner should avoid the *Koran* although it can be bought cheaply and translations (Rodwell, Palmer) are available. The oriental editions are lithographed and are not easy to read ; the matter is often difficult because it is the record of the spoken word without the help of tone and gesture to make it intelligible. Consequently it is not typical of Arabic prose.

The *Arabian Nights* (Beirut, five vols. ; volumes can be had separately) is a good stand-by ; no translation corresponds exactly to this text. For modern Arabic any volume of Mahmud Taimur's stories can be recommended. *al-Ayyam* by Taha Husain, the story of the blind professor's childhood, is good reading and there is a translation, *An Egyptian Childhood* by Paxton.

Daily papers are hard to read when they have been folded. The Egyptian illustrated *al-muṣvwwir* caters for various interests.

[1] A new edition is just out, clear and legible.

TABLE 1
STRONG VERB—STEM 1—ACTIVE

	Perfect	Indicative	Imperfect Subjunctive	Jussive	Energetic	Imperative
sing.						
3 m.	كَتَبَ	يَكْتُبُ	يَكْتُبَ	يَكْتُبْ	يَكْتُبَنَّ	
f.	كَتَبَتْ	تَكْتُبُ	تَكْتُبَ	تَكْتُبْ	تَكْتُبَنَّ	
2 m.	كَتَبْتَ	تَكْتُبُ	تَكْتُبَ	تَكْتُبْ	تَكْتُبَنَّ	اُكْتُبْ
f.	كَتَبْتِ	تَكْتُبِينَ	تَكْتُبِي	تَكْتُبِي	تَكْتُبِنَّ	اُكْتُبِي
1 c.	كَتَبْتُ	أَكْتُبُ	أَكْتُبَ	أَكْتُبْ	أَكْتُبَنَّ	
dual						
3 m.	كَتَبَا	يَكْتُبَانِ	يَكْتُبَا	يَكْتُبَا	يَكْتُبَانِّ	

TABLE 1

225

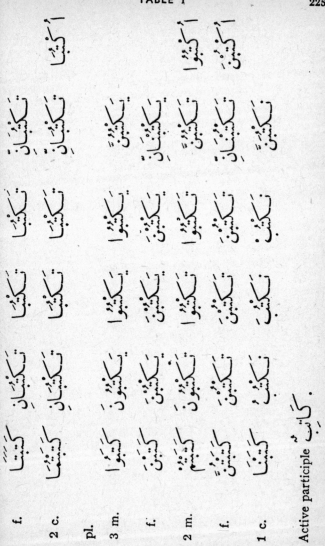

f.

2 c.

pl.

3 m.

f.

2 m.

f.

1 c.

Active participle مُكَتِّبٌ.

TABLE 2
STRONG VERB—DERIVED STEMS

	II	III	IV	V	VI
Active					
Perf.	كَتَّبَ	كاتَبَ	أَكْتَبَ	تَكَتَّبَ	تَكاتَبَ
Imperf.	يُكَتِّبُ	يُكاتِبُ	يُكْتِبُ	يَتَكَتَّبُ	يَتَكاتَبُ
Imp.	كَتِّبْ	كاتِبْ	أَكْتِبْ	تَكَتَّبْ	تَكاتَبْ
Part.	مُكَتِّب	مُكاتِب	مُكْتِب	مُتَكَتِّب	مُتَكاتِب
Inf.	تَكْتِيب	مُكاتَبة	إِكْتاب	تَكَتُّب	تَكاتُب
Passive					
Perf.	كُتِّبَ	كوتِبَ	أُكْتِبَ	تُكُتِّبَ	تُكوتِبَ
Imperf.	يُكَتَّبُ	يُكاتَبُ	يُكْتَبُ	يُتَكَتَّبُ	يُتَكاتَبُ

TABLE 2   227

	VII	VIII	IX	X	XI
Active					
Perf.	اِنْكَتَبَ	اِكْتَتَبَ	اِحْمَرَّ	اِسْتَكْتَبَ	اِحْمَارَّ
Imperf.	يَنْكَتِبُ	يَكْتَتِبُ	يَحْمَرُّ	يَسْتَكْتِبُ	يَحْمَارُّ
Imp.	اِنْكَتِبْ	اِكْتَتِبْ	اِحْمَرِرْ	اِسْتَكْتِبْ	اِحْمَارَّ
Part.	مُنْكَتِب	مُكْتَتِب	مُحْمَرّ	مُسْتَكْتِب	مُحْمَارّ
Inf.	اِنْكِتَاب	اِكْتِتَاب	اِحْمِرَار	اِسْتِكْتَاب	اِحْمِيرَار
Passive					
Perf.	اُنْكُتِبَ	اُكْتُتِبَ		اُسْتُكْتِبَ	
Imperf.	يُنْكَتَبُ	يُكْتَتَبُ		يُسْتَكْتَبُ	
Part.	مُنْكَتَب	مُكْتَتَب		مُسْتَكْتَب	

TABLE 3

STRONG VERB—STEM 1—PASSIVE

	Perfect	Indicative	Imperfect Subjunctive	Jussive
sing.				
3 m.	كُتِبَ	يُكْتَبُ	يُكْتَبَ	يُكْتَبْ
f.	كُتِبَتْ	تُكْتَبُ	تُكْتَبَ	تُكْتَبْ
2 m.	كُتِبْتَ	تُكْتَبُ	تُكْتَبَ	تُكْتَبْ
f.	كُتِبْتِ	تُكْتَبِينَ	تُكْتَبِي	تُكْتَبِي
1 c.	كُتِبْتُ	أُكْتَبُ	أُكْتَبَ	أُكْتَبْ
dual				
3 m.	كُتِبَا	يُكْتَبَانِ	يُكْتَبَا	يُكْتَبَا

TABLE 3 229

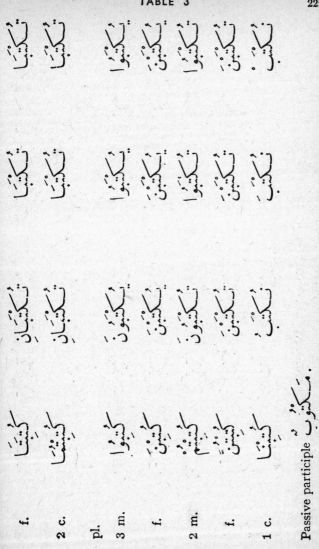

TABLE 4
HOLLOW VERB—MIDDLE W—STEM 1

	Perfect	Imperfect Indicative	Imperfect Subjunctive	Imperfect Jussive	Energetic	Imperative
sing. 3 m.	كانَ	يَكُونُ	يَكُونَ	يَكُنْ	يَكُونَنْ	
f.	كانَتْ	تَكُونُ	تَكُونَ	تَكُنْ	تَكُونَنْ	
2 m.	كُنْتَ	تَكُونُ	تَكُونَ	تَكُنْ	تَكُونَنْ	كُنْ
f.	كُنْتِ	تَكُونِينَ	تَكُونِي	تَكُونِي	تَكُونِنْ	كُونِي
1 c.	كُنْتُ	أَكُونُ	أَكُونَ	أَكُنْ	أَكُونَنْ	
dual 3 m.	كانا	يَكُونانِ	يَكُونا	يَكُونا	يَكُونانِّ	

TABLE 4   231

	تَكُونَا		تَكُونَا	تَكُونَانِ	كُنَّ
f.	تَكُونَانِ	تَكُونَا	تَكُونَا	تَكُونَانِ	كُونَا
2 c.					
pl.	تَكُونُوا	تَكُونُوا	تَكُونُوا	تَكُونُونَ	كُونُوا
3 m.	تَكُونِي	تَكُونِي	تَكُونِي	تَكُونِينَ	كُونِي
f.					
2 m.	تَكُونُوا	تَكُونُوا	تَكُونُوا	تَكُونُونَ	كُونُوا
f.	تَكُونِي	تَكُونِي	تَكُونِي	تَكُونِينَ	كُونِي
1 c.	تَكُونَ	تَكُونَ	تَكُونَ	تَكُونُ	كُنْ

Active participle كَائِنٌ .

TABLE 5
HOLLOW VERB—MIDDLE Y—STEM I

	Perfect	Imperfect Indicative	Imperfect Subjunctive	Imperfect Jussive	Imperfect Energetic	Imperative
sing. 3 m.	سَارَ	يَسِيرُ	يَسِيرَ	يَسِرْ	يَسِيرَنْ	
f.	سَارَتْ	تَسِيرُ	تَسِيرَ	تَسِرْ	تَسِيرَنْ	
2 m.	سِرْتَ	تَسِيرُ	تَسِيرَ	تَسِرْ	تَسِيرَنْ	سِرْ
f.	سِرْتِ	تَسِيرِينَ	تَسِيرِي	تَسِيرِي	تَسِيرِنْ	سِيرِي
1 c.	سِرْتُ	أَسِيرُ	أَسِيرَ	أَسِرْ	أَسِيرَنْ	

Active participle سَائِر.

TABLE 5 233

MIDDLE W OR Y—INTRANSITIVE FORM

	Perfect	Imperfect Indicative	Imperfect Subjunctive	Imperfect Jussive	Imperfect Energetic	Imperative
sing. 3 m.	نَامَ	يَنَامُ	يَنَامَ	يَنَمْ	يَنَامَنَّ	
f.	نَامَتْ	تَنَامُ	تَنَامَ	تَنَمْ	تَنَامَنَّ	
2 m.	نِمْتَ	تَنَامُ	تَنَامَ	تَنَمْ	تَنَامَنَّ	نَمْ
f.	نِمْتِ	تَنَامِينَ	تَنَامِي	تَنَامِي	تَنَامِنَّ	نَامِي
1 c.	نِمْتُ	أَنَامُ	أَنَامَ	أَنَمْ	أَنَامَنَّ	

Active participle نَائِم

TABLE 6

HOLLOW VERBS W OR Y—DERIVED STEMS

	IV	VII	VIII	X
Active				
Perf.				
3 s. m.	أَقَامَ	اِنْقَادَ	اِخْتَارَ	اِسْتَقَامَ
2 s. m.	أَقَمْتَ	اِنْقَدْتَ	اِخْتَرْتَ	اِسْتَقَمْتَ
Imperf.	يُقِيمُ	يَنْقَادُ	يَخْتَارُ	يَسْتَقِيمُ
Imp.	أَقِمْ	اِنْقَدْ	اِخْتَرْ	اِسْتَقِمْ
Part.	مُقِيم	مُنْقَاد	مُخْتَار	مُسْتَقِيم
Inf.	إِقَامَة	اِنْقِيَاد	اِخْتِيَار	اِسْتِقَامَة
Passive				
Perf.	أُقِيمَ		اُخْتِيرَ	اُسْتُقِيمَ

TABLE 6

235

STEM 1—PASSIVE

	Jussive	Imperfect Subjunctive	Indicative	Perfect
Imperf.	يُقْتَلْ	يُقْتَلَ	يُقْتَلُ	
Part.	مُقْتَلْ	مُقْتَلْ	مُقْتَلْ	
sing. 3 m.	يُقْتَلْ	يُقْتَلَ	يُقْتَلُ	قُتِلَ
2 f.	تُقْتَلِي	تُقْتَلِي	تُقْتَلِينَ	قُتِلْتِ
pl. 3 f.	يُقْتَلْنَ	يُقْتَلْنَ	يُقْتَلْنَ	قُتِلْنَ
2 m.	تُقْتَلُوا	تُقْتَلُوا	تُقْتَلُونَ	قُتِلْتُمْ

TABLE 7

VERBS. FIRST W AND Y

Active	IV		VIII		X	
Perf.	أَوْعَدَ	أَيْسَرَ	اِتَّعَدَ	اِتَّسَرَ	اِسْتَوْعَدَ	اِسْتَيْسَرَ
Imperf.	يُوعِدُ	يُوسِرُ	يَتَّعِدُ	يَتَّسِرُ	يَسْتَوْعِدُ	يَسْتَيْسِرُ
Imp.	أَوْعِدْ	أَيْسِرْ	اِتَّعِدْ	اِتَّسِرْ	اِسْتَوْعِدْ	اِسْتَيْسِرْ
Part.	مُوعِدٌ	مُوسِرٌ	مُتَّعِدٌ	مُتَّسِرٌ	مُسْتَوْعِدٌ	مُسْتَيْسِرٌ
Inf.	إِيعَادٌ	إِيسَارٌ	اِتِّعَادٌ	اِتِّسَارٌ	اِسْتِيعَادٌ	اِسْتِيسَارٌ
Passive Perf.	أُوعِدَ	أُوسِرَ	اُتُّعِدَ	اُتُّسِرَ	اُسْتُوعِدَ	اُسْتُوسِرَ

TABLE 7

237

Imperf.	يُوعَد	يُوسَر	تُشَكَّل	يُنْسَر	يُسْتَوْعَد	يُسْتَنْسَر
Part.	مَوْعُود	مَوْسُور	مُشَكَّل	مُنْسَر	مُسْتَوْعَد	مُسْتَنْسَر

STEM I—PASSIVE

Perf.	وُعِدَ	بُوسِرَ	نُسِرَ
Imperf.	يُوعَد	يُوسَر	يُنْسَر
Part.	مَوْعُود	مَوْسُور	مَنْسُور

TABLE 8
DOUBLED VERBS—STEM 1—ACTIVE

	Perfect	Imperfect Indicative	Imperfect Subjunctive	Jussive	Imperative
sing.					
3 m.	رَدَّ	يَرُدُّ	يَرُدَّ	يَرْدُدْ	
f.	رَدَّتْ	تَرُدُّ	تَرُدَّ	تَرْدُدْ	
2 m.	رَدَدْتَ	تَرُدُّ	تَرُدَّ	تَرْدُدْ	رُدَّ
f.	رَدَدْتِ	تَرُدِّينَ	تَرُدِّي	تَرُدِّي	رُدِّي
1 c.	رَدَدْتُ	أَرُدُّ	أَرُدَّ	أَرْدُدْ	اُرْدُدْ
dual					
3 m.	رَدَّا	يَرُدَّانِ	يَرُدَّا	يَرُدَّا	اُرْدُدْ
f.	رَدَّتَا	تَرُدَّانِ	تَرُدَّا	تَرُدَّا	اُرْدُدِّي

3 m.	رَدُّوا	يَرُدُّونَ	يَرُدُّوا	يَرُدُّوا
f.	رَدَدْنَ	يَرْدُدْنَ	يَرْدُدْنَ	يَرْدُدْنَ
2 m.	رَدَدْتُمْ	تَرُدُّونَ	تَرُدُّوا	تَرُدُّوا
f.	رَدَدْتُنَّ	تَرْدُدْنَ	تَرْدُدْنَ	تَرْدُدْنَ
1 c.	رَدَدْنَا	نَرُدُّ	نَرُدَّ	نَرْدُدْ

	رُدُّوا	أُرْدُدُوا		
	أُرْدُدْنَ			
Active participle رَادٌّ.				

TABLE 8

PASSIVE

sing.

3 m.	رُدَّ	يُرَدُّ	يُرَدَّ	يُرْدَدْ
2 f.	رُدِدْتِ	تُرَدِّينَ	تُرَدِّى	تُرَدِّى

pl.

3 f.	رُدِدْنَ	يُرْدَدْنَ	يُرْدَدْنَ	يُرْدَدْنَ
Passive participle مَرْدُودٌ.				

TABLE 9

DOUBLED VERB—DERIVED STEMS

	III	IV	VI	VII	VIII	X
Active						
Perf.	رادَّ	أرَدَّ	تَرادَّ	اِنْرَدَّ	اِرْتَدَّ	اِسْتَرَدَّ
Imperf.	يُرادُّ	يُرِدُّ	يَتَرادُّ	يَنْرَدُّ	يَرْتَدُّ	يَسْتَرِدُّ
Imp.	رادَّ	أرْدِدْ / أرِدَّ	تَرادَّ	اِنْرَدَّ	اِرْتَدَّ	اِسْتَرِدَّ
Part.	مُرادٌّ	مُرِدٌّ	مُتَرادٌّ	مُنْرَدٌّ	مُرْتَدٌّ	مُسْتَرِدٌّ
Inf.	مُرادَّة	إرْدادٌ	تَرادٌّ	اِنْرِدادٌ	اِرْتِدادٌ	اِسْتِرْدادٌ
Passive						
Perf.	رُودَّ	أُرِدَّ	تُرودَّ		اُرْتُدَّ	اُسْتُرِدَّ
Imperf.	يُرادُّ	يُرَدُّ	يُتَرادُّ		يُرْتَدُّ	يُسْتَرَدُّ

TABLE 9

241

STRONG VERB—STEM IX

Part.	Perfect			Imperfect		
	S	D	P	S	D	P
3 m.	احمرّ	احمرّا	احمرّوا	يحمرّ	يحمرّان	يحمرّون
f.	احمرّت	احمرّتا	احمرّنّ	تحمرّ	تحمرّان	يحمرّنّ
2 m.	احمررت	احمررتما	احمررتون	تحمرّ	تحمرّان	تحمرّون
f.	احمررتي		احمررتنّ	تحمرّين		تحمرّنّ
1 c.	احمررت		احمررنا	احمرّ		نحمرّ

Participle محمرّ.

Infinitive احمرار.

TABLE 10
VERBS FIRST HAMZA

	I	II	III	IV
Active				
Perf.	اَسَرَ	أَوَّرَ	آوَرَ	أَوْرَ
Imperf.	يَأْسِرُ	يُؤَوِّرُ	يُؤَاوِرُ	يُؤْوِرُ
Imp.	اِيسِرْ	أَوِّرْ	آوِرْ	أَوِرْ
Part.	آسِرٌ	مُؤَوِّرٌ	مُؤَاوِرٌ	مُؤْوِرٌ
Inf.	اَسْرٌ	تَأْوِيرٌ	مُؤَاوَرَةٌ / إِيوَارٌ	إِيوَارٌ
Passive				
Perf.	اُسِرَ	أُوِّرَ	أُوِرَ	أُوْرَ
Imperf.	يُؤْسَرُ	يُؤَوَّرُ	يُؤَاوَرُ	يُؤْوَرُ
Part.				

TABLE 10   243

	V	VI	VIII	X
Active				
Perf.	تَفَعَّلَ	تَفَاعَلَ	اِفْتَعَلَ	اِسْتَفْعَلَ
Imperf.	يَتَفَعَّلُ	يَتَفَاعَلُ	يَفْتَعِلُ	يَسْتَفْعِلُ
Imp.	تَفَعَّلْ	تَفَاعَلْ	اِفْتَعِلْ	اِسْتَفْعِلْ
Part.	مُتَفَعِّل	مُتَفَاعِل	مُفْتَعِل	مُسْتَفْعِل
Inf.	تَفَعُّل	تَفَاعُل	اِفْتِعَال	اِسْتِفْعَال
Passive				
Perf.	تُفُعِّلَ	تُفوعِلَ	اُفْتُعِلَ	اُسْتُفْعِلَ
Imperf.	يُتَفَعَّلُ	يُتَفَاعَلُ	يُفْتَعَلُ	يُسْتَفْعَلُ
Part.	مُتَفَعَّل	مُتَفَاعَل	مُفْتَعَل	مُسْتَفْعَل

TABLE 11
VERBS MIDDLE HAMZA

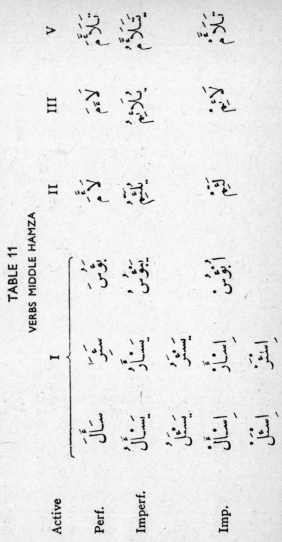

Active		I		II	III	V
Perf.						
Imperf.						
Imp.						

TABLE 11   245

مُتَشَكِّلٌ	تَشَكُّلٌ	تَشَكَّلَ		
تَشَكَّلَ	تَشَكُّلٌ			
تَخَالُمٌ	تَخَالُمٌ	تَخَالَمَ		
تَخَالَمَ	تَخَالُمٌ			
مُتَخَلِّطٌ	تَخَلُّطٌ	تَخَلَّطَ		
تَخَلَّطَ	تَخَلُّطٌ			
بَايَسَ	بَايَسَ			
سَايَرَ	سَيْرٌ			

Part.	سَائِلٌ
Inf.	سُؤَالٌ
Passive	سُئِلَ
Perf.	سَأَلَ
Imperf.	يَسْأَلُ
Part.	مَسْؤُولٌ

TABLE 12
VERBS THIRD HAMZA

Active	I					II	III
Perf.	بَرَأَ	هَنَأَ	خَطِئَ	جَرُؤَ		بَرَّأَ	بَارَأَ
2 s. m.	بَرَأْتَ	هَنَأْتَ	خَطِئْتَ	جَرُؤْتَ		بَرَّأْتَ	بَارَأْتَ
Imperf.	يَبْرَأُ	يَهْنَأُ	يَخْطَأُ	يَجْرُؤُ		يُبَرِّئُ	يُبَارِئُ
Imp.	اِبْرَأْ	اِهْنَأْ	اِخْطَأْ	اُجْرُؤْ		بَرِّئْ	بَارِئْ
Part.	بَارِئٌ	هَانِئٌ	خَاطِئٌ	جَارِئٌ		مُبَرِّئٌ	مُبَارِئٌ

TABLE 12   247

نِزَّ	هِنَّزَ	خِطَابَة	حِرِّزَارَة	تَنْزِيرَة	مِنْزَارَة
نِرْكِي	هِنِّي	خِطَّى		نِرْكِي	يُورْدِي
اِتِنْرَ	تِنْهَا	تِخِطَّلَا		تِيَنْرَ	تِيَارَا
مَنْزُرُوظَة	مَهْنُوزَ	مَخْطُوبَة		مِنْزَرَّة	مِنْزَارَا

Inf.	
Passive	
Perf.	
Imperf.	
Part.	

TABLE 13
VERBS THIRD W—CHARACTERISTIC A

	Perfect	Imperfect Indicative	Imperfect Subjunctive	Imperfect Jussive	Imperfect Energetic	Imperative
sing.						
3 m.	دَعَا	يَدْعُو	يَدْعُوَ	يَدْعُ	يَدْعُوَنْ	
f.	دَعَتْ	تَدْعُو	تَدْعُوَ	تَدْعُ	تَدْعُوَنْ	
2 m.	دَعَوْتَ	تَدْعُو	تَدْعُوَ	تَدْعُ	تَدْعُوَنْ	اُدْعُ
f.	دَعَوْتِ	تَدْعِينَ	تَدْعِي	تَدْعِي	تَدْعِنْ	اُدْعِي
1 c.	دَعَوْتُ	أَدْعُو	أَدْعُوَ	أَدْعُ	أَدْعُوَنْ	
dual						
3 m.	دَعَوَا	يَدْعُوَانِ	يَدْعُوَا	يَدْعُوَا	يَدْعُوَانِّ	

TABLE 13   249

f.	2 c.	pl.	3 m.	f.	2 m.	f.	1 c.
أَتَنَادَوْا	تَنَادَوَانِ تَنَادَوَانِ	اتَنَادَوْا اتَنَادَوْا	تَنَادَوْا تَنَادَوْا	تَنَادَوَانِ تَنَادَوَانِ	اتَنَادَوْا تَنَادَوْنَ	تَنَادَوْنَ تَنَادَوْنَ	نَتَنَادَ
اتَنَادَوْنَ							

Active participle مُتَنَادٍ ـ الْمُتَنَادِي

Passive participle مُتَنَادًى

TABLE 14
VERBS THIRD Y—CHARACTERISTIC A

	Perfect	Imperfect Indicative	Imperfect Subjunctive	Imperfect Jussive	Energetic	Imperative
sing. 3 m.	رَمَى	يَرْمِي	يَرْمِيَ	يَرْمِ	يَرْمِيَنَّ	
f.	رَمَتْ	تَرْمِي	تَرْمِيَ	تَرْمِ	تَرْمِيَنَّ	
2 m.	رَمَيْتَ	تَرْمِي	تَرْمِيَ	تَرْمِ	تَرْمِيَنَّ	اِرْمِ
f.	رَمَيْتِ	تَرْمِينَ	تَرْمِي	تَرْمِي	تَرْمِنَّ	اِرْمِي
1 c.	رَمَيْتُ	أَرْمِي	أَرْمِيَ	أَرْمِ	أَرْمِيَنَّ	
dual 3 m.	رَمَيَا	يَرْمِيَانِ	يَرْمِيَا	يَرْمِيَا	يَرْمِيَانِّ	

TABLE 14   251

Active participle مُعْرَاً — كُتْ مُعْرَاً.   Passive participle مُعْرَى.

	f.
2 c.	
pl.	
3 m.	
f.	
2 m.	
f.	
1 c.	

TABLE 15

VERBS THIRD W OR Y—CHARACTERISTIC I

	Perfect	Indicative	Subjunctive	Jussive	Energetic	Imperative
sing.			**Imperfect**			
3 m.	رَضِيَ	يَرْضَى	يَرْضَى	يَرْضَ	يَرْضَيَنَّ	
f.	رَضِيَتْ	تَرْضَى	تَرْضَى	تَرْضَ	تَرْضَيَنَّ	
2 m.	رَضِيتَ	تَرْضَى	تَرْضَى	تَرْضَ	تَرْضَيَنَّ	اِرْضَ
f.	رَضِيتِ	تَرْضَيْنَ	تَرْضَيْ	تَرْضَيْ	تَرْضَيِنَّ	اِرْضَيْ
1 c.	رَضِيتُ	أَرْضَى	أَرْضَى	أَرْضَ	أَرْضَيَنَّ	
dual						
3 m.	رَضِيَا	يَرْضَيَانِ	يَرْضَيَا	يَرْضَيَا	يَرْضَيَانِّ	

TABLE 15

253

	اِرْضَيَا			اِرْضُوا	اِرْضَيْنَ
f.	تَرْضَيَا	تَرْضَيَانِ	تَرْضَيْ		
2 c.	تَرْضَيَا	تَرْضَيَانِ	تَرْضَيْنَ		
pl.				يَرْضُوا	يَرْضَيْنَ
3 m.	يَرْضَيَا	يَرْضَيَانِ	يَرْضُوا	يَرْضَيْنَ	
f.	تَرْضَيَا	تَرْضَيَانِ	تَرْضُوا	تَرْضَيْنَ	
2 m.	تَرْضَيَا	تَرْضَيَانِ	تَرْضَوْا	تَرْضَيْنَ	
f.	تَرْضَيَا	تَرْضَيَانِ	تَرْضَيْنَ		
1 c.			نَرْضَى		

Active participle رَاضٍ – مَرْضِيّ.   Passive participle مَرْضِيّ.

The passive is inflected like verbs with characteristic 'i' in the perfect.

TABLE 16
VERBS THIRD W AND Y—DERIVED STEMS

	II	III	IV	V
Active				
Perf.	قَصَّى	قَاصَى	أَقْصَى	تَقَصَّى
Imperf.	يُقَصِّي	يُقَاصِي	يُقْصِي	يَتَقَصَّى
Imp.	قَصِّ	قَاصِ	أَقْصِ	تَقَصَّ
Part.	مُقَصٍّ	مُقَاصٍ	مُقْصٍ	مُتَقَصٍّ
Inf.	تَقْصِيَة	مُقَاصَاة	إِقْصَاء	تَقَصٍّ
Passive				
Perf.	قُصِّيَ	قُوصِيَ	أُقْصِيَ	تُقُصِّيَ
Imperf.	يُقَصَّى	يُقَاصَى	يُقْصَى	يُتَقَصَّى
Part. m.	مُقَصًّى	مُقَاصًى	مُقْصًى	مُتَقَصًّى

TABLE 16

255

	VI	VII	VIII	X
Active				
Perf.	تَقاضَى	اِنْقَضَى	اِقْتَضَى	اِسْتَقْضَى
Imperf.	يَتَقاضَى	يَنْقَضِي	يَقْتَضِي	يَسْتَقْضِي
Imp.	تَقاضَ	اِنْقَضِ	اِقْتَضِ	اِسْتَقْضِ
Part.	مُتَقاضٍ	مُنْقَضٍ	مُقْتَضٍ	مُسْتَقْضٍ
Inf.	تَقاضٍ	اِنْقِضاء	اِقْتِضاء	اِسْتِقْضاء
Passive				
Perf.	تُقُوضِيَ	اُنْقُضِيَ	اُقْتُضِيَ	اُسْتُقْضِيَ
Imperf.	يُتَقاضَى	يُنْقَضَى	يُقْتَضَى	يُسْتَقْضَى
Part. m.	مُتَقاضًى	مُنْقَضًى	مُقْتَضًى	مُسْتَقْضًى
f.	مُتَقاضاةٌ	مُنْقَضاةٌ	مُقْتَضاةٌ	مُسْتَقْضاةٌ

KEY

Most English sentences can be translated into Arabic in several ways, all equally right.

1

a big river — the gracious king — the house is clean — a beautiful garden — good bread — the poor man — an ugly man — the meat is good — the street is spacious — I am rich — a dirty boy — is he beloved ? — an old castle — are you speaking the truth ?

2

بَيْتٌ صَغِيرٌ ـ اَلْبَيْتُ صَغِيرٌ ـ رَجُلٌ فَقِيرٌ ـ اَلْحَبِيبُ
صَادِقٌ ـ هُوَ قَبِيحٌ ـ أَنَا رَجُلٌ ـ أَنْتَ لَطِيفٌ ـ اَلْبُسْتَانُ
اَلْوَاسِعُ ـ نَهْرٌ عَرِيضٌ ـ اَلْبَحْرُ حَسَنٌ ـ اَلشَّارِعُ
اَلْقَبِيحُ ـ اَلْوَلَدُ الصَّغِيرُ وَسِخٌ ـ اَلْخُبْزُ طَيِّبٌ .

3

a little girl — a big (elder) sister — the town is clean — the mother is beautiful — a new house — the wind is strong — a truthful old woman — the tall chief (old man) — the market is far off — the tree is small — an extensive island — is the girl (daughter) beloved ? — oh boy ! — oh mighty queen ! — a neighbouring land — are you (fem. sing.) rich ?

4

اَلشَّمْسُ الْحَارَّةُ ـ اَلْجَزِيرَةُ بَعِيدَةٌ ـ أُمٌّ طَوِيلَةٌ ـ
اَلْأُخْتُ الْكَبِيرَةُ ـ اَلْعَجُوزُ لَطِيفَةٌ ـ اَلنَّارُ حَارَّةٌ ـ

اَلشَّيْخُ الْعَزِيزُ ـ اَلْبَيْتُ جَدِيدٌ (اَلدَّارُ جَدِيدَةٌ) ـ
اَلْقَصْرُ الْقَدِيمُ ـ أَهِىَ فَقِيرَةٌ ـ أَنْتِ لَطِيفَةٌ .

5

a door of a house — the door of the garden — the window
of the house is open — the land is extensive — the tribe is
rich — does the book belong to the daughter of the chief? —
no, it belongs to the sister of the merchant — the street of
the town is wide — the big courtyard of the house of the
king — the key of the door is in the lock — the costume
of the chief is clean — the girl's face is beautiful — the
safety of man is in the guarding of the tongue — the
neighbour before the house and the companion before the
road (journey) — power belongs to God — the head
(beginning) of wisdom is the fear of God — the caliph is
the shadow of God on the earth.

6

بُسْتَانُ مَلِكٍ ـ عِزُّ الْإِنْسَانِ فِى اللِّسَانِ ـ وَجْهُ
الْبِنْتِ الْحَسَنَةِ الْحَسَنُ ـ مِفْتَاحُ الْبَابِ ثَقِيلٌ ـ
اَلْبَيْتُ الصَّغِيرُ فِى ظِلِّ شَجَرَةٍ كَبِيرَةٍ ـ اَلرَّفِيقُ
الْحَسَنُ رَأْسُ السَّلَامَةِ عَلَى الطَّرِيقِ ـ اَلتَّاجِرُ عِزُّ
الْأَرْضِ ـ إِنَّ الْكِتَابَ الصَّغِيرَ لَخَفِيفٌ ـ لِلْبِنْتِ
كِسَاءٌ خَفِيفٌ وَلِلْعَجُوزِ كِسَاءٌ ثَقِيلٌ .

7

is the baker rich ?— no, he is poor — the bakers and the carpenters are busy — there are many bakers and carpenters in the town — the two eyes and the two ears are in the head — the two boys (children) are playing — two playing girls — the two hands of the boy are dirty — the old man and the old woman are sitting beside a short and shady tree — two horses and two donkeys — the two sisters of the merchant are in the little room — are you two speaking the truth ? — yes, we are speaking the truth — the few sheep belong to the owner of the little house.

8

بَابَا اَلْبَيْتِ مَفْتُوحَانِ ـ هُوَ صَاحِبُ فَرَسَيْنِ ـ هِىَ

صَاحِبَةُ بَيْتٍ وَبُسْتَانٍ فِى اَلْمَدِينَةِ ـ اَلْحِمَارُ فَرَسُ

اَلْفَقِيرِ ـ فِى اَلْمَدِينَةِ طَبِيبَانِ ـ لِكُلِّ حُجْرَةٍ فِى

اَلْبَيْتِ شُبَّاكَانِ ـ أَأَنْتُمْ فَرَّاشُونَ ـ لَا نَحْنُ

طَبَّاخُونَ ـ إِنَّ فِى اَلْبَيْتِ قِطْعَتَىْ لَحْمٍ وَخُبْزًا كَثِيرًا ـ

[قِطْعَتَا لَحْمٍ وَخُبْزٌ كَثِيرٌ فِى اَلْبَيْتِ] ـ اَلْبُسْتَانُ

لِصَاحِبَىِ اَلْمَلِكِ ـ هُنَّ خَيَّاطَاتٌ مَشْغُولَةٌ

[مَشْغُولَاتٌ] .

9

relatives are scorpions — the learned are the heirs of the prophets — the carpenter has partners — the cook has the eatables in the kitchen — the windows of the great house are many — there are many schools in the town — has the watchman the keys of the town? — no, the governor has them — the old men and the old women are sitting in the shade of the trees — an Arab tribe has many dogs — the vices of the elect are the virtues of the mob — the loaves are from the shops of the bakers — the nobles are the associates of the governors in guarding the towns — the shops of the greengrocers are in a special market.

10

اَلْفَلَّاحُونَ وَالتُّجَّارُ أَعْمِدَةُ الْأَرْضِ ـ أَصَابِعُ الْوَلَدِ
وَسِخَةٌ ـ الْعَبِيدُ عِبَادٌ ـ الْحِنْطَةُ طَعَامُ الْأَشْرَافِ
وَالشَّعِيرُ طَعَامُ الْفُقَرَاءِ ـ أَصْحَابُ الْكِسَاءِ الْحَسَنِ
فِي بُيُوتِ الْمُلُوكِ ـ فَوَاكِهُ الشَّامِ طَيِّبَةٌ ـ أَوْلَادُ
الْأَشْرَافِ فِي مَدَارِسَ خَاصَّةٍ ـ إِنَّ أَظْفَارَ الْبِنْتِ
نَظِيفَةٌ وَأَظْفَارَ الْوَلَدِ وَسِخَةٌ ـ الْكِلَابُ حُرَّاسُ
الْعَرَبِ ـ إِنَّ الرِّيَاحَ عَلَى الْجَزَائِرِ بَارِدَةٌ ـ قُلُوبُ
النَّاسِ بَيْنَ أَصَابِعِ اللَّهِ .

11

my hand is clean — your two hands are clean — his fine horses are swift — Zayd, his daughter is beautiful — his cattle have much milk — my weight (worth) in his opinion

is as the weight of a dog — the strength of a man is in his
intelligence and his tongue — the poets and knights of the
Arabs are many — he has two boys, the elder of the two is
short and the younger of the two is tall — the honour of
a man is his sons and his care his house and his neighbour
— your graceful poems are known among men, all of them
— my poor friend has two donkeys and your woman
friend has many horses — your big box is light and her
little box is heavy.

12

حِنْطَتِى وَشَعِيرِى فِى صَنَادِيقِى الْكَبِيرَةِ ـ إِنَّ
يَدَيْهَا لَنَظِيفَتَانِ ـ وَطَنُنَا حَبِيبٌ إِلَيْنَا ـ يَا أَوْلَادُ
أَعِنْدَكُمْ كُتُبُكُمْ ـ رَسَائِلُكَ اللَّطِيفَةُ فِى حِفْظِ
صَاحِبِى [رَسَائِلُكُمُ اللَّطِيفَةُ] ـ يَدَاىَ وَرِجْلَاىَ ـ
أُخْتُكَ وَخَادِمَاتُهَا جَالِسَةٌ عِنْدَ طَبَّاخِى ـ شُيُوخُهُمْ
أَصْحَابُ الْحِكْمَةِ ـ يَدَا الْعَجُوزِ وَعَيْنَاهَا ضَعِيفَتَانِ ـ
وَزْنُ الْإِنْسَانِ وَزْنُ عَقْلِهِ ـ حِكْمَةُ الشَّيْخِ مِنْ كَثْرَةِ
تَجَارِبِهِ .

13

the old man hit the boy's head — the old woman understood the girl's words — did you seek food from the
kitchen ? — I fetched meat from the butcher's shop —
the boys came out from the mosque and went into the

school — the sempstresses went away from our town and returned to their native land — girls, have you drunk water? — no, we drank milk — did you two hear the voices (song) of the birds on the trees? — I cut the meat into small pieces — my mother sent me to you — the men came down from the top of the mountain and captured the town.

14

أَكَتَبْتَ الرَّسَائِلَ ـ هَلْ كَتَبْتُمُ الرَّسَائِلَ ـ كَسَرَ
الْوَلَدُ قَدَمَ الْكَلْبِ بِحَجَرَةٍ ـ سَمِعُوا كَلَامَ الْأَمِيرِ
وَرَجَعُوا إِلَى بُيُوتِهِمْ ـ دَخَلَ الْمُلُوكُ الْأَرْضَ وَفَتَحُوهَا ـ
فَتَحَتُ الشَّبَاكَ وَدَخَلَ كَلْبٌ ـ صَرَخَ حُرَّاسُ الْبَقَرِ
هَلْ سَمِعْتُمُوهُمْ ـ قَطَعَ الْأَطِبَّاءُ يَدَ الرَّجُلِ وَرِجْلَهُ ـ
أَدَخَلْتُمُ الْحُجْرَةَ ـ يَا بَنَاتُ هَلْ لَعِبْتُنَّ مَعَ الْكَلْبِ
الْكَبِيرِ ـ قَطَعَ رِجَالٌ قَبِيحَةٌ آذَانَ الْبَقَرِ ـ يَا بِنْتَانِ
أَيَعْتُمَا تُحْفَةً إِلَى أُخْتِكُمَا .

15

the boys went into the sea to swim — the carpenter sent to me to ask for wood — we sat by the spring drinking and laughing — the commander of the army came out, went up the mountain and looked at the ranks of the enemy — the companions went from Syria to Jerusalem stopping every night in a village — men in summer go away from the hot towns and put up in towns near the sea

— the merchant progressed to the king's city collecting the dinars from his clients — you will hear the sound of the drums.

16

سَيَفْتَحُ اللهُ الْمَدِينَةَ عَلَى يَدِ نَبِيَّهِ ـ خَرَجَ الْكِلَابُ يَنْبَحُونَ [تَنْبَحُ] ـ يَلْبَسُ النَّاسُ [الْإِنْسَانُ] ثِيَابًا ثَقِيلَةً فِى الشِّتَاءِ ـ جَلَسْتُمْ تَسْمَعُونَ كَلَامَ الشَّاعِرِ ـ أَتَصْنَعُ الْبَنَاتُ ثِيَابَهُنَّ [ثِيَابَهَا] ـ يَضْرِبُ الْمَلِكُ دَنَانِيرَ طَيِّبَةً ـ خَرَجَ الْأَوْلَادُ يَلْعَبُونَ ـ قَدِمَ الْجَيْشُ يَضْرِبُونَ طُبُولَهُمْ ـ صَنَعَ لَنَا النَّجَّارُ كُؤُوسًا مِنْ خَشَبٍ نَشْرَبُ مِنْهَا ـ سَمِعْنَا الْحُرَّاسَ يَصْرُخُونَ عَلَى الْعَدُوِّ ـ نَظَرْتُ إِلَيْهِ وَهُوَ يَغْضَبُ عَلَى كَلَامِى .

17

these two men are the two chiefs of the tribe — this is the truthful slave girl — this estate of mine is renowned in the country — these girls are playing in the court of the school — those men have camped at the entry of the town — I heard that dog of yours barking — this is your bed — whose are these jewels? — they belong to the agent of the owner of this estate — those are slave girls from the household of the chief — who made those cups and dishes of yours? —— whom did you send to me? — from whose statement is this?

18

اَلْأَشْعَارُ ٱلْقَصِيرَةُ هِيَ ٱلْمَشْهُورَةُ ـ أَغْضَبُ [أَنَا] عَلَى مَا فَعَلْتَ ـ لِذٰلِكَ ٱلْوَكِيلِ فِضَّةٌ كَثِيرَةٌ وَذَهَبٌ كَثِيرٌ ـ لِمَنْ تِلْكَ ٱلضَّيْعَةُ ـ صَعِدَ ٱلْحَارِسُ فِى مَنَارَةِ ٱلْمَسْجِدِ ذٰلِكَ يَصْرُخُ ـ سَيَكْتُبُ ٱلْأَوْلَادُ عَلَى تِلْكَ ٱلْأَوْرَاقِ بِهٰذِهِ ٱلْأَقْلَامِ ـ ذَهَبَ صَاحِبُكَ ٱلْفَقِيرُ ذٰلِكَ يَطْلُبُ ٱلْقُوتَ ـ جَمَعَ وَكِيلُكَ هٰذَا مَالًا كَثِيرًا ـ أَوْرَاقُ ٱلشَّجَرِ هٰذِهِ قُوتٌ لِلْغَنَمِ ـ اَلْمَخْرَجُ مِنْ جَهْلِهِ عَسِيرٌ عَلَى ٱلْجَاهِلِ ـ مَالِى هُوَ سَيْفِى وَكُتُبِى.

19

that dog of yours is white — this horse is black — the black
slave is in the red room — this tree is green in summer —
the two eyes of the girl are blue — the Path is sharper than
a sword and thinner than a hair — the colour of this flower,
what is it? — it has two colours, blue and yellow — the
leaves of the trees are brown and red in autumn —
gold is heavier than silver — prayer is better than sleep —
best of gifts is understanding and the worst of calamities
ignorance — a dumb slave girl is the best — my daughter
is taller than I.

20

لَهُ إِمَاءٌ طُرْشٌ وَسُودٌ ـ جَيْشُنَا أَقَلُّ مِنْ جَيْشِ
أَعْدَائِنَا ـ اَلْغَنَمُ فِى بِلادِ الْعَرَبِ سُودٌ [سَوْدَاءُ] ـ
اَلْقُوتُ الْأَحَبُّ إِلَى الْعَرَبِ الْأَسْوَدَانِ اللَّحْمُ والتَّمْرُ ـ
اَلنَّخْلُ أَطْوَلُ مِنَ الزَّيْتُونِ ـ ضَيْعَتُكَ أَصْغَرُ مِنْ ضَيْعَتِى ـ
إِنَّ لِهٰذَا الطَّائِرِ صَدْرًا أَصْفَرَ وَجَنَاحَيْنِ أَحْمَرَيْنِ ـ
بَعَثَ إِلَىَّ أَصْدِقَائِى مَوَاهِبَ كَثِيرَةً وَمَوْهَبَتُكَ هِىَ
الْحُسْنَى ـ بَعَثَ اللهُ نَبِيَّهُ لِكُلِّ النَّاسِ السُّودِ
وَالْبِيضِ وَالْحُمْرِ ـ إِنَّ أُخْتَكَ الصُّغْرَى هِىَ الْطَفَهُنَّ .

21

my father and your brother heard the noises of the riding
beasts — the daughter looked for her father in the market
— the old man gathered his sons round his bed before his
death — the greengrocer's daughter took the white papers
away from her brother's hand — the woman with her sons
went into the presence (between the hands) of the caliph
— boys, do you know the names of the flowers ? — yes,
we know the name of every flower in the garden — I
followed your brother in the road writing his name on the
wall of every house — your parents rejoice at your success
— a man is in the two smallest (parts) of him, his heart and
his tongue — the beauty of a man lies in his tongue and
the beauty of a woman in her understanding.

22

أَفَهِمْتُمَا أَنْتَ وَأَخُوكَ كَلَامِى ـ يَلْعَبُ أَخَوَاىَ

وَأُخْتَاىَ مَعْ إِخْوَانِكَ وَأَخَوَاتِكَ ـ أَبَعَثَ أَبُوكَ أَخَاكَ

إِلَىَّ ـ بَعَثَتِ الْمَرْأَةُ أَبْنَاءَهَا يَطْلُبُونَ الْمَالَ فِى

بُلْدَانٍ بَعِيدَةٍ ـ مَا اسْمُكَ ـ اِسْمِى مَشْهُورٌ هُوَ

أَشْهَرُ أَسْمَاءِ الْعَرَبِ ـ يَا امْرَأَةُ أَلَكِ أَوْلَادٌ ـ نَعَمْ

إِنَّ لِى ابْنًا وَابْنَتَيْنِ ـ لِهَذَا الرَّجُلِ أَبَوَانِ أَبُو

جِسْمِهِ وَأَبُو عَقْلِهِ ـ هَلْ نَزَلْتَ عِنْدَ أَبِى صَدِيقِى ـ

ذَوُو الْعِلْمِ وَالْمَالِ هُمْ أَقَلُّ النَّاسِ.

23

women, listen to the noise of your infants — the going into this business is easier than the coming out from it — maid, go to the market and ask for my new clothes from the dressmaker — the hider of a secret is a faithful friend — self conquest is the greatest conquest — general, dismount from your horse and enter my house ; this will be a great honour to me — what is required from you is to return from the far country to the house of your parents — he who is served, in your opinion, is the servant of you all — we belong to God and to him we return — a man's serving his brother is honour.

24

يَا اُبْنَتِى اُسْمَعِى قَوْلِى ـ اُطْلُبِ الْعِلْمَ مِنَ الْكُلِّ

الرِّجَالِ وَالنِّسَاءِ ـ دُخُولُ الْمَالِ عَسِيرٌ وَالْخُرُوجُ

مِنْهُ يَسِيرٌ ـ مَعْرِفَةُ نَفْسِكَ الْمَعْرِفَةُ الْكُبْرَى

وَالْعُسْرَى ـ فَرِحَ الْمَلِكُ بِرُجُوعِ جَيْشِهِ بَعْدَ فَتْحِهِ

أَعْدَاءَهُ ـ قَطْعُ الْيَدِ عَذَابُ السَّارِقِ ـ يَفْرَحُ الْكَرِيمُ

بِقُدُومِ الْأَضْيَافِ ـ حِفْظُكَ اللِّسَانَ مِنَ الْقَبِيحِ

مَخَافَةُ اللهِ ـ مَطْلُوبُ بَعْثِى هَذَا الْغُلَامَ إِلَيْكَ دُخُولُهُ

فِى خِدْمَتِكَ.

25

he who hurries repents — the government sent its servants
to measure the fields — the doctor wanted me to drink
much milk — had you been at the war, you would know
which of the two armies was the braver — let him take its
prey from the mouth of the lion that we may know his
strength and courage — I do not like that you should look
on the faults of your neighbours — the caliph wrote to the
commander of his army ; do not kill old men and infants
and do not cut down trees — if you get out of this affair,
you will be glad all your life — it is part of courage to put
up with calamities and the unpleasant — the father called
for two doctors to find out his son's illness.

26

لَا تَلْعَبْ بِذَلِكَ السَّيْفِ الْحَدِيدِ ـ لَأَكْشِفَنَّ عَنْ
سِرِّهِ ـ لِيَسْكُتِ الْغُلَامُ بَيْنَ يَدَيْ أَكْبَرَ مِنْهُ ـ
لَأَدْخُلْ دَارَكَ لِأَنْظُرَ إِلَى فُرُشِكَ ـ كَسَرُوا الْكَأْسَ
لِيَسْقُطَ السَّمُّ فِيهَا عَلَى الْأَرْضِ ـ ابْعَثِ الْغُلَامَ
لِيَجْمَعَ التَّمْرَ السَّاقِطَ عَلَى الْأَرْضِ ـ تَخْرُجُ نِسَاءُ
الْقَبِيلَةِ كُلَّ يَوْمٍ لِيَجْمَعْنَ حَطَبًا [لِجَمْعِ الْحَطَبِ] ـ
لَا تَغْضَبْ عَلَى الصَّدِيقِ ـ مِنَ الشَّرَفِ أَنْ تَكْرَهَ
عُيُوبَ نَفْسِكَ .

27

do not beat your children — my father did not send me
to look for a book for you (a book of yours) — he will never
be noble who does not hide secrets — we have never heard
the like of this story — God is one, nothing is like him —
we do not return from our work in the fields while the sun
is in the sky — we were not glad at this news and not
sorry — there is no poverty and no trial like greed grasping-
ness and no wealth like contentment — there is no
intelligence like good management, no piety like self
control and no beauty like the beauty of character —
running away in the time for it is better than holding on
when it is not the time for it — two are not satisfied, the
seeker after knowledge and the seeker after wealth.

28

إِنَّ أَعْدَاءَنَا لَا رَحِمَهُمُ اللهُ كَثِيرَةٌ ــ لَا تَفْزَعْ مِنَ
الشُّغْلِ ــ لَمْ يَشْبَعِ النَّبِىُّ لَحْمًا فِى حَيَاتِهِ ــ لَا تَقْنَعْ
بِقَلِيلٍ مِنَ الْعِلْمِ ــ لَنْ يَرْجِعَ الْأَيَّامُ الذَّاهِبَةُ ــ مَا
أَطْلُبُ تُحَفًا مِنَ الْحُكُومَةِ الْيَوْمَ ــ لَا تَفْزَعْ إِلَى
غَيْرِ اللهِ ــ يَا بُنَىَّ لَا تَضْحَكِى عَلَى مُصِيبَةِ الْفَقِيرِ
وَلَا تَغْضَبِى عَلَى نَجَاحِ ذِى مَالٍ ــ هُوَ ذُو مَالٍ
وَضِيَاعٍ وَبُيُوتٍ وَلَا يَقْنَعُ ــ لَسْتَ ذَا حِكْمَةٍ [بِذِى
حِكْمَةٍ].

29

it is yellow in colour (he is fair of complexion) — Zayd is
stupid but Umar is more stupid than he — the wind to-day
is stronger than it was yesterday — he fled from the
country for fear of the wrath of the sultan — he went right
and left looking for food — they waited for no long time —
I stayed away from the war out of cowardice — the peasants
planted their fields with barley — I am more afraid of him
than he of me — I aimed at (entering) the service of some
great man for the sake of getting rich — I was glad but
hid my feelings in sorrow for the sick man — I bowed down
to God for joy at his sending the prophet.

فَزِعَتْ فَزَعًا عَظِيمًا ـ لَمْ يَهْرُبْ أَحَدٌ هَرَبِى ـ
سَكَنْتُ فِى تِلْكَ الْمَدِينَةِ سِنِينَ كَثِيرَةً ـ إِنَّ لَهُ
مَالًا قَلِيلًا وَيَقْنَعُ بِفَقْرِهِ [هُوَ ذُو مَالٍ قَلِيلٍ] ـ اَلْحَرُّ
الْيَوْمَ أَشَدُّ مِنْهُ الْبَارِحَ ـ شَجَاعَتُهُ شَجَاعَةُ الْأَسَدِ ـ
إِنَّهُ أَشْجَعُ مِنَ الْأَسَدِ ـ سَكَتَ طَوِيلًا ـ لَا أَذْهَبُ
إِلَى الْبُلْدَانِ الْحَارَّةِ خَوْفًا مِنَ الْمَرَضِ ـ لَبِسَ ثِيَابَ
الْحَرِيرِ فَرَحًا فِى جَمْعِهِ مَالًا كَثِيرًا ـ هُوَ قَوِىٌّ
ذِرَاعًا وَضَعِيفٌ قَدَمًا.

31

whose argument is short, his tongue is long (much verbiage
instead of a good case) — stand up, my boy, and go to
your grandfather — the children were playing in the street —
the girl feared the violence of the wind — the caravan came
back through fear of brigands — my daughter, be not
afraid ; you will not go alone — let him say what he
thinks — I was the son of my father then I became the
father of my son — the colour of the snake is dark (a
darkness) inclining to blackness — the bedouin were
selling the skins of sheep and goats to the peasants — the
army will have overcome its enemies before sunset.

32

قَامَ مِنْ فِرَاشِهِ وَالشَّمْسُ قَدْ مَالَتْ لِغُرُوبِهَا ـ إِنْ
مَاتَ شَيْخٌ مِنْ قَوْمِنَا قَامَ شَيْخٌ [يَمُتْ ... يَقُمْ] ـ
يَـكُونُ الْقَافِلَةُ سَارَتْ أَيَّامًا كَثِيرَةً ـ قَدْ سَمِعَ
الْجَمَاعَةُ كُلُّهَا مَا أَقُولُ ـ يَقِيلُ كُلُّ النَّاسِ فِى
أَيَّامِ الصَّيْفِ الْحَارَّةِ ـ يَقُولُ كَثِيرٌ غَيْرَ مَا فِى
قَلْبِهِ ـ لَا تَخِفْ مَكَارِيهَ الطَّرِيقِ ـ قَدْ كَانَتِ
الْمَرْأَةُ تَصْنَعُ ثِيَابًا لِأَوْلَادِهَا ـ لَا يَـكُونُ الْأَضْيَافُ
قَامُوا مِنْ فُرُشِهِمْ قَبْلَ ذَهَابِكَ ـ يَا جَدَّتِى هَلْ
تَسِيرِينَ مَعَ النِّسَاءِ الْأُخَرِ إِلَى الْقُدْسِ .

33

I spoke to him and did not speak to any other — the
rich man fed many poor men so they went away grate-
ful — boys, do not oppose your parents — we were
following the peasant and got separated from our fellows
— wait for me in the market and do not go away — the
inhabitants of the town were perturbed on the arrival of
the news of the defeat of the army — all you approve in
a dog, demand it in a horse — the woman were crowding
round the gate of the palace to receive the queen's gifts —
the brigands overpowered the town and destroyed all that
was in it — I asked my farm labourers to store up the

snow in chambers under ground — I do not wish you to
compare my boasts with my acts — the leader surrendered
the fortress to the besiegers.

34

اِسْتَغْفَرْتُ اللهَ فَيَغْفِرُ لِى ـ أَنْظِرْنِى إِلَى قُدُومِ
الْأَضْيَافِ لِأَسْمَعَ أَخْبَارَهُمْ ـ سَأَنْتَظِرُكَ بَعْدَ غُرُوبِ
الشَّمْسِ ـ قَدْ يُنَازِعُ الْإِخْوَانُ أَخَوَاتِهِمْ ـ سَأُعَذِّبُ
اللُّصُوصَ وَكُلَّ فَاعِلِى الشَّرِّ ـ غَالَبَنِى وَغَلَبْتُهُ ـ لَا
يَسْتَقْبِحُ وَلَدٌ أُمَّهُ ـ اِخْتَلَفَ الْجَمَاعَةُ فِى مَا يَفْعَلُونَ ـ
اِسْتَخْلَفَ الْأَمِيرُ اِبْنَهُ فِى غَيُوبِهِ ـ يُلْبِسُ كُلُّ
النَّاسِ أَوْلَادَهُمْ ثِيَابًا جَدِيدَةً عَلَى الْعِيدَيْنِ
الْـكَبِيرَيْنِ ـ أَبُوكَ أَقَدْ يُدْخِلُ فَقِيرًا الْبَيْتَ وَيُطْعِمُهُ .

35

that coin was struck in Stamboul — a man is known
by his companions — it was gone two miles (two miles
were traversed) — if you are killed, being killed is the
noblest mode of death — I was burdened with the care of
my younger brothers after our father's death — he was
doubted about his pedigree, attacked for it (the genuine-
ness of his descent was suspected and attacked) — he,
who has been forbidden kindness, has been forbidden all
good — this is a matter wherein there is difference (of

opinion) — Ramadan was fasted (the fast of Ramadan was kept) — the caliph died and the youngest son of his uncle succeeded — entry is forbidden — he was carried on government horses to Egypt — have you learnt engineering ? yes, the teacher taught it to us — the fields were sown with flowers.

36

يُنْشَدُ شِعْرُهُ بَيْنَ يَدَىْ كِبَارِ الْبِلَادِ ـ زُرِعَ الْمَزَارِعُ

حِنْطَةً وَشَعِيرًا وَذُرَةً ـ دُخُولُ الْمَسَاجِدِ مَمْنُوعٌ ـ

قُتِلَ الرَّئِيسُ وَانْهَزَمَ الْجَيْشُ ـ صُنِعَتِ الْأَرْضُ فِرَاشًا

لَكُمْ ـ صُرِفَ وَجْهُهُ عَنْ قَصْدِهِ ـ فَخْرُهُ مَشْكُوكٌ

فِيهِ ـ قُتِلَ أَبُوهُ قَتَلَهُ رَجُلٌ مِنْ مِصْرَ ـ يُقَدِّمُ قُدُومَ

الْجَمَلِ الْمَحْمُولِ عَلَيْهِ ـ لِيمَ (كَانَ يُلَامُ) عَلَى صَوْمِهِ

الْكَثِيرِ ـ سَيُكْشَفُ عَنْ سِرِّهِ .

37

do you want to go away ? — let a writer not be unwilling to write — get down out of paradise for it is not for you to act proudly in it — we did not busy ourselves with mentioning that, that the book might not be too long — I do not believe that anyone is superior to Zayd in learning and manners — the beautiful forgiveness is that you do not blame him whom you pardon — your blood is tabu to you (murder is an unholy act) till you stand before your lord — someone asked a woman in marriage and she said, No, until you divorce your wife — I do not fear for you that you should be afraid ; I only fear for you that you should not be afraid — the child is so heavy that its mother cannot carry it — a bedouin heard a man say : I testify that Muhammad the apostle of God ; so he said, does what ?

38

طَالَ خُطْبَتُهُ حَتَّى يَنَامَ السَّامِعُونَ ـ نَعْتَقِدُ أَنَّ اللهَ
أَحَدٌ وَأَنْ يَغْفِرَ لِلنَّادِمِينَ ـ كَرِهَ الزَّوْجُ أَنْ يُطَلِّقَ
زَوْجَتَهُ الْعَجُوزَ رَحْمَةً عَلَيْهَا ـ اِسْتَمَعَتْ كُلُّ السَّمْعِ
خَوْفًا أَنْ يَسْقُطَ عَنِّى شَيْءٌ مِمَّا يَقُولُ ـ مَا مَنَعَكَ
أَنْ تَسْجُدَ [مَا مَنَعَكَ مِنَ السُّجُودِ] ـ يَبْعَثُ غِلْمَانَهُ
لِيُنْزِلُوا الثَّلْجَ مِنَ الْجِبَالِ لِحِفْظِ طَعَامِهِ فِى الْأَيَّامِ
الْحَارَّةِ ـ نَخَافُ أَنْ يُنَازِعَ الْجَمَاعَتَانِ بَعْضُهُمَا
بَعْضًا ـ أَخْبِرْهُ أَنِّى صَنَعْتُ هٰذَا الصَّوْتَ لَهُ .

39

he will soon come back from his journey — the sick man scarcely moves on his bed — you always benefited me by your advice and example — if he talked to us, he talked well ; if we talked to him, he listened attentively — can a man like this compose poetry or make good poetry — a number of nights befell us when we did not sleep from the cold and almost died — the shop-keeper was in the morning and people crowding in front of his shop (the shop-keeper woke to find, etc.) — learn knowledge for if you are unimportant in one people perhaps you may become important in another — if he marries you to her, perhaps you may be granted a child like me — I am almost afraid of the noise of the wind.

40

كِدْتُ أَعْتَقِدُ مَا يَقُولُ ـ هَرَبُوا هَرَبًا سَرِيعًا ـ

أَسْرَعُوا ٱلْهَرَبَ ـ لَمْ يَلْبَثْ أَنْ يَدْخُلَ ـ عَسَى أَنْ

يَرْجِعُوا غَدًا ـ لَعَلَّهُمْ يَرْجِعُونَ غَدًا ـ لَمْ تَكَدْ تَلُومُ

أُبْنَهَا عَلَى أَنْ يَسْبَحَ فِي ٱلنَّهْرِ ٱلْكَبِيرِ وَهُوَ لَا

يُحْسِنُ ٱلسِّبَاحَةَ ـ يُوشِكُ ٱلْمُتَكَبِّرُونَ أَنْ يَنْدَمُوا

عَلَى تَكَبُّرِهِمْ ـ إِنَّ ذَلِكَ ٱلْغُلَامَ كَادَ يَعْكِسُ

ٱلدُّنْيَا ـ هَزَمُونَا مَرَّةً وَلَا يَعُودُونَ يَهْزِمُونَنَا ـ حَرَّكَ

رَجُلَانِ ذَوَا قُوَّةٍ عَظِيمَةٍ ٱلْحَجَرَ وَلَمْ يَكَدْ يَتَحَرَّكُ ـ

لَا تَعُدْ تَفْعَلْ هَذَا [تَفْعَلْ] .

41

God is one ; he does not beget and is not begotten — he is a man, his description cannot be described (supremely

ordinary) — he did not let his younger son inherit with the
elder — leave excuses alone for most of them are sins
(lies) — God's knowledge embraces the acts and thoughts
of his servants (of men) — justice is that you should put
things in their places — who is the worst of men as to
position ? he said : he whose knowledge is wide, his power
narrow, and his ambition far-reaching — they suspected
him of unbelief for his studying the books of the
philosophers — it is necessary for the learner that he
should seek the truth — I expected the arrival of the news
and it has not yet come — the two doctors will soon agree
on the treatment of the invalid.

42

صِفْ أَحْوَالَ مَرَضِكَ (صِفِى أَحْوَالَ دَاءِكِ)۔ كَانَ

أَخْبَارٌ جَدِيدَةٌ تَصِلُ كُلَّ سَاعَةٍ ۔ ضَاقَتْ عَلَيْهِ

اَلْأَرْضُ وَقَدْ كَانَتْ وَسِعَتْ۔ وَجَّهْتُهُ إِلَيْكَ وَلَمْ يَتَوَجَّهْ۔

سَمِعْنَاكُمْ تَصِفُونَ مَا فَعَلْتُمْ ۔ سَنَجِدُهُمْ يَقِفُونَ فِى

اَلشَّارِعِ ۔ لَا يُوجَدُ كُفْرَانٌ [لَا كُفْرَانَ] كَكُفْرَانِ

اَلْوَلَدِ اَلْكَافِرِ۔ سَمِعْتُ أَصْدِقَاءَهُ يُوَدِّعُونَهُ۔ أَوْجَبَ

عَلَيْكَ أَنْ تَكِلَ هٰذَا اَلْأَمْرَ لِغَيْرِكَ ۔ ضَعْ يَدَكَ عَلَى

كِتَابِ اَللهِ وَاَحْلِفْ .

43

he had cousins who inherited from him — you are not
those who run away from the truth (duty) — what a man
sows to-day he will reap to-morrow — I got down from the
couch on which I had been thrown — that was the seal
(last) of his good deeds which surpass description — how
are you not pleased with a plan which will combine for you
health of body, acuteness of mind, and much wealth ? —
the two girls, whom I sent to the girls' school, have turned
out learned and cultured — be to them as a doctor who
does not hurry with a remedy before knowing the disease
— did you sell the two slaves with whom you were dis-
pleased ? — describe to me (the man) who spoke to you.

44

وَكَّلْتُ أَحَدًا أَتَّكِلُ عَلَيْهِ ـ يَزْعَمُ أَنَّ مَا نَزَلَ بِهِ

لَمْ يَنْزِلْ عَلَى غَيْرِهِ ـ مَنْ لَا يَعْرِفُ ٱلدَّاءَ لَا يَعْرِفُ

ٱلدَّوَاءَ ـ لَا يُرِيدُونَ أَنْ يَبِيعُوا ٱلْكِتَابَيْنِ ٱلَّذَيْنِ

وَرِثُوهُمَا مِنْ عَمِّهِمْ ـ زَرَعْنَا ٱلْمَزَارِعَ ٱلَّتِي وَجَذَنَاهَا غَيْرَ

مَزْرُوعَةٍ ـ هٰذَانِ هُمَا ٱلِاثْنَانِ ٱلَّذَانِ وَجَدَا ٱلْمَجْرُوحَ

وَحَمَلَاهُ إِلَى مَنْزِلِي ـ خَرَجْتُ مِنَ ٱلْبَابِ ٱلَّذِي

دَخَلْتُ فِيهِ ـ إِنَّ ٱلْحُقُوقَ ٱلَّتِي وَجَبَتْ عَلَيَّ جَاوَزَتْ

قُوَّتِي ـ وَدَّعْتُ ٱلشُّغْلَ ٱلَّذِي أَرْغَبُ فِيهِ وَتَوَجَّهْتُ

إِلَى شُغْلٍ أَرْغَبُ عَنْهُ.

45

I love her, she loves me, and my camel loves her she-camel — I thought that he was preparing to climb mountains — do not think that I oppose you — he who is moderate, the meeting with him is light on his friend; the man of (many) requests, his face is loathed — a different story is told about Musaab and his brother's dismissing him from Basra and sending him back to it — the quickest to (take part in) civil strife are the least of them as to shame at running away — I perceived the noise of the passing of a snake; did you not perceive it? — stretch out your hand to the rope of God and he will help you — count the sick and get ready the medicines for treating them — he passed by the boys telling them the stories of the prophet.

46

دُلّنِى لِمَا يَسُرُّنِى ـ ظَنَنْتُ أَنَّكَ تَدُلّنِى وَأَصْلَلْتَنِى ـ
كَانَ الْوَلَدُ يَسْتَمِدُّ الْمُعَلّمَ وَيُمِدُّهُ ـ تُحِبُّ أَنْ تَصِيرَ
شَيْخَ الْقَوْمِ فَاسْتَخِفَّ مَا يَقُولُ النَّاسُ ـ ظَنَنَّا
النّسَاءَ يَفْرِزْنَ خَوْفًا وَهُنَّ يُسْرِعْنَ لِلِقَاءِ أَزْوَاجِهِنَّ ـ
لَا نَعْرِفُ مَا نَظُنُّ ـ ضَلَّ الْكَافِرُونَ وَيُضِلُّونَ
غَيْرَهُمْ ـ سَلَّمْتُ عَلَى الْجَمَاعَةِ وَرَدُّوا سَلَامِى ـ
أَتَظُنُّهُمْ سَيُقِرُّونَ بِحُقُوقِى ـ لَا رَادَّ لِمَا يَفْعَلُ اللّهُ.

47

the noble's promise is cash down, the ignoble's is postponement — we went hunting and made a bag — my sister did not wish to obey the orders of her teacher — why do you not wish to leave your work ? — bats hide in the daytime for fear lest they should be hunted for their beauty — my father wanted to buy what his family needed — some one heard a man asking God's help for his mother. He said to him, What about your father ? He said, He is a man and can fend for himself — Did your father give you any choice in your marriage ? — No, my mother chose a wife for me — we heard a Jew threatening his servant — you must answer (obey) the call of the government — greed led those women to incline from the path of kindness and they let themselves be led.

48

سَكَتَ وَأَطَالَ ٱلسُّكُوتَ ـ يَمِيلُ ٱلْبُخْلُ ٱلنَّاسَ
عَنِ ٱلصِّرَاطِ ٱلْمُسْتَقِيمِ ـ اِسْتَغْنَاهُ وَأَعَانَنَا ـ أَقَامَ
حَجَرًا كَبِيرًا ذِكْرًا لِمَا أَصَابَ ٱلْقَوْمَ مِنَ ٱلشَّرِّ ـ
أَخَافَ ٱللُّصُوصَ سُكَّانَ ٱلْبُيُوتِ ٱلْبَعِيدَةِ ـ يُمِيتُنِي
عِنَايَةُ أَهْلِي وَبَيْتِي ـ يَفْعَلُ ذَلِكَ ٱلْيَهُودِيُّ مَا يُرِيدُ
وَيُصَوِّبُهُ ٱلْيَهُودُ وَٱلنَّصَارَى ـ يَتَعَلَّمُ ٱلْحَكِيمُ مِمَّا
يُصِيبُ غَيْرَهُ مِنَ ٱلشَّرِّ ـ اِحْتَاجَتْ إِلَى ٱلْعَوْنِ وَلَمْ
تَجِدْ مُعِينًا ـ اِحْتَلْتُ كُلَّ ٱلِٱحْتِيَالِ لِأَخْرُجَ مِنَ

ٱلْحِصْنِ ٱلَّذِى أَنَا أَسِيرٌ فِيهِ وَلَمْ أَجِدْ مَخْرَجًا ـ

اِبْتَاعَتِ اُمْرَأَتِى ثِيَابًا مِنَ ٱلْحَرِيرِ وَٱلصُّوفِ .

49

who trains his child when young will find pleasure in him when grown up — I believe in God, in his angels, in his apostles, in his books, and in the last day — does the commander allow me to question the prisoners ? — I rented my house from a merchant and paid him the rent for it every month — they began the festival with the reading of the noble Koran ; then one of the women preached telling the story of the apostle — the old man was friendly with the beggars and refugees — he earned a great reward by composing a book in defence of the religion of the Christians — people congratulated him on his return safe from the war — greet him (from me) and inform him that I will meet him to-morrow — I am not the man to prefer anyone with my share from you (I will not give up to any what you have given me) — is anyone safe from misfortune ?

50

آكِلُ هٰذَا ٱلسَّائِلَ وَأَمْرُهُ بِٱلذَّهَابِ ـ لَمْ يَأْمَنْ مَا

يَحْتَالُ ٱلْحَاسِدُ ـ أَسْتَأْجَرْتَ رِجَالًا يَحْصُدُونَ

مَزَارِعَكَ [هَلِ اسْتَأْجَرْتَ رِجَالًا أَنْ يَحْصُدُوا] ـ آنَسْتُ

هٰذَا ٱلْقَوْمَ فَيُكَافِئُونَنِى مُكَافَأَةً عَظِيمَةً ـ

سَيَؤُوَا كِلْنِى أَصْدِقَاؤُكَ وَيُشَارِبُونَنِى ـ سَأُوكِلُهُ
خُبْزًا وَتَمْرًا ـ ثُمَّ يَسْتَأْذِنُ ٱلشُّعَرَاءُ ٱلْأَمِيرَ أَنْ يَبْتَدِئُوا
إِنْشَادَ أَشْعَارِهِمْ ـ أَثَّرَ ٱلشَّمْسُ فِى وَجْهِ ٱلْفَلَّاح
وَلَمْ يَتَأَثَّرْ قُوَّةُ جِسْمِهِ ـ تَأَخَّرَتِ ٱلْقَافِلَةُ أَخَّرَهَا
ٱلْمَطَرُ.

51

when you do a man a good turn, forget it — there is
no good in kindness when it is counted — a man hid what
(kindness) he did and published what was done to him —
the Arabs say, a turbaned chief, meaning that every
crime one of his tribe commits is bound on his head (he
takes the responsibility for it) — why do you not make
lampoons long ? he said, what goes round the neck is
enough of a necklace for you — what I like does not come
to me, and what comes to me I do not like — make me
independent by my need of you and do not make me poor
by my being able to do without you — what is little and
sufficient is better than what is much and distracts —
why do you not go to war? he said, I hate cordially death
in my bed, how can I go to it with a run ? — buy dates
from Mosul and carry them to Basra ; that will destroy
your fortune.

52

سَأَكْفِيكَهُ ـ مَا أَنْسَ لَا أَنْسَ مُؤَانَسَتَكَ ـ
أَشْتَرَيْتَ مَا تَحْتَاجُ إِلَيْهِ [هَلِ ٱشْتَرَيْتَ] ـ يَا ٱبْنَتِى

خُذِي مَا أُعْطِيكِ وَاشْتَرِى مَا تُرِيدِينَ ـ بَكَتِ
النِّسَاءُ عَلَى الْمَقْتُولِينَ [الْقَتْلَى] ـ مَنْ يَبْكِى الآنَ
سَيَضْحَكُ ـ أَظُنُّ أَنَّهُمْ سَيَبْقَوْنَ عَلَى مَا هُمُ الآنَ
عَلَيْهِ ـ لَا يُلْهِكَ لَعَبٌ عَنْ دُرُوسِكَ ـ نَهَيْتُهَا
وَانْتَهَتْ ـ أَلْهُوا عَمَّا يَصْنَعُونَ ـ أَلْهِينَ عَمَّا يَصْنَعْنَ ـ
إِنَّ الْخَلِيفَةَ أَبْقَاهُ اللهُ لَا يَنْسَى مُكَافَأَةَ مَنْ
يَسْتَحِقُّهَا.

53

he said, let me make my will, and he said, make it — they
held the views of the philosophers — are you not ashamed
that this should be the measure of your kindness to your
son ? — when you feel no shame (at it) then act as you
please — why do you hear and not understand ? — they
made him rich and he made them little return — may
God let you see in your sons what he let your father see
in you and may God let your sons see in you what he let
you see in your father — when he promised something
good, he performed ; when he threatened, he did not
perform and forgave — prefer what you will meet to-morrow
to what you will never see — I used to find those who
promise and perform, those who promise and do not perform
wearied me — I was ashamed (of my treatment) of him
and sent (one) to him with the jewels — we have what you
want ; go to your house and it will come to you — let one
of you guard his face from the Fire — the caliph appoints
whom he will.

54

أَمَرَهُمْ أَنْ يَأْتُوا بِكُتُبِهِمْ ـ كَيْفَ رَأَيْتَ مِصْرَ ـ
هَؤُلَاءِ النِّسَاءُ هَلْ تَفِينَ مَا وَعَدْنَ ـ اِتَّقُوا الاِتِّهَامَ ـ
حَيَّوْنَا تَحِيَّةَ الْكَرِيمِ ـ أَرِنِى كَيْفَ ذٰلِكَ يَنْفَعُنِى ـ
سَلِ الْحَافِظَ أَنْ يُرِيَكَ مَا فِى الصَّنَادِيقِ ـ اِتَّقُوا
اللهَ وَأَكْرِمُوا الْمَلِكَ ـ أُوثِرُ أَنْ يَخَافَنِى النَّاسُ مِنْ
أَنْ يَتَّقُوا اللهَ ـ اِيتِنِى سَهْمِى مِنَ الطَّعَامِ فَاٰكُلَهُ
عِنْدَ النَّهْرِ ـ أَلَمْ تَرَوْا كُلُّكُمْ مَا كَتَبَتْ عَمَّتُكُمْ ـ
إِنَّ الدَّرْسَ الْكَثِيرَ يُعْيِى الصِّغَارَ.

55

if you do not kill him, I shall certainly marry him;
then he will have killed your father and married your
mother; so he killed him — had avarice been a shirt,
I would not have put it on; had it been a road, I would
not have travelled it — if what keeps me alive is in heaven,
send it down; if it is in the earth, bring it out; if it is
far off, bring it near; and if it is near, make it easy —
if you sit with the learned, be more eager to hear than to
speak — were it not that his deeds do not make necessary
(make impossible) the forgiving of him, he would deserve
to be left alive for this excellence — there is no strength
except under the garment of hard work — why do you not
compose long lampoons? I have not found a poem (longer)
than one verse to travel — he deposited this money with

several men ; they made off with it, except one Jew —
I have come only on business which concerns the minister
and myself alone ; discussion of it is useful only in strict
privacy — there is a remedy for every disease except
death — you are nothing but a thing to which nobody
pays any attention — they are infidels ; they shall be asked
to repent ; if they repent (well and good) ; if not, their
heads shall be cut off.

56

مَنْ لَمْ يُخْطِئْ لَمْ يَصْنَعْ شَيْئًا ـ جَاءَ كُلُّ السُّكَّانِ

إِلَّا أَبَاكَ ـ إِنْ صَوَّبْتُمُوهُ فَاتَّبِعُوا أُسْوَتَهُ ـ إِنْ وَجَدْتَ

أَنِّى جِئْتُ فِى أَمْرٍ يَخُصُّنِى وَلَا يَعُمُّ الْقَوْمَ جَمِيعًا

فَأَذْهِبْنِى ـ مَا أَيْقَظَنِى إِلَّا حَرُّ الشَّمْسِ عَلَى

ظَهْرِى [لَمْ يُوقِظْنِى] ـ أَيْنَمَا سَكَنْتَ لَقِيتَ أَصْدِقَاءَ ـ

لَا يُشَابِهُ مِنَ الْأَوْلَادِ أَبَاهُمْ إِلَّا مُحَمَّدٌ ـ إِنْ صَدَّقْتُمْ

مَا يَقُولُ وَجَبَ عَلَيْكُمْ أَنْ تَفْعَلُوا عَلَيْهِ ـ لَمْ يَدَعْ

مِنَ الْبِرِّ شَيْئًا إِلَّا فَعَلَهُ ـ إِنْ أَبْطَأْتَ الْأَكْلَ كُلَّ أَطَلْتَ

الْعُمْرَ ـ إِذَا مَاتَ تَقَاتَلَ وَرَثَتُهُ عَلَى الْوِرَاثَةِ ـ لَوْلَاهُ

لَهَلَكَ الْجَيْشُ.

57

he knew that when he refused them civil strife would
flare up, from the consequences of which he would not be
safe, and that the (right) policy made gentleness to them
necessary — while we were burying him another body was
carried — I felt acute pain and when it was in the night
it became quiet and I slept — when your fathers made
mistakes no one did right except you — when the illness
grew strong upon him he kept his bed — there did not
pass over this except less than a month until (less than
a month after this) the caliph summoned his cousin and
invested him with the ministry — I was talking to him
when some young men appeared ; he called the eldest of
them and whispered to him something apart from me and
his fellows (which we could not hear) — he went with him
until they reached the house like horses racing — his friends
had evil forebodings and feared for him, yet the first thing
they knew was that he was there driving the camels and
they two drove them with him — he stayed in the town
till, when the heat of summer fatigued him, he went to
his estate.

58

لَمَّا اشْتَرَكُوا فِى الشُّغْلِ اشْتَرَكُوا فِى الرِّبْحِ ـ لَمَّا
أَقْبَلَ سَهْمِى مِنَ الْأَجْرِ ـ مَتَى رَأَيْتُمْ أَحَدًا يُشَابِهُهُ
وَجْهًا ـ أَشْرَكَنِى مَعَ نَفْسِهِ فِى طَلَبِهِ مِنَ الْحُكُومَةِ ـ
إِذَا ذَهَبْتَ إِلَى بِلَادٍ غَرِيبَةٍ فَاتَّخِذْ عَادَاتِهَا ـ لَمَّا
أَعْطَوْنِى سَهْمِى لَمْ أَرْضَ عَنْهُ ـ أَصَابَهُ الْفَقْرُ وَإِذَا

KEY 285

أَصْدِقَاؤُهُ مَعَهُ [يُسَاعِدُونَهُ] ـ لَمَّا رَأَتِ النُّهَى غَيْرَ
نَافِعٍ بَكَتْ ـ كَانَ يَشْتَغِلُ بِالْكِتَابَةِ حَتَّى إِذَا
قَدْ كَتَبَ أَوْرَاقًا كَثِيرَةً أَعْيَا بَيَاضُ الْوَرَقِ عَيْنَيْهِ ـ
إِنَّ الْوَعْدَ إِذَا لَمْ يَصْحَبْهُ إِنْجَازٌ يُحَقِّقُهُ كَكَلَامٍ لَا
مَعْنَى لَهُ .

59

I stayed in the land of polytheism 4 months and 11
days — she bought one cock and 15 hens — his caravan
consisted of 100 camels and 25 donkeys — he was born
in the year 1932 — the war lasted two years and a half —
the government takes one-tenth of all the goods of the
merchants who come into its country from outside —
I have not eaten anything for three nights (days) and
I want you to stay with me that we may eat and talk —
his death was two years before the great earthquake — he
is 65 years old — a kind act is only perfected by 3 qualities,
doing it quickly, making light of it, and keeping it secret.

60

إِنَّ أَنْوَاعَ التَّمْرِ هِيَ اثْنَانِ وَسَبْعُونَ نَوْعًا ـ هِيَ
بِنْتُ سَبْعٍ وَعَشْرَةَ سَنَةً ـ كَانَ ذَلِكَ الشَّيْخُ أَبَا قَوْمِهِ
كَانَ لَهُ سِتَّةَ عَشَرَ ابْنًا وَاثْنَتَا عَشْرَةَ ابْنَةً ـ قَطَعَتِ
اللَّحْمَ اثْنَى عَشَرَ سَهْمًا ـ انْصَرَفَ الْأَضْيَافُ اثْنَيْنِ

أَثْنَيْنِ ـ سَافَرَ تِسْعَةَ عَشَرَ يَوْمًا يَعْبُرُ ثَلَاثَةَ أَنْهَارٍ
وَيَصْعَدُ فِى سَبْعَةِ جِبَالٍ ـ أَعْفُ عَنْهُ سَبْعِينَ مَرَّةً ـ
وَصَلَ رَسُولِى بَعْدَ وُصُولِى بِثَلَاثِ سَاعَاتٍ ـ وَرِثَتْ
أُبْنَتُهُ رُبْعَ رُبْعِ مَالِهِ ـ هُوَ الْاِبْنُ السَّابِعُ لِأُبْنِ
سَابِعٍ .

61

he sat like a tired man — have you ever heard the like
of this? he said, no, the like of it has never torn my
ears — Moses hit the stone once and water came out
enough for all the people — the woman of the house drove
out the thief, hitting him with the broom — cause them
to hear the word of God and bring them to their place of
safety — we journeyed some stages and reached a place
where lions were numerous where we feared for our horses
— let us now mention the history from the birth of the
apostle of God to (the time of) his mission — they tried
me with questions of which I understood nothing — we
crossed the river, some by a ferry and some by a ford —
he was the most remembering of men for what he heard,
the least of them in (need of) sleep, and the most enduring
of wakefulness.

62

اِشْتَهَرَ اسْمُهُ فِى الْمَشْرِقِ وَالْمَغْرِبِ ـ دَخَلَ اللُّصُّ
دِخْلَةَ الْأَسَدِ وَخَرَجَ خِرْجَةَ الشَّاةِ ـ يَسْبَحُ أَوْلَادُهُ
جَمِيعًا سِبْحَةَ السَّمَكِ ـ مَا دَامَتِ الْحَيَاةُ لَا أَتْرُكُ

اَلْمُقَاتَلَ ـ قَطَعَ الطِّفْلُ إِصْبَعَهُ بِمِقَصِّ الْخَيَّاطِ ـ يَغْسِلُ
كَلْبَهُ كُلَّ يَوْمٍ غَسْلَتَيْنِ ـ إِنَّ الْعَقْلَ لِلْإِنْسَانِ مِبْرَدٌ
يَبْرُدُ بِهِ خُشُونَةَ الْقَلْبِ وَمِكْنَسَةٌ يُزِيلُ بِهَا أَعْمَالَ
السُّوءِ وَمِدَقٌّ يَدُقُّ بِهِ رَأْسَ الشَّيْطَانِ وَمُنْخُلٌ يُنَظِّفُ
بِهِ أَفْكَارَهُ ـ يَفْتَخِرُ الشَّامِيُّ بِثَلْجِ جِبَالِهِ وَفَوَاكِهِهَا
وَالْمِصْرِيُّ بِمَاءِ نَهْرِهِ ـ مَا كَانَ لِلنَّجَّارِ أَنْ يَجْهَلَ
كَيْفِيَّاتِ أَنْوَاعِ الْخَشَبِ الْمُخْتَلِفَةِ .

63

the judge decided against the plaintiff and acquitted the
defendant — he began asking a loan of me and I lent
him 500 dinars to get quit of him — he saw a sick fox
which could not move and said, this fox must die of hunger
— lead us in the straight path, the path of those to whom
you have given bounty, who were not the object of your
anger and have not gone astray — man wants by nature
the things forbidden — some people fell into an argument
and looked for a passer-by to decide between them ; when
he asked about the matter in dispute they could not
explain the point of difference — then the unbelievers will
drop their heads in fear of what they may see and will
wail — you cannot defend yourselves, you must submit —
misfortunes happen inevitably ; some of them are mercy
and grace from God to his servant and others are punishment (vengeance) — be rich if you will or poor, care is
unavoidable in the world.

64

اِحْمِلُوا الْوَلَدَ الْمَغْشِيَّ عَلَيْهِ إِلَى الْمُسْتَشْفَى ــ إِنَّ
الْمُدَّعَى عَلَيْهِ فِى الْمَحْكَمَةِ وَأَيْنَ الْمُدَّعِى ــ كَانَتْ
بِنْتٌ زَمِنَتْ نَحْوَ خَمْسَ عَشَرَةَ سَنَةً لَا يُمْكِنُهَا أَنْ
تَتَقَلَّبَ مِنْ جَنْبٍ إِلَى جَنْبٍ أَوْ يُقَلِّبَهَا غَيْرُهَا ــ مَا
ظَنَنْتُ أَنَّهُ أَمْكَنَهُ أَنْ يَذْكُرَنِى حَتَّى دُعِىَ بِى ــ
مَا كَانَ مَعَكَ ثَمَنُ هَذَا الْبَطِّيخِ مَا قَدَرْتَ تَمْنَعُ
نَفْسَكَ مِنْهُ ــ أُتْرَكُ مَشْدُودًا عَلَىَّ وَثَاقِى ــ لَمْ نَجِدْ
مِنْ دَفْعِ ذَلِكَ إِلَيْهِ بُدًّا ــ حَسْبِىَ الَّذِى بِى ــ كَيْفَ
أَصْبَحَ زَوْجُكِ قَالَتْ لَا حَيًّا فَيُرْجَى وَلَا مَيِّتًا
فَيُنْسَى ــ لَا تُعْطِى مَا لَيْسَ عِنْدَكَ.

65

I saw (thought) the wisdom of the poor despised —
I shall wash disgrace off me with the sword though God's
providence brings on me what it may — I know, the
command (business) of the apostle of God is more blessed
than mine — it is as if al-Husain was advancing towards
you — the army feared death till the hearts of most of
them were as air — you speak the words of one whose

character it is not to keep truth — the importance of the
world in the eye of Abd al-Rahman and that he thought
the beggar who came to him the angel of death made him
small in my sight — the gifts of the sultan were only for
the poor and those whose hearts had been won over —
take us out of this land the people of which are evil-doers
— I seem to see you pretending to be ignorant — I have
suffered from time (fate) all my life till I cannot hope for
prosperity — the king of Egypt devotes his attention to
the improvement of agriculture especially cotton.

66

وُلِدَ ٱلرَّجُلُ ٱلشَّرُّ لَيْلَةَ مَاتَ فِيهَا ٱلرَّجُلُ ٱلْخَيْرُ ـ
كَأَنِّى بِكُمْ تَكْرَهُونَنِى ـ إِنْ تُعِيدُوهَا نُعِدْ لَكُمْ
مِنْ هِجَاءٍ سَائِرٍ كَلَامُهُ ـ يَا سَامِعَ ٱلدُّعَاءِ
خَلِّصْنِى مِمَّا يَحْتَالُونَ عَلَىَّ أَعْدَائِى ـ كَأَنِّى بِكُمْ
تُرَاهِنُونَ عَلَى فَرَسٍ لَا يَسْبِقُ فِى ٱلسِّبَاقِ ـ أَرَتْنَا
ٱلْخَيَّاطَةُ ثِيَابًا مُخْتَلِفَةَ أَلْوَانِهَا ـ مَنْ عَلَّمَ شَيْخًا
فَكَأَنَّهُ يَبَّضَ أَسْوَدَ ـ مَا رَأَيْتُ أَحَدًا مِنَ ٱلْخُلَفَاءِ
أَكْرَهَ إِلَيْهِ ٱلدِّمَاءِ مِنْ هِشَامٍ ـ كَانَ يَتَعَشَّى وَلَا
يَتَغَدَّى فَحَسْبُهُ ذَلِكَ أَرْبَعِينَ سَنَةً .

67

beware of begging from men, for it is man's last way of earning — how vigorously he is washing himself — we ask you by God to observe towards us the testament of the apostle of God — what a bad decision they have arrived at — know that God is your lord, what a lord, what a helper — worthy Musaab! whose ancestors are noble — how careless she is in her own affairs, how busy about those of others — how thirsty the boy is, I cannot satisfy him — beware of those who make excuses — I swore extravagant oaths, he shall not thirst so long as I live — lack of money and opportunity made me unable to help him.

68

نِعْمَ ذلِكَ الْوَلَدُ سَابِحًا ـ أَكْذِبْ بِهِ وَالْعَجَبُ أَنَّ

كُلَّ وَاحِدٍ يُصَدِّقُهُ ـ مَا أَعْطَشَ الطِّفْلَ مَلَأْتُ لَهُ

ثَلَاثَ كُؤُوسٍ لَبَنًا وَيُفَرِّغُهَا جَمِيعًا ـ مَا أَسْرَعَ

مَا يَأْتِيكُمُ الْعَدُوُّ ـ إِذِ انْقَطَعَ عَنْهُمُ الْمِيَاهُ قَالُوا

أَهْلَكْتَنَا قَالَ قَدْ بَلَغْتُمُ الْمَاءَ مَا أَقْرَبَكُمْ بِهِ ـ

بِئْسَ زَوْجُ الْمَرْأَةِ الْحُرَّةِ أَنْتَ ـ وَالَّذِي نَفْسِى بِيَدِهِ

لَيَنَامَنَّ عُرْيَانًا فِى الثَّلْجِ ـ وَرَبِّ الْكَعْبَةِ إِلَّا

بَيَّنْتَ لِى رِسَالَتَكَ ـ وَاللهِ لَا شَمَّ قَاتِلُ مُسْلِمٍ رَائِحَةَ

الْجَنَّةِ ـ يَجِبُ أَنْ أُعَرِّفَكَ أَنَّكَ أَنْتَ الْأَحْمَقُ لَا أَنَا.

69

I shall not come in and not go away until you ride to the mosque — either I go to Syria, and how unpleasant that will be, or I stay ; and therein is a reward for me — we claim that men are graded in excellence not by their fathers but by their acts, their characters, their magnanimity, and their high ambitions — the Arabs say of one who is asked to give and cannot and refuses, my house is stingy not I — I was alone with her and the moon showed her to me ; when it disappeared she showed it to me — do not speak of what you do not know lest you be suspected in what you do know — do not forbid a quality (mode of behaviour) and come to (do) something like it — the Arabs will not consent to put you in authority as you are not one of them — this poem is something which happened in youth ; I made it about my wife. I was inclined to (in love with) her, she was my slave and ruled my heart ; but now, I have had no truck with such things for years and have not made poetry for a long time.

70

لَيْتَنِى لَمْ تَلِدْنِى أُمِّى وَلَمْ أَرَ نُورَ النَّهَارِ ـ كُنْتُ

أَسْتَتِرُ فِى بَيْتِهَا وَهِىَ تَصْعَدُ إِلَىَّ كُلَّ يَوْمٍ تَسْأَلُ

مَا أَحْتَاجُ إِلَيْهِ ـ حَلَفَ أَلَّا يَبْدُلَ هَذَا الْقَمِيصَ أَوْ

يَفْرَغَ مِنْ أَمْرِ مَنْ شَتَمَهُ ـ وَرَدَتِ الْكُتُبُ إِلَى

مَحْمُودٍ وَهُوَ عَامِلُ الشَّأْمِ أَنْ يَجْمَعَ بَيْنَنَا فِى الْمَسْجِدِ

وَلَا نَبْرَحَ أَوْ يُرْضِيَنَا ـ رُبَّ آكِلٍ شَاكِرٍ أَعْظَمُ

أَجْرًا مِنْ صَائِمٍ ـ أَمَرَ الْأَمَةَ بِغَسْلِ الثِّيَابِ وَتَنْشِيفِهَا

تَنْشِيفًا تَامًّا ـ رُبَّ صَحْرَاءَ قَطَعْتُهَا وَذَخِيرَةٍ وَجَدْتُهَا

وَمُشْكِلَةٍ حَلَلْتُهَا ـ سَأَلَنِي ابْنُ كَمْ أَنْتَ [كَمْ عُمْرُكَ

ـ كَمْ سَنَّةً لَكَ] ـ لَيْتَكَ تَدْخُلُ فَتُسَلِّمُ عَلَى الْأَمِيرِ

وَ تُخْبِرُهُ بِحَقِيقَةِ الْأَمْرِ فَيَسْكُنَ غَضَبُهُ عَنَّا ـ أَبْطِئِ

الْأَكْلَ فَتَهْضِمَ الطَّعَامَ هَضْمًا كَامِلًا.

71

I love you for yourself more than my loving you for myself (profit) — how do you find yourself? I find myself not finding what I desire and desiring what I do not find. I am in a very bad age among very bad men; he who is generous does not find (anything to give) and he who does find is not generous — by the excuse we make God has enabled you to dispense with excusing yourself and by our love to you God has enabled us to dispense with thinking badly of you — to whom did your father give his dying charge about you? he gave his charge to me, not about me — liberal of tongue without action! would that the liberality of the tongue was in your hands — but God has saved me by you; no one has consoled me with a more useful than your consolation — satisfy my brother and my ally who between them took the captive — a sultan wanted to build a palace and estimated for this millions of dirhams; the expenditure was above the estimate several times and he required the minister to send money for this although the income (of the country) came short of the outgoings — he picked out those who sold in the markets things like cooking pots and old shirts

and what one would be compelled to think unsaleable
except from dire distress and old women who sold what
they had spun and gave them several times the price of
it (the goods) and left it (the goods) with them.

72

مَا أَعْرِفُ لِهٰذِهِ الثِّيَابِ ثَمَنًا وَلَا رَأَيْتُ مِثْلَهَا قَطْ

وَلَوْلَا أَنِّى شَهِدْتُهَا لَكَذَّبْتُ بِوُجُودِ مِثْلِهَا. وَلَوْ

قُلْتُ أَنَّ ثَمَنَ كُلِّ وَاحِدٍ مِائَةُ أَلْفِ دِينَارٍ مَا خِفْتُ

الْبُعْدَ ـ وَاللهِ مَا كَانَ فِى نَفْسِى أَنْ أُعْطِيَهَا إِلَّا

مِائَتَىْ دِرْهَمٍ وَلٰكِنَّ اللهَ أَجْرَى لَهَا عَلَى يَدِى

مِائَتَىْ دِينَارٍ فَلَا أَرْجِعُ فِى ذٰلِكَ أَعْطِهَا ـ كَانَ

الْوَزِيرُ يَسْتَخِفُّ صَاحِبَ دِيوَانِ الْخَرَاجِ وَإِذَا أَرَادَ

عَمَلًا مِنَ الدِّيوَانِ أَوْ حِسَابًا غَفَلَ عَنِ الصَّاحِبِ

وَاسْتَدْعَى الْكُتَّابَ وَاسْتَشَارَهُمْ وَالصَّاحِبُ حَاضِرٌ

فَإِذَا أَرَادَ عَمَلًا يَعْلَمُ أَنَّ صِنَاعَةَ الصَّاحِبِ لَا تَقِى

بِهِ وَلَا يُمْكِنُهُ الْكَلَامُ فِيهِ شَاوَرَهُ بَيْنَ يَدَىِ النَّاسِ

لِيُبَيِّنَ نَقْصَه ـ قَالَ ٱلْنَبِىُّ فِى ٱلْنِّسَاءِ شَاوِرْهُنَّ
وَخَالِفْهُنَّ وَإِنِّى عَصَيْتُهُ وَأَطَعْتُ صَاحِبَتِى فَٱشْتَرَيْتُ
غُلَامًا فَسَرَقَ ـ لَا يُغْنِى حَذَرٌ مِنْ قَدَرٍ ـ مَا ٱلْزُّهْدُ
فِى ٱلْدُّنْيَا قَالَ أَنْ لَا يَغْلِبَ ٱلْحَرَامُ صَبْرَكَ وَلَا
ٱلْحَلَالُ شُكْرَكَ ـ عَلِّمْ أَوْلَادِى ٱلْسِّبَاحَةَ قَبْلَ
ٱلْكِتَابَةِ فَإِنَّهُمْ يُصِيبُونَ مِنْ يَكْتُبُ عَنْهُمْ وَلَا
يُصِيبُونَ مَنْ يَسْبَحُ عَنْهُمْ.

INDEX

(Supplementary to the Table of Contents)